JULIAN BOND:
Black Rebel

JULIAN BOND:

BLACK REBEL

by John Neary

WILLIAM MORROW
AND COMPANY, INC.
NEW YORK · 1971

To Joan

Acknowledgments

Thanks:

—to Julian Bond, for never once putting anything off the record in our conversations, for opening his files, for permitting me to quote his poems, and for enduring my intrusions as I tried to glimpse his life

—to his wife, Alice, and their children for their hospitality

—to Dr. and Mrs. Horace Mann Bond for their many kindnesses, and their memories

—to James Bond and Jane Bond Moore for their thoughts about their famous brother, and to Attorney Howard Moore for his insights into his brother-in-law

—to Noe Baldwin, Julian Bond's secretary, for countless rescues

—to Charles Morgan and Mrs. Ruste Kitfield of the American Civil Liberties Union for their advice and the use of their library

—to the Atlanta *Constitution* and the Atlanta *Journal* for access to their morgues

—to Tony Heffernan, Atlanta bureau chief of Reuters, for wise counsel

—to George P. Hunt, Roy Rowan and David Snell, all formerly of *Life* magazine, for their permission to pursue this project and their encouragement

—to Charles Elliott, of *Life*, Susanna McBee, of *McCall's*, and my brother, Steve Neary, of the Washington *Post*, for their reading of the manuscript and their helpful comments.

* * *

Although Julian Bond cooperated in the preparation of this biography, it is in no sense an "authorized" version of his life and all responsibility for errors of fact or judgment lies with me.

John Neary

Port Washington, N.Y.

1970

JULIAN BOND:
Black Rebel

I

EVERY morning that he was home in the little crackerbox of a house where he used to live, on Euharlee Street in Atlanta, Georgia, Julian Bond would stretch out of bed and, looking all ashy and sleepy and a little cold there in his underwear and bare feet, paddle out through the living room, past the gigantic color television set and the sideboard packed high with books and the brass plaques on the wall, and walk out through the little front porch he had turned into an office. There, on the front steps of the little house he used to have, he would find a whole new episode, an entire new chapter for him to savor in that real-life drama he so enjoys, The Saga of Julian Bond. His victories in that ongoing adventure have brought him fame—and a bigger house. But each morning still brings its invitations to new episodes.

There, jamming the mailbox and cluttering the top step, Bond would find offers from people wanting to sell transcriptions of his soft, laconic voice, who wanted him to sign book contracts, who wanted him to appear on television shows, who wanted to write magazine stories about him, who wanted him to write magazine stories for them, who wanted to engrave his name on their business letterheads, who wanted him to join the governing councils of their foundations, who wanted him to join in starting magazines and newspapers, sign ads condemning racism and oppression, who wanted to give him more brass plaques for his wall, who wanted him to come and speak, who had all conceivable manner of schemes, profit-making and charitable, which, they believed, would flourish if only Julian Bond would consent to lend the magic of his name to their endeavors. Bond would pick them up off the steps, riffle through them, and shove them into the cardboard box next to the portable electric heater, the box where he kept the offers to make him rich and famous. Bond, in fact, accepted quite a few of the invitations, enough so that his profits enabled him, a little more than a year after the Democratic Convention—which set off this flurry of attention in the first place—to leave the little house for a larger, more comfortable home. There, too, every morning brings a tide of invitations to his mailbox. Bond picks them up, inspects them, puts them in the box. Then he goes back inside to change the baby's diaper and get dressed and catch an airplane to some place where he must make a speech or get a plaque, or just go down the street to Paschal's motel and drink coffee, or go to the cleaner's, or over to the House of Representatives, where, to the mortification of some of his colleagues and the delight of his constituents, he is a bona fide legislator. It has always been this way for Julian Bond, finding things out in front of his house. He doesn't know why. He doesn't think about it much.

Bond of Georgia: infamous, anathema, poison, troubador of the old darky dreams, hero at large. Politicians are what people say they are, and Bond as a professional Negro politician is not only said to be all these protean things—he in fact *is* all of those things, and he got that way because things just have a way of happening to him. One morning it was the civil rights movement sitting out there, staring him smack in the eye, and it never went away; on another morning, it was Viet Nam come to his door to raise merry hell. Trouble and sadness have perched there, con-men and near-saints. People who wanted a handout—and those others, the people who started coming to his door to wangle Bond into going all the way to the Chicago convention in 1968 and all the way into history.

Bond got himself ousted from the Georgia House of Representatives back in the early part of 1966 by enthusiastically endorsing opposition to the war in Viet Nam, and not until he won three more elections and the unanimous support of the Supreme Court of the United States did he get back in. But despite that impressive escort into the House chamber, Bond remains a pariah there and in Georgia politics statewide as well. For all the antipathy he encounters at home, however, Bond nationally is a hero, the man who was nominated for vice-president by some Democrats in Chicago after he and his ragtag slate of challenging delegates wrested half the Georgia seats from Governor Lester Maddox and the machine bhoys.

For all the attention this got him, Bond even to his closest friends remains pretty much a riddle. His life, despite its movie-script quality, is generally devoid of much direction by him. Horace Julian Bond would like to see himself, in his more serious moments, as the kind of politician who is an organization man, efficient, focused clearly on the issues, abjuring the cult of personality. Bond gets downright uncomfortable when he is asked how it feels to be a symbol, because he doesn't think it's proper to be one—in spite of the obvious facts that he is one, and that his main value politically, to himself, to his constituents and to the many who seek to bask in his glow or plug into the near-mystical power that generates it, is *as* a personality, not an ideologist.

Although he was a published poet by the time he dropped out of Morehouse College in Atlanta, Bond doesn't spend much time writing any more, except for the speeches he recites a half-dozen or so times each week—when the Legislature is not in session. Since the 1968 Democratic Convention, he has turned into a kind of modern-dress goliard, bringing the news to the boondocks, appearing hundreds of times before hundreds of thousands of students on campuses around the country. In his now-spoken words, Bond the former poet remains the articulator of the *is*ness of things, the concretizer of the abstract, which is about half of what it takes over the long haul to make it as a politician. By civics-book standards, though, the other half consists of going beyond what *is* to propose what *ought* to be, and suggest some way of getting there. (It should be pointed out, however, that some highly successful politicians, among them Richard Nixon, have spent long years in public service despite legislative records largely devoid of any such proposals.) Bond just shrinks from this chore of prescribing programmatic solutions to the maladies he sees afflicting his society. Partly he's lazy, partly he doesn't have the legal know-how to convert problems into legislation readily, and mainly he senses that the answers ought to come not from him so much as from the people—that it has been, in fact, the abortion of their simple horse sense from which much of the malaise upon us has arisen, and that those most keenly affected and most often not consulted must now have their turn.

Bond has moved far beyond the strictures of his own past, breaking with traditions molded by his own family and the black academic aristocracy it belongs to, abandoning the old habits of mind, the old fights, the old etiquettes, the old values. Having done so, it became impossible for him to accept any of the rest of America unquestioningly. As this is written, Bond is young, and to be young is to know with an immanent poignancy the hypocrisy, the persiflage in the face of tragedy and the pain of promises made only to be broken; to be young and black at the same time is to know all this and not be known oneself. Which puts Bond in a tough spot as a politician: as a sworn officer of the state and a sought-after leader, he must be officially part of society but personally, as a black man, he is in fact excluded from it. Bond's grandfather, an indefatigable dynamo of a man who got himself from slavery to being a guest at the White House by strength of character, called this kind of divided existence "life on the margin."

Living in the same margin has caused Julian Bond to know —and know well—that America from which his black genes exclude him. He grew up on black campuses, in a highly stylized caricature of white society oddly free of the internal racist harshness of that paradigm. Then he lived in Atlanta, in a university enclave surrounded, like many universities, by a slum. There are at least several Atlantas, one of them isolated, unventilated, paranoid, self-deluding, guilt-ridden, laboring under an inferiority complex as big as its drawl; another is courtly, boisterous, exciting in its ferment, a gentle island in a red-clay zoo of bigotry and brutality. Atlanta was for a long time a place where being black meant being invisible and when that stopped, being black came to mean being suspected of fomenting insurrection, agitation and advocating treason. As Julian Bond acquired an easy familiarity with the intellectualities of the campus, got accustomed to being invisible, learned grace under suspicion, and came to understand the dreams and specters of blacks, he found he was in fact getting a kind of weapon few Americans truly have: a passport enabling him to journey safely and leisurely through all the warring camps on the American scene from angry black militant to baffled and fearful white.

So today, national reporters stop off and chat easily with him on their swings through the South; national politicians court his support—and all those propositions come in the mail every day. While just a century or so ago a well-to-do white farmer could have bought Julian Bond outright for the going price of a healthy field hand—about $800 for one on the skinny side, like Bond—today it costs around $1000 plus expenses for just a few hours of his time; and groups everywhere, eager to hear what Bond has to say about how things are in those warring camps, seem eager to pay it.

Few along his peripatetic route find Bond completely satisfying or reassuring and few are more baffled than the disbelieving and outraged men who surround him in the Georgia House. To their way of looking at Bond's rise in affairs, they are responsible for him; they *created* him, a realization which causes them unholy and bitter chagrin. By jubilantly expelling him in 1966, they launched him; and now, under the gold-plated dome of the Georgia capitol building, Bond is excoriated tirelessly by them as a traitor to his state, his race and his country.

A traitor. Even those who consider themselves his friends stand off from too close a public link with him, lest it mean political defeat for their causes and themselves as well. To the blacks who sit with him in the chambers of the Georgia Legislature, Bond is a *wunderkind*, not to be trifled with and not altogether to be trusted either—because he is not their kind of *dependable* politician.

Bond moves through the swirl of emotion he evokes with little visible concern. He tries to get to work on time, dressing for the job as he chooses, usually with studied Ivy League conservatism embellished with a dandyesque watch-chain dangling in a nonchalant parabola across his tweedy vest. Sometimes he comes clad as a sport, in slacks and turtleneck. He generally sticks around the capitol until the legislative day has ended. He is amiably willing, his constituents have learned, to execute all those tiresome leaps through hoops that taxpayers have devised for their representatives: he will come out of the House chamber and pose for pictures with squadrons of schoolchildren—he will even amuse them with a short talk on citizenship and arrange for some of them to serve as pages. There remain, however, those certain other, more serious, legislative tasks that Julian Bond finds it difficult to bring himself to perform. In his first several sessions as a seated member of the House, Bond never once rose to utter so much as a question in the House chamber. No stinging speech, such as those he has delivered to eager audiences in the North, was heard from Bond in the well of the Georgia House of Representatives. Not once did Bond submit legislation requiring the approval of the entire House. Instead, in the legislature, Julian Bond behaved entirely like a chastened schoolboy on academic probation—odd behavior indeed, considering the lengths to which he had gone to win that seat.

Why?

Because Julian Bond got stomped on once by these men who are now his colleagues in the House and does not trust them, he therefore is not willing to expose himself to them again, cannot bring himself to run the risk of another repudiation, and so he will relinquish his ideas—and his hopes—to the mouths of other men less controversial than he. That's what Bond says. Because he's so busy off lallygagging around the country bad-mouthing Georgia and the South he lacks the time to do the hard work and the buttonholing it takes to get legislation passed. That's what his adversaries declare. Whichever way it really is, his constituents seem not to mind much that their legislator contents himself with getting potholes fixed and streetlights installed by making judicious phone calls to City Hall: Bond was unopposed in his most recent bids for reelection.

It is Bond himself, moving laconically about the capitol, or hurrying home to baby-sit while his pretty wife, Alice, goes off to shop, or pausing in his answer to a question at a political meeting to think it over, who of course is mainly responsible for the puzzlement about himself. In an age where quite ordinary politicians have successfully assumed the mantle of statesmanhood, and thus become as carefully screened, prompted, coached, and shellacked with the sleek sheen of success as any Hollywood mannequin, Bond has somehow managed genuinely to stay just Bond. It is an act of faith in himself that no normally apprehensive politician of major aspiration could dare affect. Having no one but himself to do his editing for him, Bond is as contrarily contradictory as any other cussed human being—and therein lies his charm. But, more: another reason for the bafflement that Atlantans feel toward him is the fact that they are much, much too close. In pondering their mercurial Mr. Bond, a walking collage of mannerisms and moods, they miss the obvious fact that what they've got on their hands is something few people—and certainly few Georgia blacks—ever become: a genuine poster-size American folk hero.

The timing was simply perfect for Julian Bond to come along. If there had not been a Julian Bond to magnify on picture tubes and magazine covers, then whole detachments of writers would have contrived one. Americans needed a Super-negro. Bill Cosby in a cape. James Brown in boots and tights, masked, horsed, riding hard against injustice and inequity wherever they exist. If, in the heyday of American radio and movie serials, the audience had been black, there would have been a Captain Ebony, a Black Avenger, an Onyxman up there on the screen on Saturday afternoons. In fact, in the early 1960's, Julian Bond and the other young workers in the Student Non-Violent Coordinating Committee once admired a cartoon panel drawn for their private amusement by Claude Weaver, entitled "Super Snick." By day, Super Snick was a shuffling shambles of a janitor who cleaned up around the *Daily Scimitar* building—but when wrongdoers struck, he emerged as Super Snick, a mesomorphic caped black Galahad hustling off to the rescue.

And now America needed a real one. We all had wept—for a bearded French reporter found shot to death on the tear-gas-shrouded Ole Miss campus, for a slain President, for his brother, for a raffish daredevil trio named Schwerner, Chaney and Goodman found buried in an earthdam, for a basso preacher whose ringing voice still echoes in our minds evoking there a dim and fading memory of his dream, to vie with our living nightmares. Even the most callous had stirred and then, with mounting apprehension as Watts, Detroit, Newark, Washington exploded, had yearned for an answer and an end to the tragedy.

Who could tell us what that tragedy was, define the actuality of what had happened to these men and women, these cities, and to us? Was the tragedy the events, or was it instead that we really were weeping for ourselves, for a lost and illusory tranquillity that had in itself brought on these horrible events, things never again to be the same? Who—whom we could trust—knew?

Then Bond was heard, his soft voice, a man who seemingly could perceive the fact behind the illusion and lay it bare for us to behold. Part Negro, part Cherokee, part white, Bond appeared with, some of us hoped, what was the beginning of a start toward an answer.

Well . . . he didn't just appear. He was seized upon, dragged out, hauled up to the rostrum. Lyndon had picked up his chips and pulled out of the game. Bobby Kennedy got shot. Martin King was gone. Secret Service agents, for the first time, guarded all the candidates as they went through the now-dreary ceremony of campaigns and conventions. The parties met in armed camps, the one in Miami an embattled island festival, disturbed only fitfully by the rattle of nearby gunfire, the one in Chicago breached by an invasion of distraught children bent on bringing their elders to their senses.

It scared the hell out of people who were scared to begin with. This nation of people who relish novelizing, poeticizing, hymning, painting, sculpting on mountainsides, composing and shooting movies by the garbagecanful attesting to their belief that theirs is the land of the free and the home of the brave, was just plain scared to death. And, being scared, they were beginning to applaud the oppression they hoped would quell what they feared. The cops who groin-slugged kids in the streets of Chicago were toasted at cocktail parties in Port Washington, N.Y., as having given the little bastards what

they asked for; and the kids who wanted to assemble to petition their grievances were condemned by folks in Alexandria,
Va.—where are enshrined, in marble and bronze, the memories
of other young men who assembled on far bloodier battlefields
like Manassas and Gettysburg.

America had got itself turned around; there was a hunger
for somebody to come along and set it right. The U.S. turned
back to the good book in the meantime—not the Bible, but the
one written by squadrons of anonymous writers about the
days when men were hillbillies and proud of it; the country-
and-western singers moved back into the movies and onto
television and people said Strom Thurmond ran Washington
with a courtly hand almost quicker than the eye. The White
House came snickeringly to be known as Uncle Strom's
Cabin. In New York the Mayor took to reading Yeats' "The
Second Coming" over television. Hardly a more sinister clue
to the condition of the country is imaginable. "The best lack
all conviction, while the worst," he quoted Yeats, "are full of
passionate intensity. . . ."

Lacking conviction, a good many citizens chuckled at
Humphrey's anguish, and full of passionate intensity, others
set about festooning the car windows with flag decals and
cheered for men whose innocence was long gone. There was
George Wallace, and, watching Wallace with a cold and
measuring eye, adjusting his own ailerons to soar on those
shifting thermals of fear and hate, there was Richard Nixon.
Eugene McCarthy came to Chicago and learned that he was
not the one. Before that knowledge dawned, however, his
teeming retinue of youthful disciples filled the streets.

Julian Bond, too. But Bond came, it could be said, for other
causes as well: for the Georgia voters squashed for years under
the dead weight of the machine now headed by Maddox, and
for Georgia black men and black men everywhere, to show
that a black man did not have to be a showpiece, but that he
could slug it out in the bear-pit with the best of whites and

win. It could be said, too, that Bond came to oppose the war that, even if Americans did not understand it, was getting them killed by the thousands. And there was the dream that Bond came for, the dream shot in the head in Dallas, in California, in Memphis, on reservations, in the baking Harlem streets, in the gullies of Appalachia.

Mainly, though, Bond came because some people showed up on his front steps, talked him into going and hauled him off, and when he appeared, unheralded, at the convention, his effect upon a nation sick of charades by charlatans was electrifying. The convention should have been held on an aircraft carrier far at sea, but instead it was held in a barbed-wire camp under martial law. Somehow, though, the enemy had got through: Bond was there, and by sheer force of personality, he got them to stop and listen, got them to yield to his suasion and give his people their seats on the convention floor, and although the cameramen were stymied on the streets outside, the country watched as Julian Bond led his delegation down from the gallery to claim those chairs and listened as Bond easily explained his victory. McCarthy and his people might have lost but somehow one of them in the end had made it over the wall, and they could savor a small taste of triumph, nonetheless.

Pap Finn would have known all about how Bond's opponents felt. Long ago Twain had Pap say, "And to see the cool way of that nigger—why, he wouldn't 'a' give me the road if I hadn't shoved him out of the way. I says to the people, why ain't this nigger put up at auction and sold?"

Pap would have known all about Bond.

And Bond, knowing all about Pap, had been the victor.

II

BOND eyed my little carry-on suitcase admiringly and said, as we shook hands for the first time, in the lobby of Democratic National Headquarters, "You like to travel light, too."

We were standing on the sixth floor of the Watergate—now ironically a Republican stronghold, a luxurious apartment building wherein lived Spiro Agnew, John Mitchell and a host of other high administration officials. Julian Bond was there that morning in the fall of 1968 to discuss the forthcoming national elections and the role he might play in securing the election of Hubert Horatio Humphrey as the next president of the United States of America. With Bond was Ben Brown, his seat-mate in the Georgia House of Representatives, an old friend from the early days of the civil rights movement nearly a decade before.

The elevator plunged down from the carpeted lobby, adorned with portraits of Democratic greats past and present, to the main floor of the Watergate, where we decided to get some lunch before getting a cab out to National Airport and the short flight south to Atlanta. Bond, as I was to learn in the time I have spent with him, traveling and in Atlanta, is constantly being hailed by old friends real and imagined, and our drinks had hardly been ordered when a man approached our table to say hello. Say his name was Larry. He worked for Georgia Governor Lester Maddox. To my surprise, he and Bond and Brown seemed on the most cordial of terms; Larry wound up joining us for lunch and we soon were sitting there in the carpeted dining room like old Kiwanis buddies, talking easily about the frustrations of Washington, the perils of air travel and the upcoming national election. Like Bond himself, Larry was one of the new breed of Southerners, not the slightest bit ill at ease sitting there at the same table with two black men, a social integration that would have been unthinkable only a few years before anywhere in Washington or Atlanta— and which, in fact, would still be out of the question in some places not very far outside of Georgia's or the nation's capital city. Crisply tailored in a dark, hard-finish suit, neatly barbered, Larry could have been a young IBM executive. He exuded none of the evangelistic zeal one might expect of an aide to one of the South's leading bigots.

Bond told me later and many times afterward that he and the governor get along surprisingly well, that Maddox had, in fact, turned out to be a much better governor for the state of Georgia than his opponents had feared and than many of Maddox's own supporters had actually expected. He had, as governor, looked into prison conditions and had moved to place blacks on Georgia draft boards, something nobody could recall his ostensibly more liberal predecessors ever doing, and Georgia black people were aware of this and grateful. This sort of gallant acknowledgment, of course, did not deter Bond from cudgeling his old foe at every opportunity on other grounds as often as he could. The occasions are few when Bond mounts the podium to speak before an audience of liberals and blacks and fails to tell the audience his version of why it is that Lester Maddox was not able to join him on that particular evening. "The governor," Bond says archly, "wanted to be here, but there was a fire at the mansion." A slight gasp never fails to tremor through the audience, and Bond quickly adds, "Don't be alarmed; nobody was injured. The fire did, however, destroy the library . . . and both of the books were burned." The audience roars, and as the laughter subsides, Bond adds, gravely: "And the governor was particularly upset, because one of them hadn't even been colored in yet!"

And Julian Bond enjoyed as much as any other Atlantan the story that was circulating around the city of the nightclub comedian who interrupted his show one evening to inquire of his startled audience whether anyone there was from Georgia. When nearly everyone said he was, the comic said, "Well, don't be alarmed, but we've just got word that there's been some kind of emergency, and Governor Maddox has just been rushed to the hospital. We'll bring you further bulletins as they arrive." Later in the show, the comic again interrupted his routine to say, "The governor has just been taken to the operating room and everything is expected to proceed normally." Later he said, "Don't be alarmed, but the hospital now says things have reached a critical point: the governor has just had a rectum transplant and there is always the danger in a transplant operation of tissue rejection. In this case, there is some fear that his new rectum *may* reject Governor Maddox."

Anecdotal, crude, and coarsely funny, these stories are nonetheless told with a gentle fondness for the man who is, so to speak, their butt. These qualities are basic in the politics of the South, too, and although Julian Bond is a black interloper in that previously all-white field of endeavor, he has quickly picked up the hang of the game. Not only that, but Bond is loath to leave it, having developed, over the years that he has lived there, a deep and pervasive fondness for this area so traditionally hostile to people of his race.

We sat, jammed together in the back seat of the taxi as it raced down the George Washington Parkway toward National Airport, and Bond and Brown talked laughingly about the November campaign. "Wouldn't a Bond-Brown ticket look great?" Brown asked.

After our jet had climbed steeply to altitude and was hurtling southward across Virginia toward Georgia, I asked Bond if the drift of the civil rights effort over the past several years—from direct action such as his old organization, the Student Non-Violent Coordinating Committee, had engaged in so effectively throughout the South, to more legalistic attacks on discrimination—had brought him any problems of adjustment. "What it ought to be," he said, talking about SNCC, "is a *political* organization." He paused, and then said, "I used to think the problems of the South were peculiar to the South. And then I thought the problems were the same all over. Now, I think they *are* peculiar. In the South, where Negroes are voting for the first time, the opportunities are fantastic—to control school boards, city halls. Up North, the Democratic machine has got everything all sewed up; but there is no machine in Jackson, Mississippi."

We were making this trip shortly after Bond's triumph at the Chicago convention, and he was not then the veteran air traveler that the speaking invitations he received as a result of that victory caused him to become. As the pitch of the jet engines changed, or as the huge plane banked, Bond's knuckles whitened under his caramel skin from the force with which he gripped the arms of his seat. We ordered some drinks from the stewardess and Bond leafed through a copy of *Life*. The magazine had assigned me to write a profile of this Georgia politician who had attracted so much attention. At every advertisement, Bond and Brown noted the number of black faces shown in the photographs of happy beer-drinkers, auto-buyers, cigarette smokers—and then brusquely commented on how well the ad agency had or had not done in representing their race as consumers.

Thinking of Brown's joke in the taxi, I asked Bond what his long-run hopes were, and true to form, he answered me as any politician could be expected to: "I don't like to make long-range plans. I'm beginning to get a bit of mail from people saying, 'We'll vote for you in 1976,' but I don't even like to think about it.

"More and more, I have been looking at things two ways, the Georgia way and the national way. In the Georgia way, that convention was just wonderful, because it destroyed the unit rule, and the way Georgia picked delegates. In unseating the regular delegation and creating the new delegation, splitting seats between regulars and us, Governor Richard Hughes [chairman of the credentials committee] indicated that never again would delegates selected the Maddox way be seated."

But what about the national "way"? How did that look to him? Some insiders, like Frank Mankiewicz, who had long been close to Senator Robert Kennedy, and who, along with Pierre Salinger and many of the slain Senator's staff, had shifted over to work for Senator George McGovern, had left Chicago feeling that the Democratic Party had shaken itself apart there in Chicago. "No," Bond said. "You had two groups, in and out. The McGovern and McCarthy and Ted Kennedy people are new, and are going to stay in politics and stay in the party. They'll work from now until November for local candidates. I don't think the party has destroyed itself. It might have been a good thing if it had destroyed itself, but I don't think it has. I heard somebody say that people in Virginia think they're better than Wallace. But most Southerners think Wallace is their guy. *He's* their man."

Somewhere, I told Bond, I had read that he consciously aimed his every act at the betterment of the condition of the Negro in American life. Was that true? "No," he said, flashing his little smile. "I don't *try* to do it. If you're black, you just have to be conscious of your race. You're made conscious of it, every hour of every day, no matter who you are, where you live. And you have to ask yourself, 'What does it mean, racially? Is it good for us, racially?' That's what I try to do."

I asked Bond if he had any explanation for why the nation's

ghettos had, by comparison to their turmoil of several years before, largely quieted down, and he said, "I guess people realize it just hurt them. They've got four years of experience to draw on, now, since 1964, and I think it'll stay that way. Of course, we could land in Atlanta and find a big riot going on there."

We got off the airplane, however, to find the airport clear of civil disturbance. Bond was going to deliver a speech that evening in tiny Carrollton, an hour or so outside the city by car, and would not have time for dinner; we stopped at a sandwich counter in the airport to get something to eat. There and at the car rental desk on the concourse below, Bond was approached by several people who wanted to congratulate him on his victory at Chicago. He has several ways of handling this; the usual one is simply to smile and say thanks. Another is to deny that he is Julian Bond at all, and to insist that he is actor Sidney Poitier, thus reducing the flustered celebrity chaser to baffled confusion; and once in the airport at Newark, N.J., I saw him coolly autograph a copy of Eldridge Cleaver's book, *Soul on Ice*, for a pert stewardess who knew he was *somebody* famous but couldn't quite place the name. Bond is a shy man, and he does have an iron sense of his own privacy, as well as a whimsical sense of humor that compels him to indulge the people who buttonhole him to extend their salutations on what a credit to his race he is.

We got into our car and drove the short distance from the airport to the tiny house Bond was then living in on Euharlee Street in Atlanta's West Side Negro district, a one-story four-room place that was indistinguishable from the others around it. Out in front sat Bond's aging ruin of a car, inoperable because of some mysterious ailment. The house was locked, and after pounding on the door and front window and calling, "Alice! Alice!" Bond gave up and we sat in the car to await his wife's return. When at last she did arrive, driving his father's car, it was immediately clear that Alice Bond was mightily displeased about something. She got out of the car, left the front door of the sedan open, and marched past us without a word, straight to the front door, opening it and entering, a tiny, pretty woman, her jaw set and her mouth tight. Bond followed her, and returned about a half-hour later, looking like a chastised husband. His wife, as she told me later, has absolutely no use whatsoever for the life of a politician. On this particular occasion, Alice was made angry by her husband's weekend stay in New York, where he had been taping a television interview show, and his stopover in Washington, D.C.

It took us nearly an hour to drive from Atlanta to Carrollton, where Bond was to speak at the First Baptist Church. The tiny red brick church was crowded, with every pew occupied and some people standing at the rear and spilling out onto the front porch. Children were playing in the dusty red clay outside as the host introduced Bond, declaring, "He is 'Mr. Wonderful' throughout the nation."

"Mr. Wonderful" easily swung into his standard appraisal of the course of civil rights in recent years, saying in his low voice, unamplified in the little church, "We believed—we were very wrong—but we believed that if we could only integrate lunch counters, then we'd never have any problems at all. But we found out two things: the food wasn't that good and even though eating at integrated counters is nice, it is not the nicest thing in the world. It's very important, but it's not the most important thing. Then those buses . . . if only we could sit in the front of the bus, there would be no more problems. Finally the federal government decided it would enforce its own laws, and then we found that sitting in the front of buses was nice, but it was not the most important thing in the world. Then the right to register and vote. Now we are starting to vote in larger and larger numbers and we are starting to discover something that sounds too terrible to be true: we are discovering that the right to vote, by itself, is not the most important thing in the world."

To underline his point, when the uneasy laughter had ended,

Bond told a little story about one of the legislators who sits behind him in the state House of Representatives. "He told me," Bond said, "that he just couldn't make up his mind between Lester Maddox and Bo Callaway [Maddox's Republican opponent]," when the two were running against each other for the governorship of Georgia. "He said he went around to all the white people in his district and asked them, 'Should I vote for Lester Maddox or for Bo Callaway?' and it turned out that half of the people were for Maddox and half of them were for Bo. Finally, he came upon two farmers arguing with each other. One farmer said that Lester Maddox was a good man because he wants to keep the Negroes in their place. The other farmer said Bo was a good man because he wants to keep the Negroes in their place. The first farmer then said that they both are good men, but there is one difference between them: Lester Maddox is the best man. The other farmer asked what the difference was, and the first farmer said, 'Bo is a millionaire, and he thinks that anyone who makes less than fifteen thousand dollars a year is a Negro!' "

The mere right to vote, Bond told the people crowded into the church, is "meaningless if we don't also have the right to participate in politics." Citing the Mississippi Freedom Democratic Party and the early Black Panther Party begun by Stokely Carmichael in "Bloody" Lowndes County, Alabama, Bond said that "in different parts of the South, Negroes are getting involved in politics like they've never been before."

Bond felt he ought to say something about the local factionalism that he had been told by one of his hosts was dividing blacks in Carrollton, so he said, "None of us is going to get anywhere unless we all go together, and unless we start spending as much time fighting our problems as we spend fighting each other. We are chasing ourselves like a cat chasing his tail, arguing over leaders and who is an Uncle Tom and who is not."

Then Julian Bond told them a brief and pointed story, about a "friend of mine, who began to look at himself in a different light when he became twenty-one years of age. He went to Albany State College and he had never been anywhere else in his life but Albany. He graduated from college and his parents said he ought to get a chance to see the rest of the United States, to see the big city. They told him to take a bus to Atlanta, the plane to New York and to go around in New York and see the big buildings and the streets and the cars and the theater and then to come back.

"When the plane got over the airport, the stewardess announced the airport was crowded down below and the plane couldn't land. 'Ladies and gentlemen,' she said, 'we are going to circle New York for ten minutes and so you won't get bored, if you'll look out the windows, I'll point out the sights to you.'

"My friend," said Bond, "was excited. He didn't mind circling, because it would give him a chance to see New York City from the air. She pointed out the Brooklyn Bridge, and his heart beat fast. She pointed out the Empire State Building, and my friend felt his heart beat just a little bit faster, and his breath grow short, and he said, 'This is fantastic; this is beautiful; I've never seen anything so wonderful.'

"Then he saw a statue of a woman with a long robe on, reaching to her ankles; she had a crown on top of her head, some books in her right hand and a torch in her left hand, on an island. He called the stewardess over and asked what it was, and she looked at him for a long time and said, 'Well, I thought everybody knew what that is—that is the Statue of Liberty!'

"My friend said, 'I'm sorry; I've never been here before; I'm really sort of ignorant. I didn't know what it was. I hope you can explain it to me.'

"She said, 'The Statue of Liberty was put there so that people who come in from England, or France, or Germany see it and know they are in the land of the free and the home of the brave, the land of freedom and justice, democracy, equality, brotherhood and fair play.'

"My friend said, 'That is the most beautiful thing I've ever heard in my life, but isn't something wrong with it?' She looked over and said 'No.'

"He said, 'Don't you think they ought to put it on a turntable, so it would turn around, so those of us who are inside the country would know we are in the land of the brave?'

"The stewardess got angry, and the plane came in low, at three hundred miles per hour, and he read, 'Give me your tired, your poor, your huddled masses yearning to breathe free,' and my friend said:

" 'Baby, here we are!' "

Bond enjoys telling that story, has told and retold it many times, adjusting the timing and phrasing until it has become a regular part of his lecture-podium repertoire, and his presentation did not fail him that evening: it brought the laughter and applause he had come to expect of it. As it engulfed him, Bond kept his noncommittal expression, a serious, almost gloomy deadpan; only his flashing eyes, and the trace of a tiny cat smirk revealing the deep bitterness of his own that made him recount the tale once again.

Afterward, Bond and I drove to the home of one of the whites in the area who had attended his speech; not a few had done so, teachers at a nearby college for the most part and keenly interested in maintaining a good liaison with their black neighbors. The house, low and long, sat well back on a cropped lawn, hardly more than a dark silhouette in the gloomy Georgia night; several cars pulled into the driveway off the quiet road, and people got out, standing self-consciously around making conversation. Gradually we became aware of the sound of a truck engine, and then the crunch of tires on the gravel shoulder of the road as a pickup truck rolled to a tentative halt. Someone dove into the bushes by the carport, a man shouted for us to get down, and several of the people in the yard hurried into the house. A man got out of the truck, leaving the headlights on and the engine running, and as he neared the lights from the house, those few remaining in the yard called sheepish and relieved hellos to him. Another faculty member, unsure that he had the right house; his arrival revealed the trigger-tension when biracial groups met in rural Georgia in 1968. Bond had remained in the yard.

Inside, our hosts laughed nervously about the scare outside; somehow, pickup trucks connoted rifles slung across the rear windows or under the dashboards, stood as some symbol of the region's bloody past, and the response to that faculty member's unexpected arrival had been embarrassingly reflexive.

We were out in red-clay Georgia, but except for the false alarm the party otherwise could have been in New York. Drinks were passed around, and the folks pressed in close for a chance to talk with Julian Bond about the convention. Bond, tired from his air trip and the long ride out from Atlanta, gave his fundamental shyness and reticence full sway and he quickly retired into the dining room to attack an enormous plate of ham and olives and potato salad. After a quick drink or two, we left.

We drove fast on the way back to Atlanta, roaring down the winding two-lane blacktop at sixty-five, seventy, catching only murky glimpses of the nighttime countryside rushing past us. In an hour or so we were back in Atlanta, at the crisp and sparkling new Hyatt House hotel, where we met Vernon Merritt, the photographer working with me on the story for *Life* magazine. Merritt and Bond were old friends, and they talked easily, Merritt sprawled on a bed surrounded by his cameras and aluminum cases of equipment, Bond sitting in a straight chair, tipping it back against the wall, as they recalled the days of the Movement, and Julian pondered the future.

He was trying to decide, he said, what he wanted that future to be like. Tomorrow, though, he would take us to see the seat in the Georgia House of Representatives that he had fought so hard to win.

III

ONE way out of the nightmare they found themselves born into might have been bloody and implacable resistance. And, in places and at times, that was tried. But it never achieved the impermeable solidity or the momentum necessary for a rebellion to catch fire and sweep across the slaveland to victory or annihilation. A white man might ask why that never happened, why those people chose instead to endure oppression and ignominy without attempting that racial paroxysm that might have been expected and that was—has been—feared.

Part of the answer lies simply in the numbers, and in some atavistic urge toward survival, and in sheer human compassion, partly for they were not without blood kin among the enemy. And the answer lies, too, in simple hope.

So another way was found out of the nightmare, and it was education and the achievement of that traditional sanctuary of the oppressed, the neutral but relatively safe middle ground of the church. It was toward that area that Julian Bond's paternal grandfather, James Bond, chose to make his struggle. Like his mother, Jane, James Bond was born a slave—not a man at all but, by legal definition, a piece of property, a chattel like a wagon or a hoe. When, by the simple presidential action of redefinition, James Bond became a man and no longer a piece of property, he was barely two years old. But still black.

Again, that specification of color was only a mere matter of definition, because James Bond's father had been a white man, a farmer in the Kentucky Bluegrass region. The facts as Dr. Horace Mann Bond, who is James's son and Julian's father, recalls them are that his paternal grandmother, Jane, was born in 1833. Her owner was a Knox County, Kentucky, farmer named Ambrose Arthur. Arthur had emancipated his slaves, but it was Jane's singular misfortune to have been born in the year he died and his son did not share his father's particular sense of conscience. So, when the younger Arthur's daughter married, in 1848, a gentleman named Preston Bond, Jane was sent along to her new home as part of the dowry. She took her new mistress's surname as her own and passed it on to the two sons sired by her mistress's husband in rural and miscegenating dalliance. At the end of the Civil War, Mammy (as she was called by the children, who distinguished between her and the white lady of the household by calling the latter "Ma")—Horace Mann Bond's "Granny"—left the Bluegrass with her two sons and traveled back up into the Kentucky mountains.

Growing up there, James Bond came to realize that a powerful and undeniable urge to learn had been somehow sparked in his young heart. He made the audacious decision that he would attend college, at Berea. "He did it," Horace Mann Bond recalls, with pride and amazement at the accomplishment of his father, "off of nothing. My father went to Berea . . . he had a story of how he went there. He drove a calf seventy-five miles to Berea to sell to pay for his entrance fee, or he gave it to the school, and he said he lived mostly on oatmeal, molasses and cornbread. . . ." So Jim Bond got to Berea and eventually acquired his coveted degree, and went on from there to Oberlin and won another. He became a minister, and the life never got much easier than that first long, tough hike across the mountains, driving that calf to Berea. He was tough and outspoken; he insisted that his sons prove to him they they could swim by swimming—across the Cumberland River. He argued hard with the Kentucky governor to call out the National Guard when the threat of lynchings demanded force to put down angry mobs. He shocked his parishioners by installing a skating rink for the kids of his church in its basement, and he shocked them again by switching his political allegiance from the Republican party to the Democrats. And in his old age, he started having second thoughts about his religion, finally taking refuge, during long discussions with his son, Horace, in the laws of thermodynamics, tracing his belief in God back to the eternal existence of matter.

In the decades—and there have not been so many—since Jim Bond's hike across the mountains, travel in Kentucky and elsewhere in the United States has become a good deal easier, not only for white people, but for black people as well. Travel has become, in fact, a booming industry. As Americans turn themselves into a mobile nation of sight-seeing gawkers, an eager and endlessly innovative automotive and petroleum industry has busily kept pace. No effort has been spared to see that travelers are guided with ease and dispatch to fine restaurants, clean restrooms and comfortable motels. So solicitous is this industry of its customers' comfort, in fact, that by 1957 the tourism industries had even accommodated themselves to America's peculiar institutions of apartheid—which, unlike the rutted roads he traveled, had not changed much since Jim Bond's day.

To help traveling blacks, American know-how had produced a little volume known as the "green book," which listed, like some *Michelin macabre*, wayside establishments willing to accept black dollars for food and lodging.

So, by the "green book," three of Jim Bond's descendants—his son, Dr. Horace Mann Bond, and his two grandsons, Julian and Julian's younger brother, James—navigated their segregated way south from Lincoln University in Chester County, Pennsylvania, to Atlanta, Georgia. Mrs. Bond and their daughter, Jane, had gone on ahead. As his grandfather had been, Julian Bond in 1957 was on his way, full of fears, apprehensions and shivery excitement, to a new place to live, a new school and a whole new life.

The Bond family's decision to move to Atlanta was prompted by sudden misfortune. Dr. Bond, after twelve years as Lincoln's first black president, from 1945 to 1957, had lost his job in a tangle with the school's directors over falling enrollment and sagging finances. Himself a Lincoln alumnus, Dr. Bond had been in the center of controversy at the tiny school almost from his arrival. The predominantly white faculty bitterly resented having a "nigger" as their boss. Learning his children would have to attend a segregated public elementary school, Dr. Bond lodged a suit against the county school system and pressed it—despite some volleys fired from passing cars into his colonnaded front porch—until he won the suit. When, in 1947, some Lincoln students staged a sit-in protesting a nearby theater's Jim Crow seating policy, Dr. Bond had—to the consternation of his faculty—joined it. Horace Bond had tried hard—even becoming an active Republican in his efforts to woo subsidies from the rock-ribbed Republican legislators—but now he was on his way to a new job as dean of Atlanta University's School of Education.

For the elder Bonds, moving South meant going home; and for both them and their apprehensive children, it meant going to a place full of old horror stories. For the children it was an almost terrifyingly distasteful adventure—seventeen-year-old Julian was certain he would never stay in the South. One of Dr. Bond's earliest recollections was the nightmares he had of being pursued by the terrifying "Lynch Law" figure that stalked editorial pages in the Negro newspapers his father would bring home. And he recalled his father's rage when, out for a stroll one day, they were asked to leave a park that was for whites only. Lastingly bitter as those incidents had been for him, Horace Mann Bond had found, in school and his studies, a refuge of sorts within the segregated South, and if white men nevertheless ran the system, well, black men had found ways around them before and no doubt he could manage to get along down South again. Once, in 1940, when he had been president at Fort Valley College and Governor Gene Talmadge, running for reelection, was cutting close to his money supply—the Julius Rosenwald fund—by bellowing from the stump that these Yankee outsiders were leading the good Georgia darkies astray, Dr. Bond ambushed him. Inviting Talmadge down to Fort Valley for ceremonies dedicating a new model farmhouse (which had been erected with Rosenwald money), Dr. Bond staked out a photographer in a second story window to record the governor's presence at the Negro festivities. Dr. Bond was offered as much as $5000 for the pictures his photographer got that day, but never accepted. Old Gene continued his campaign, and left Fort Valley alone.

Such forebearance in the face of what must have been almost overwhelming temptation to lash back in kind at the obstructions posed by the white man was, in a real sense, merely an investment in survival. For Horace Mann Bond, the example had been set again and again by his father. Even when the Tennessee state legislature in 1901 was deliberating over the passage of harshly repressive antiblack measures, Jim Bond held himself in check; speaking before his congregation in Nashville's Howard Congregational Church, he declared, with the kind of wry irony that his grandson, Julian, was later to use so effectively: "It is indeed an anomaly that I should stand today in the glorious dawn of the Twentieth Century, with all its truth and privilege and its boasted Christian civilization, and in freedom-loving and chivalrous America, to plead for justice and fair play." Reverend Bond argued for moderation, for unstinting perseverance, and he wound up by telling his flock:

"In the recent emergency what ought the Negro to do? He ought to be a man. If he would be a man under favorable conditions, he ought to be a man now. If he cannot be a man now, he will not be one then. Play the part of a man, my brother, and the recognition of a man will come to you by and by."

And, Reverend Bond said, it was no good running away, though that might understandably have sounded sensible and attractive to many a harassed Negro in Nashville. "Again," urged Jim Bond, "he ought to stay with his people. I have recently heard several prominent colored men express their purpose, in view of legislation aimed at the Negro, to move North. That is wrong. I will stay here with my people. If I am crushed, I will go down in honorable battle with my face toward the foe. I will not run or desert my people."

The hope that generated strength and stamina had been plainly stated: play the part of a man and the recognition will come by and by. That was easy enough to say, but only under the mantle of the clerical cloth or in the haven of the university could a black man both say it and stand a large chance of getting away with it. It was not for nothing that James Bond wryly titled his autobiography *Life on the Margin*. By dint of the fact of the color of his skin, by dint of his quality of mind, he did in fact live on/in the margin between black and white, between the oppressor and the oppressed, and he chose deliberately to cast his own life and work with the black oppressed in the firm hope of effecting the salvation of both black and white.

The same belief in education dwelled in James's son, Horace Mann Bond, and propelled him along all his life, a life at once bound up with the political concerns of his race yet outside the politics they involved. Old Jim Bond had died in 1929, still hard at work on the hopeful project he felt certain was the greatest instrument for the betterment of blacks since the Emancipation Proclamation: his YMCA interracial commission. His son went to Lincoln University, went to the then-segregated University of Chicago, wrote two books, taught and administrated at a host of black schools, and stayed altogether clear of becoming a political activist. Horace Mann Bond was an educator, and even this move now, as he guided the car toward Atlanta in 1957, was aimed at continuing that Bond family tradition. By going to Atlanta to teach, he would assure his children of entrance to good colleges.

Horace Bond's mother, Jane, had always wanted him to be a professor and, precocious child that he was, that ambition soon became indistinguishable from his own. He tagged along behind his mother every morning as she set off to teach school to augment her preacher husband's income, and by the time he was nine years old, he had progressed all the way up to the ninth grade in school. An aunt who had gone to medical school taught him the taxonomy of the bones in the human body; he read voraciously, every book and magazine he could get— even those that gave him nightmares. Encounters with racists were few, but they cut deep into a sensitive and intelligent little boy's mind. Dr. Horace Mann Bond still remembers keenly the first time he heard the words "Nigger, nigger, nigger" hurled at him by a taunting playmate, and he recalls vividly the white cop who cantered into the black neighborhoods of Atlanta to stop the rock fights that broke out occasionally when roving gangs of white kids had to be repulsed. But by the time he was fourteen, Horace Bond had been graduated from high school and was safely away from all that, in a deliciously calm and shady world of books up north in Pennsylvania. "My mother," he says now, in his deep and raspy voice, "always wanted me to be a professor of history and I always, really, figured that was what I was going to be."

Horace Bond met Julia Washington while he was teaching at Fiske in 1928; she had signed up for his course thinking another professor was giving it, and promptly withdrew when she discovered Bond was the teacher instead. Deciding that he thought Miss Washington, the daughter of a Nashville schoolteacher, was "real pretty," he courted her despite that initial rebuff, and they were married on October 11, 1929. As it does for her husband, the South holds some grim memories for frail, soft-spoken Julia Bond. There was the time her mother and her grandmother took her off to a park for a picnic—and were followed by a white policeman. "We walked and walked and finally left," she recalls. She can remember going home and asking her mother what the word *nigger* meant after the white druggist had leaned over the counter and asked her, "What do you want, little nigger?" And there was the time she and her mother went out one afternoon to meet her brother on his way home from school—just in time to watch him come tearing down the street just a few yards ahead of a hooting gang of white boys. Growing up black meant growing up lonesome for Julia Washington; her father had bought a house in a white neighborhood, getting it cheap because it was next door to the only other Negro family in the area. She recalls families moving out almost as quickly as they moved in upon learning there were colored folks on the street. These are long-ago incidents, muffled by years passed, but still stinging enough to move Julian Bond's mother to tears. She recalls her surprised delight when, one day, the little white girl across the street came to ask her to play. Without asking her mother's permission, she followed the girl up an alley; then, when they were out of sight of the street, between the high alley fences, "She turned around and slapped me as hard as she could, and ran. It was so devastating, because then I realized what was in her mind. I was just about seven years old."

Moving north hadn't been a complete surcease from that kind of experience for the Bonds. The tiny community at Lincoln was tense and ugly toward the family because of the desegregation suit they had filed; it resented Dr. Bond's position of power at the university, and wasn't about to relax its strict color line because of it. To go swimming meant the Bonds had to drive to Delaware, and Mrs. Bond now can manage to laugh about the time they went to a pool there and young James looked around him and muttered to Julian, "Funny thing, you know: everybody here is colored, except me and you!" That night, as her mother told the story at the dinner table, Julian's sister, Jane, reacted with outrage. "But, Mother," she wailed, "what will happen to him if you don't tell him? You should explain to him! You shouldn't just let him go around like that, not knowing any better!"

Julia Bond can't remember specifically gathering her children around her and telling them about how things were in America, about what it meant to be black in a white society, or lecturing them about civil rights. She says, "It might happen that we would talk about it at the dinner table. It's so much a part of your life that you just don't isolate it—you just sort of live it." The tensions of life in Chester County, Pennsylvania, were so pervasive, she recalls, that on the campus where her husband was president, "there was a great concern with race. We were apt to say that was what white people talked about, but it was *all* that Negroes talked about when they got together. I can remember we would sit up for nights and that's all they would talk about—the racial incidents that had happened and what could be done. They would maybe speculate about how we could gain our freedom, whether we could kill off all the white people or poison them all. It was just sort of a catharsis; that's what you did whenever you got in a group. And we'd get to times when we'd just get awfully tired of it and wish there was something else we could talk about.

"We must have talked before our children just as a matter of course, without really thinking that we were doing it," she says. "But I don't remember counseling or advising them. I think most parents just try to reassure the children, and try to insulate them as much as you could from it until you felt they would be old enough or strong enough to stand up to it."

Segregation and animosity of the community notwithstanding, Mrs. Bond sees Lincoln in her memory as a wonderful place for a little boy like Julian, with stands of virgin timber dotting its gentle acres. Streams for wading were nearby, and the playing fields were right out in front of the house. "With little boys, you just gave them their breakfast and put them out the door and that was the end of it. Oh, it was just wonderful." It did, she admits now, have some drawbacks. There was leisure and time for thought, but there was also isolation, she now feels, "a not-too-healthy environment for children, in that it was not a good representation of the whole world. It was just such a tiny ingrown community with so few people that—when they came to Atlanta—I don't think they were quite prepared for such a competitive world as you find in a city." Like his father, Julian Bond started school early, when he was four or five. Before long he was astonishing Lincoln students with his precocious ability to read. His mother still prizes a poem he wrote around that time:

> You can pull it up
> You can pull it down
> You can pull it anywhere
> 'Cept to town.

When Julian was in the sixth grade, his mother remembers, the school tested its students, and Julian got the highest score. His teacher announced this fact to his classmates and, says Mrs. Bond, it "just about literally ruined him—he's never opened a book since." But, to his parents' delight, young Julian *did* do well enough in school to indicate he was headed in the direction they wished he would take, toward scholarship and professional study. So keen was the elder Bonds' hope that, when W. E. B. Du Bois had come to visit them at Fort Valley, Dr. Bond had prevailed upon his old friend to conduct a small and memorable ceremony. The distinguished leader, reputed to be a cold and austerely aloof man, solemnly inducted the four-year-old Julian into a life of scholarship, swearing him into Academe right there in the Bond living room. And, lest their children falter from that course, Horace and Julia Bond decided to pull them out of the Chester County School and send them off to private schools. Julian at twelve went to the Quaker-run George School near Philadelphia.

Goalie on the soccer team, star swimmer, member of the wrestling team, Bond is not remembered by his classmates at George School as any shakes of a scholar; it took him, in fact, five years rather than four to finish. His mother, anxious about how her son was taking the separation and his new life in the predominantly white school, looked closely for signs of unhappiness when she and Dr. Bond drove over from Lincoln to visit him. As they sat in the car waiting for him, Julian came walking up flanked by two white boys, his arms draped over their shoulders, and Mrs. Bond exclaimed to her husband: "Look, Horace! He has his arms around *them*—they don't have their arms around him." But, she felt, Julian didn't notice the difference and was comfortably at home.

Which, in fact, was not quite true. Julian had driven no steer before him when he went off to school as his grandfather had had to do, and, also unlike old Jim Bond, Julian while in school had no onerous chores like brush-clearing to make his life tiresome. But Julian had something, just a little biting, gnawing something, there to contend with that he had never in his life encountered before. Later, much later, he decided that it must have been racism. "You'd be sitting around a room, and some kid gets a package from home and there'd be some cakes in it," Bond recalls, "and he'd pass it around and miss somebody and that kid would say: 'What am I—a *nigger* or something?' . . . then he'd say, 'Oops! Bond's here!'" That stung; but still, it wasn't as bad as his cousin's experience at Harvard around the same time, when somebody burned a cross outside his dormitory room, upsetting him and the Bond family so deeply that they still talk about it. While the cake incident hurt Julian Bond, it didn't make him leave, nor did it turn him into a handkerchiefhead who walked softly lest he offend the white folks whose school it was. On the contrary, finding that, whenever he went into nearby Newtown to go see a movie, the cashier sold him a balcony ticket whether he asked for one or not, he took to insisting on an orchestra seat, driving a one-man teen-age wedge into the local apartheid; without incident he broke it successfully.

Newtown might not have cared much where he ate his cookies and his popcorn, balcony or downstairs, but it did mind mightily the fact that Julian Bond was going steady with a white girl. Bond and the girl, a Virginian in the class behind him, would often walk from school into Newtown, and the townsfolk objected. The school hesitated about taking action, but finally decided something had to be done, subtly but effectively.

George School students when Julian Bond was there, like many students in many schools, pestered their parents, and saved up allowances to get $35 together. An enormous sum for a high school kid, this money was then taken to the local sporting-goods store and exchanged for a warm-up jacket, but one with the school colors, and far more than merely keeping you warm (which it singularly didn't) it was a suit of mail, a costume. Collar flipped up, if it had one, bottom button rakishly unbuttoned, just the right amount of sag to the shoulders, drape to the chest, if worn regularly, the jacket acquired such élan that by the time one was a senior it fairly shouted "cool." Bond wore his jacket everywhere he went—even as he strolled into Newtown with his love. Until, that is, the George School dean summoned him in one day and told Bond the school would appreciate his thoughtfulness if he would leave his school jacket in the closet when he squired his girl friend into town. "That," Julian recalls, "was really a blow to me; that was like somebody just stopping you and slapping you in the face."

Bond mentioned this incident to a magazine reporter after he had been gone from the George School campus for several years, and the school's bitter denial of the published account both amused Bond and caused him to take a second look at something else that had puzzled him about the school: where he had lived on campus. For some of the time he was a George student, Bond lived not in the student dormitories, but in the homes of faculty members, a sought-after privilege that brought with it a good deal of freedom from adult supervision. Looking back, Bond decided that by all rights, the school had no business giving him those privileges: straight-A grades were a prerequisite and his grades had been below that. "I think they did that to get me out of the dorms," he exclaimed. "What a hotbed of racism that place is!"

For all that, Bond could look back on George School, as his father's car carried him closer to the South, as a place where by and large he had been happy, the kind of community he felt most comfortable in. "You know," he says now, "an extremely sheltered life, a little in-community, everybody knowing everybody else." Now not only were those years over, but college was right off the horizon, and the South. All that Julian Bond could remember firsthand about the South was the red clay of Fort Valley, a garish and unpleasant contrast to the cool greens of Pennsylvania. He was born a Southerner in Nashville, on January 14, 1940, but with all his young heart he did not want to return. All that Julian Bond really knew about the South was what he had read in the newspapers—and it scared him. "Oh, boy," he says now, "when I came down here to Atlanta, I thought whites would just stop me on the street and beat me up. I was seventeen. For instance, my mother wanted to take me down to the department store and buy me a suit—and I said, 'No! You go; you know my measurements, *you* go ahead!' I thought that race as a problem didn't exist in the North, but that it existed viciously here, much more viciously than it really does, and that it all tended largely to be physical." What Bond thought, he said, was that if he went to that store, some white person, any white person, just for the utter hell of it, would beat him.

Bond found instead that while the brutality he feared—and still does fear—was not as rampant as he had anxiously anticipated, not in Atlanta at least, racism was. Being black and living in the black community, however, he largely escaped encountering it. "Because," he says now, "we moved *here*, just a few blocks from where we live now, and it was a nice little community. I didn't know then that some people lived some place and some people lived . . ." Bond's voice trailed off as he recalled that arrival, leaving unfinished the painful thought that even a black family as distinguished as Horace Mann Bond's was constrained to live in Atlanta's black West End, while there were other families, perhaps less noted, but white, who lived anywhere they pleased and usually they were pleased to live in white neighborhoods. "We never went *any*-place when we came here, anyway. I used to go to the Fox theater and go up in the balcony to see movies, but I never went downtown for anything. I never had any reason to."

His mother has a slightly different perspective on her older son's rapid acclimatization to Atlanta: "I think one of the things Julian found was, there were so many pretty girls. And he'd never seen so many Negro girls before." Mrs. Bond recalls that before the family moved to Atlanta, her children "had never had a relationship with so many Negroes before. When they first came, of course, they said, 'We won't stay; we'll never live here; we'll leave as soon as we can.' But I don't think you could get them to go now. I like Atlanta. I wouldn't have missed it for anything. Our lives would have been very dull if we had stayed at Lincoln, and they have been very interesting and exciting here."

Part of the Atlanta University complex where Bond's father was to teach was venerable Morehouse College, and it was at Morehouse, rather than such costly, distant and glamorous schools as Swarthmore, Princeton, and Wesleyan, where his old George School buddies were going, that Julian Bond registered as a freshman student. With his prep school poise and polish, Bond found Morehouse anything but overwhelming. He finished his placement tests first and highest, he recalls, and thereupon allowed himself to slack off. He discovered, however, that Morehouse had more than a few latter-day Jim Bonds—and where they had all of his grandfather's old dawn-to-dusk zeal, he had inherited almost none. "What I found out very quickly was that while I had all of the verbal facility and the reading ability that most of my classmates didn't have, they *all* had a greater determination than I did. College was much more important to them than it was to me. Some of them came from rural Georgia, some of them had entered college from their junior years in high school, and they just had a tremendous amount of drive that I didn't have . . . not aimed toward academic things, anyway.

"So, while I was first in the class first week in freshman year, by the end of that year I imagine I was in the middle and probably stayed in the middle. It wasn't a question of being interested in something else and not being interested in college; it just wasn't that big a thing. I thought it would be enough to get through, to pass, to get a degree . . . and make a 'career choice.' "

While his parents, and his father especially, continued to assume that Julian Bond was going to wind up a scholar, Julian himself was thinking of becoming a writer. Worse yet, a poet. Classes at Morehouse occupied only part of his year; he bussed tables in restaurants for summer money, haggling with the waiters and the waitresses for his share of the tips, gorging huge milkshakes; one summer during college he lived in Cambridge, Massachusetts, with his cousin, the Harvard man, half-heartedly taking a chemistry course at Boston University and hanging around the funky Left-Bankish joints in Harvard Square, nursing the intellectual's Holy Communion—coffee and toasted English muffins—long into the gentle nights. Already, being a black boy in a white boy's school, being a Northerner born a Southerner and dragged back down below

the Mason-Dixon line, had made him feel as his grandfather
had come to feel, that he was living in some weird marginal
world. Atlanta whites didn't beat up black kids; they ignored
them, kept them so hermetically sealed behind the invisible
walls of nonrecognition that the blacks got so they felt that
way themselves. Lonely, a little scared, full of that wistful,
winsome, half-felt ineffable yearning that is adolescence white
or black, Bond found he *could* write poetry and, moved by
the dim resonances from the amphitheater near his home, or
by the threnodies of his own jazz records, he tried to put it
all down.

> I too, hear America singing
> But from where I stand
> I can only hear Little Richard
> and Fats Domino
> But sometimes
> I hear Ray Charles
> Drowning in his own tears
> Or Bird
> Relaxin' at Camarillo
> or Horace Silver, doodlin'
> Then I don't mind standing a little longer.

Julian Bond had started coming out of adolescence, through
all the near-parodic chicaneries American life inflicted on its
children in the '50's, and, precociously, he knew who he was
and where he was. His friends call Bond aloof, shy, reserved,
cool, but in fact he is not. Bond *is* viscerally aware, tuned to
nuance, resonating to the pitches, the vibrations around him,
like some human tuning fork. Ray Charles is one of his heroes,
and only with that kind of conscious separation could Bond
have written his poetic tribute to Charles, "The Bishop of
Atlanta."

> The Bishop seduces the world with his voice
> Sweat strangles mute eyes
> as insinuations gush out through a hydrant of sorrow

Dreams, a world never seen
moulded on Africa's anvil, tempered down home
documented in cries and wails
screaming to be ignored, crooning to be heard
throbbing from the gutter
on Saturday night
silver offering only, the right Reverend's back in town
don't it make you feel all right?

Still a young man, not much more than a boy, Bond's vanity
could compel him to listen with shy pleasure as a woman told
him at a party in Boston that he ought to be a movie star, to
glow as she called her Hollywood-agent friend on the Coast
to announce the discovery of another Belafonte (if only he
would consent to a little dental work), compel him to show
up at her place the next week for the appointed interview . . .
and compel him to wait, and wait, and wait, for six hours, until
he at last admitted to himself that he had been forgotten.
Yankeeland might have gulled him but he had the last word
on that, he had Yankeeland's number:

I know you Cambridge, beard-town of New England
I have sat all night in Hayes-Bickford's in Harvard Square
I have gamboled along the grassy slopes of the Charles-bank
and I have been refused service in the Paradise Bar.
When rain comes in on little hippo feet
mewling and wetting my body, I have sneezed in Cambridge
Damn . . . I have stolen books from you, Widener, and you, Lamont
You saw me with my little green bag, and smiled
I have ferried the river (by the Brattle Street bridge)
and ventured onto Beacon Hill, where I danced
with wild and woeful wenches from B.U. My hair grew long in
        Cambridge
(shave and a haircut—$2.50) and my belly thin
when I could not pilfer pastries pastily from Schrafft's and the
        Widener book-
guards wondered at my coat on summer days

Several roads diverge at Harvard Square; I took the one most
    traveled by.
I sojourned in P-town, that haven for misbeguided males, get ye
    back to Fire
Island. A Bard girl, thinking me sweet, comforted me. I asked her
    with my
eyes to ask again, yes, yes, ask again, yesyesyesyes I will have a
    Danish
I rescued her from a pimply Yalie. P-town, O'Neillian fools
    simpering on the
beach, like an ostrich, New England has its head in the sand.
    (heard in a Boston coffee-house)
SODOMY IS A SUMMER FESTIVAL
Sweet Cindy, who had never been south of New Haven, can you
    believe it?
See you later, educator, after a while, bibliophile
You can bet your sweet life you can and will ball in Cambridge.

Quite an accomplished young man was this womanizing
bookthief of a poet, poised, articulate and without a visible
scintilla of politics in his whole makeup. Bond during his
years as a student at Morehouse, from 1957 to 1961, was fairly
content to sit around the campus drugstore, exchanging pleas-
antries with the lovelies from Spelman College, Atlanta University's girls' school, and greeting his many friends as they
arrived. "None of us knew each other," says Charles Black,
one of Bond's friends from that time, looking back at the
Morehouse days. "We had our individual concerns and we had
engaged in some discussions about needing some change. At
the time, I was working for the college newspaper and we
were always writing little editorials about student apathy on
campus. This was really about the extent of the concern of the
students. We always had the discontents, I suppose, having
been basically reared in the South and having experienced all
the routine indignations, you know: bus problems, rest-room
problems, downtown lunch counter. It was just, I suppose, a
keg of dynamite waiting for a light on the fuse."

The old ferment at work since slavery's birth in old and young blacks was still there, mounting toward some yet-unknown flash point. When it came, for reasons that neither Julian Bond nor his friends were then aware of, their lives changed irrevocably. Why it did come then, why it had not been reached long before, they still don't know. There were, perhaps, instead of just one, many causes behind it. If World War I had thrust a generation of black soldiers back into a racist pressure cooker, then so did World War II. Postwar court decisions built steadily toward the landmark *Brown* v. *Board of Education* case in 1954, in which the highest court of the land asserted that separate education was not, could not be, equal education. The kids who were entering high school in the years immediately following that decision, the classes of '60 and '61, had discovered that things didn't have to be the way they always had been, and those kids then went off to college and adult life emphatically determined that things would not so remain. Their elders had sanctioned by their inaction a national apartheid and the "Silent Generation" of the fifties, although it did a lot of blasé talking, had acceded, too. But not this succeeding one; it had a determination to join in behind Martin King and walk it down, sing it down, work it down, into the dust. And that one thing, that determination, was something their parents, either cheering or declaiming, could in their secret hearts never really forgive them for, because they had to admit the kids were right, and that they themselves were now and henceforth exposed as the hypocrites they had been and that their children now knew them for. But now no matter; the advent of the 1960's meant an end —for a delirious brief while—to the bland inertia of the Eisenhower era and a hopeful beginning, led on by a strident and urgent voice calling for the nation to move again. "I suppose," Charles Black says, "the students were ready, and just needed some kind of motivation factor." There was a daring choice: to join the spirit of the times, to give, literally, one's body to some vague stirring that came to be called the "Movement," or to stand aside. Ironically, it was the kind of call that Americans had always taken unthinking pride in believing they traditionally answered, but answering this one didn't win anybody any confetti—no bunting, no medals for bravery. Least of all Julian Bond.

For Bond, the "motivation factor" appeared in his path, on his very doorstep—or not far from it—one day in the dead of winter, in the powerfully built form of Lonnie King, a self-assured and cocky young Navy veteran who had grown up in Atlanta's West End Negro section. During a hitch in the Navy, King had run head-on into white racism in ways that few of his classmates at Morehouse had ever encountered, and he had learned that victories over it could be won. King, who was no relation to the Reverend Martin Luther King, had come back to Atlanta fiercely determined to get an education, to get a law degree after college, and then to work at winning more and bigger victories over bigotry. As did the plans of the others in his particular generation, Lonnie King's schedule for action was suddenly moved up: some students in Greensboro had abruptly decided to say to hell with Jim Crow service at a restaurant counter and camped out on the counter stools. Nothing could have been simpler. People throughout the South and some Northerners had, of course, been acutely aware for generations of the segregationist customs that kept Negroes drinking out of different water fountains from whites, riding in the back of buses, using different rest rooms, and getting their food through the little sliding windows at the sides of diners. Oddly, however, the existence of this situation was not vividly realized elsewhere in the nation.

Even in the capital, Washington, D.C., Jim Crow ruled, and its pervasive effects went unchallenged. The citizens of Washington, bereft of any real political power, sublimated their normal electoral energies into pitiful imitation pressure groups, tiny neighborhood associations—with a crisp distinction between white and black groups. The whites called theirs *Citizens* Associations and the black outfits called theirs *Civic* Associations. In Washington, showcase of a nation parodying its founding charters, it was possible for the city fathers in the early 1960's to throw themselves a Brotherhood Luncheon—and have as the only nonwhites present the Filipino waiters.

What this situation needed was something galvanic, something to get headlines with, something so huge and undeniable that it would ignite the repressed outrage in every conscientious American who believed that pledge of allegiance he had recited from his very first day in first grade, and move him to bring unbearable pressure on the only men in the entire country who could *do* something about this charade of equality: the Congress. While only the people could, really, do something, they first had to come to feel they *should* do something, that they would not be scorned for letting black men sit down next to them, or in front of them, or even instead of them. And for that feeling to grow, it had to be legitimized by Congress assembled. The Greensboro students had taken a small, immensely potent, step toward obtaining that sanction.

The headline that Julian Bond was supposed to read, that day in early February of 1960, as Lonnie King thrust the newspaper toward him in the drugstore, announced the Greensboro sit-ins were entering their third day.

"Have you seen this?" King demanded.

"I read the papers," Bond replied.

"Don't you think that's *great?*" asked King. "Don't you think something like that ought to happen here?"

"I'm sure it will," replied Bond, still trying to hang onto his cool.

"Don't you think," King persisted, "that we ought to *make* it happen?"

Julian groaned to himself, "Why me?"—but he got up out of his seat and while Lonnie King covered one side of the store, Bond took the other, and together they urged everybody there to attend a noon meeting to start planning their own student demonstrations. That afternoon, the Atlanta Committee on Appeal for Human Rights, COAHR, was born on the Morehouse campus. Just as students up and down the eastern seaboard were coalescing, often under the auspices of the Congress of Racial Equality, an established civil rights group, to prepare their placards and to file into department stores and chain lunch counters, the Morehouse students, too, realized the power of the magic discovered at Greensboro and got ready to apply it themselves. First, upon the advice of the university president, Dr. Rufus Clement, Bond and his friends decided to take out a full-page advertisement in the Atlanta newspapers to announce their formation—and their progress. Julian Bond, who wrote most of it, can still recall the wording of the ad *verbatim*: "We, the students of the six affiliated institutions of the Atlanta University Center, Clark, Morehouse, Morris Brown, Spelman, Atlanta University and the Interdenominational Theological Center, have joined our hearts, minds and bodies in the cause of human rights. . . ." The advertisement, appearing during the first week of March, 1960, was harshly critical of the city of Atlanta, citing among other statistics revealing the effects of discrimination in the Georgia capital, that although Negroes constituted 35 percent of the city's population in 1960, they occupied just 16 percent of its residential land.

Atlanta was shocked at this affront to its image as a forward-looking city; the newspapers which had carried "An Appeal for Human Rights" dispatched reporters to find out what white Atlantans thought of the ad's claims. "They said," Bond recalls, " 'I didn't know the lunch counters were segregated— I just thought *they* liked to eat over there.' " Savoring the stir they had caused, Bond and his friends decided to carry their efforts further: they organized, King becoming executive secretary, Bond the group's publicity agent. Each of the Atlanta University schools had representatives on the committee, and churches near the campus were included, too. The results of the advertisement were pleasing—the governor said it sounded to him as though it had been written in Moscow and the mayor said he felt, on the contrary, that it was perfectly honorable—but just creating conversation was not enough. Now the young people of COAHR wanted results. Arming themselves with clipboards and yellow lined legal pads, Lonnie King and Bond reconnoitered the downtown lunch counters, counting seats—while the restaurant managers followed them, painfully aware of their intentions.

"But then we decided, because of the question of the legality of sit-ins, that we would put ourselves on absolutely safe ground," Bond recalls, "and only go to public places, government-owned places, the cafeteria in the state capitol, in the city hall, in the bus stations, in the train station, in the Federal Building. We had that first sit-in on March 15, 1960; I led the group into City Hall. That was the only time I've ever been arrested."

The civil rights movement was really a children's crusade; the Atlanta sit-in was launched, in fact, because Bond, King and the others were certain their elders and particularly their advisers on the university faculties were merely trying to divert them into talk and thus avert a dangerous clash. As Bond's mother recalls, "When the sit-ins started, there was great consternation, and most people like us were opposed to it. I knew that Julian had been going to meetings, but they didn't tell us anything. They didn't talk to us because they didn't trust us; they thought that we would tell the wrong people and that they would be stopped."

The atmosphere in black Atlanta on March 15 was electric and apprehensive, particularly in the Bond home. Young James was still in high school and his mother was afraid he might be hurt in the riot she feared would happen. Then came news over the radio that the sit-ins had taken place and that arrests had been made. The community mobilized to try to raise bail money. Cars rolled past the Bond house, she remembers, as "all the Negroes who thought they might help at all went down to the police station." That night, when Horace Bond returned home from a business trip to New York, his wife greeted him by bursting into tears and sobbing out the news: "Julian got arrested!"

To her enormous surprise, when they were released from jail, the kids seemed not chastened at all, but strangely, jubilantly happy, and even more surprising, some in the black community held an impromptu dinner toasting them, full of speeches and interviews explaining how they had planned the assault on Jim Crow. To a friend who asked her at the time how she felt now about having a son with a police record, Mrs. Bond said, "You know how it is with some white people who tell their children that they want them to be tolerant of Negroes and to like Negroes and when the child comes home married to a Negro they're just amazed? They say, 'Well, we didn't mean *that!*' And, we'd always told our children that we believed in democracy and that there shouldn't be any discrimination, but we didn't have any idea they were going to take it so literally, the way they did!"

IV

LOOKING back, the time, the end of the fifties and the beginning of the sixties, has the same kind of immediate, winsome familiarity as an old yearbook, full of events and people we recognize, whose names, perhaps, don't spring right to mind, but whose style we will never forget. Reporters out on the street got urgent pressroom phone calls from excited deskmen at the office, telling them of demonstrations, or they got hushed advance tips from new friends in the Movement. At the scenes of the demonstrations, at the appointed place and hour, they found tense cops, flustered store officials, empty floors in department stores, inquisitive bystanders waiting for something to happen. The groups had a sameness about them: mild, earnest young blacks and whites, a scattering of divinity students, the inevitable young women with loose hair and dirty white raincoats over their baggy skirts and saggy sweaters. They had an enviable certainty and clarity and terrible intensity about them there on the scene that the others milling about them somehow lacked. One shared their sympathies, perhaps, but one feared for them.

They had grabbed onto a vine that snaked through the foundation stones into the walls of American society. The lunch counters were just one part of it, one visible tendril of the whole root system they were tugging at: here in these Southern towns, there were no blacks in public office, no Negro cops, no Negro firemen, no blacks on school boards, no blacks teaching whites, no blacks on juries, no blacks on bar associations who might have censured courts that let off white men transgressing against blacks with only a mild chuckle and a warning; the chambers of commerce had no black men among them and had no one to stir their consciences.

Some of these kids had knowledge of the task they had taken on, knew enough to afford them a glimpse of what lay ahead, the inevitable clashes to come, knew what a long haul theirs was going to be. And what bravery would be required. Looking back, against, say, the events of Chicago, 1968, they now seem the very model of decorous protest compared to the wild and hysterical kids who battled the cops in the streets of convention-town. But then . . . then, they seemed abandoned guerrilla forces, these young ministers and their followers. On the very last spread of *Nothing Personal*, a book he did with James Baldwin, Richard Avedon has captured their spirit in a photograph, posed, of some of the Atlanta members of the Student Non-Violent Coordinating Committee. They seem almost luminous standing there, massed, placid but implacable, devoted, waiting. There in his shetland sweater beneath his tweed jacket, his button-down shirt open at the throat, gaunt and intense, is the group's press agent, Julian Bond.

The group he and Lonnie King helped start, the Committee on Appeal for Human Rights, responded to an invitation to come to Raleigh, North Carolina, in April of 1960 to talk about where the Movement would go next. In all, about three hundred students went, answering the call which had come from the Southern Christian Leadership Conference, the Reverend Martin Luther King's group. There in Raleigh, the students from Atlanta joined with others from all over the Eastern seaboard to form the Student Non-Violent Coordinating Committee, SNCC—which its members and its jeering opponents alike came to call "Snick." Just as these kids themselves were something new and different on the American scene, they needed a new outfit, a new acronymic name to hold out in front; the others seemed old and tired. The National Association for the Advancement of Colored People just didn't do it; the middle-aged men and women who ran the NAACP chapters too often seemed content to sit there in their little store-front offices, softly explaining why nothing could yet be done. The Urban League was up north somewhere. The Congress of Racial Equality, CORE, was tougher, more active, but still it belonged to somebody else, as did SCLC. SNCC belonged to the kids themselves.

Perhaps because it was located in an urban center with an attitude of relative tolerance and because it could draw manpower from the universities like Morehouse and Clark, the Atlanta group became one of the best-organized, best-financed and most stable of the loosely knit units making up the Movement. At one time, Bond recalls, "We had nearly $6000 in the bank, and we had almost 4000 people picketing in downtown Atlanta, a masterpiece of precision. Oh, man," he says, "we had waterproof picket signs and football parkas for the girls to wear to keep the spitballs off. Martin Luther King got arrested with us one time—and the lunch counters were integrated."

The Committee on Appeal for Human Rights gradually lost its separate identity and blended into the larger group, SNCC. It mounted demonstrations, mostly picketing, which eventually led to a near-total boycott by Atlanta blacks of the city's downtown businesses until a *detente* was worked out with businessmen. As a result, one by one the barriers excluding blacks from restaurants, theaters and other establishments began to fall. At the same time, Bond and his fellow SNCC workers carried on voter-registration campaigns; during the summer of 1960 alone they claimed to have signed up nearly

10,000 new black voters. But beyond the formal victory over apartheid and the statistics, the real victory was not the one scored over the white community's policies of segregation, but the one accomplished within the black community. "I think the big success," says Charles Black, whose friends took to calling him "Sit-Down" for his service on the front line, "was not the tangible things, but the whole change in attitude of the black community toward accepting the kinds of things they had experienced all their lives."

Bond's role in effecting this change was at once inconspicuous but extremely valuable. As a public relations man, he was of necessity in the background, in the office—and by nature he shrank from exposing himself on the picket line. Because the efforts of the Movement were primarily aimed not at isolated victories, but at getting newspaper headlines, at galvanizing what latent support there was dormant in the larger community, Bond's job as interpreter of the purposes of the group was crucially important to its success. The old fear of violence, moreover, was still too strong within Bond to permit him to perform on the picket line with ease; he literally broke into hives whenever he tried. "I always viewed Julian as being a bit fearful of becoming too directly involved," recalls Charles Black. "We had a little joke about Julian—we were on a picket line on the West End section of Atlanta once, and he had to go back into the office because he broke out in hives. He explained that then as being a reaction to the sun, and I never knew until several years later, when I was down at the state capitol—the time his case was being argued on the floor there and he broke out in hives and I had to carry him home for some pills, and he revealed it for the first time—that it was his *nerves*. Julian would break out all over; I know his face would be covered with 'em, little red bumps."

Bond the would-be poet became Bond the newspaperman when Atlanta's major Negro paper, the *Daily World*, began to attack the Appeal for Human Rights group as ill-advised in their demonstrations. To provide themselves with a voice of their own, the students and some of their faculty supporters launched the Atlanta *Inquirer*. Thinking it could become a useful political tool in molding the opinions of the city's fragmented Negro community, Bond went to work for it. He had written his poetry, he says, "because there was just something in me that had to come out. I just wanted to. I thought I had a little message there. It wasn't for the world, just a poetical way of saying things." Bond became equally serious about journalism, not in the way so many college editors do, foreseeing careers that leapfrog from their campus papers to national magazines and then beyond toward pundithood, but, he now recalls, rather as a way of genuinely serving the black community. Instead of aiming toward the mainstream of journalism—which means trying to break into white newsrooms—Bond says he stuck with the *Inquirer* because "I enjoyed much more working on this small paper because I was much more in control. In fact, I was writing two or three different columns and making up the paper, too."

More or less simultaneously, Bond was working on his COAHR projects, making certain the office was clean, sending out press releases, cajoling students into showing up for scheduled demonstrations, and at the same time charging around Atlanta covering stories for the *Inquirer*, too. Investigating harassment of blacks who had tried moving into white neighborhoods and checking out rumors of a school bombing were some typical assignments. Once, Bond and fellow *Inquirer* newsman John Gibson investigated the fatal shooting of a Negro by an Atlanta bondsman, who had claimed self-defense, stating the man he shot had advanced upon him with a knife. Bond and Gibson went to the funeral parlor, and, Bond recalls, "John, with a tremendous stroke of brilliance, turned the dead man's body over and said, 'There's the bullet hole, see!'" But the discovery that the dead man had been shot in the back led to the bondsman's indictment for murder.

In addition to working on the street as a reporter, Bond took time to ghostwrite Lonnie King's "Let Freedom Ring" column for the *Inquirer*, a sports column and advice to the lovelorn.

Bond was himself lovelorn. In spite of college work, the paper and COAHR, he had met Alice Clopton, the shy daughter of a chef at Columbia Theological Center in nearby Decatur, Georgia. A student at Spelman, pretty Alice planned to become a fashion designer upon her graduation. They met at the same corner drugstore where Lonnie King had shown Bond the newspaper announcing the success of the Greensboro sit-ins, and Julian recalls his first meeting with Alice as a casual encounter. Alice, on the contrary, remembers that she learned of Julian's fondness for her long before he managed to overcome his shyness enough to introduce himself. Before long, when Julian worked on the lyrics for a student benefit production called *Sit-In Showdown* to raise money for the Movement, Alice tried out for a part. When Julian worked at the *Inquirer* office, Alice was there, too, taking phone calls and helping out, long into the nights.

When he was finished with his work on the paper, and had seen Alice home, Bond would head for the bars along Hunter Street, the main drag through Atlanta's ghetto, where he would sit up and talk the rest of the morning away, before going home himself. M. Carl Holman, then a faculty member at Clark and an editor on the *Inquirer* and now a Washington official of the Urban Coalition, recalls that this hectic pace soon took its inevitable toll on Bond's academic life. "In the morning," Holman discovered by making some discreet inquiries, "he'd get up and go over to the Morehouse campus and go over to one of the rooms and go to sleep. The result was, by the time we found out about it, Julian was punching out." Bond's plan to quit school shocked Holman and his colleagues, who felt not only an obligation to Bond but to his mother and father to see that he stayed on course. "I felt that

Julian had such gifts that he should really get the degree, whether he needed it or not," Holman says, adding, "I must say I haven't found the lack of that degree has hampered him very much."

Julian Bond was trying to decide whether to take that gamble, to forego getting his degree and instead work full time at civil rights and the newspaper business—and also to get married. On July 28, 1961, he and Alice Clopton made their third trip to nearby Dallas, Georgia, to have the ceremony performed. They chose that town because by being married there, the event would not be covered by the Atlanta *Daily World*—and thus, they hoped, their parents would not learn of it. On their first trip to Dallas, they had forgotten to get their blood test; on the second, they forgot to bring proofs of their ages; but on the third, three months after their first try, they made it, returning to Atlanta and the student movement office as man and wife. "Where have you been?" their friends asked; when Bond announced what they had just done, he recalls, his fellow activists responded with wordless sputterings. "And I said, 'I'll see you, Alice—I'm going home.'" The newlyweds lived apart for the next six months, reasoning that if they lived together they would have to give up their parents' support. When they did acknowledge their wedding, they moved into a room in Bond's parents' house.

Meanwhile, the Student Non-Violent Coordinating Committee was picking up momentum, working now out of a makeshift headquarters in Atlanta; James Forman, a veteran civil rights activist who had joined to become SNCC's headquarters director, flipped through his files and found Bond's name. Bond recalls Forman growling over the phone, "It says in here that you are a public relations man. Come down and publicly relate." Bond's reaction was an immediate acceptance.

"I knew," he recalls, "that I had a chance to grow with the firm. Snick was really exciting because, first, the work was interesting and secondly, it was all people your own age running the show—except Forman, who was lying about his age. So I went over there to organize it; in fact, I started going over there rather than going to school. After a little while, it got so good to me, as they say, I just left school."

This decision, radical departure that it was from the direction his whole life had previously taken, came as a tremendous shock to his parents. His father still only barely manages to conceal his distaste for his son's departure from Academe. "Well, he just did it," says the elder Bond of his son's move. "I told him I was agin' it, but it had no effect. He never talked to *me* about Snick. I asked him once, 'What are you folks up to?' But they were really very secretive, you know. He said to me, 'You look like one of those Uncle Toms that's going to tell the white folks,' and that was it. . . . He was kidding."

Dr. Bond's dismay was shared by his wife, who says, "We were very disappointed; we wanted him to go on with school; we just felt that he had thrown his life away. We just despaired of any future for him at all, which is really very strange now, isn't it? If he *had* stayed in school and had done as we counseled him to do, his life would have been very routine."

Nonetheless, with a mother's intuitive understanding of her son, she thinks she knows why Julian was compelled to go to work for SNCC. "Once he got into it, it was the drama of it and the cops and robbers part of it that he really loved. I think it was like the games that he played as a child. There were always the goodies and the baddies; they were always outwitting somebody. I'm sure that appealed to him. I'm sure he had deeper values, too, but that was something that he loved."

There was, however, almost less derring-do required of Julian Bond in his chores at SNCC than there had been at COAHR. The organization had no mimeograph machine of its own, and in order to get his press releases out, Bond three times each week went to the stationery supply store, bought his mimeograph paper—in different colors so that busy newspaper deskmen could readily distinguish one story from another—then walked the five blocks to the National Students Association office and ran off the stencils which he had typed and corrected himself. He would clean the machine, get the porter to let him out, walk back to SNCC headquarters, fold the releases by hand ("until I convinced Forman that for five dollars a month he could rent a little folding machine"), stuff them into their envelopes, lick the envelopes, and then, "on my way home at night, *if* I had my father's car, take them by the post office and mail them."

Bond also edited the SNCC newspaper, the *Student Voice*, and produced occasional topical pamphlets. The one he is proudest of, a leaflet titled *Southern Students Face Danger— For You*, detailed assaults on SNCC workers in Mississippi, where during some few months of 1961 no fewer than twenty-one incidents of harassment or worse had taken place. "It was a beautiful piece, swell layout," Bond says. "To this day, Forman pretends he wrote it. But *I* wrote it.

"I spent *all* my time down there, from early morning to late at night. I finally asked Forman why couldn't he give me a little bread. My wife was pregnant; I was living with my folks and it was very uncomfortable. He started paying me $40 a week. *He* was making $60; he was married, too. He said they had a rule that all married people made $60. I said, 'Why am *I* not getting $60?' and he said, 'Ahhh; man, *you* live with your parents—you don't *need* it!' Forman was like that."

Bond came to be trusted by reporters as a reliable and intelligent spokesman for a group which, because it was so far-ranging and fragmented, was not always easy to figure out. And he came to be admired by his fellow civil rights workers as a soft-spoken, shrewd young man who steered clear of the strident factionalism that always threatened to shake the organization apart from within. He worked hard at mastering the fine art of flackery, learning how to reach upward along the editorial chain of command to insure coverage if, for example, a SNCC worker was beaten and there was a likelihood the local press would overlook the story.

Gifted as he is at handling words, however, Julian Bond cannot *really* invest the job of being a flack with supercharged drama. He liked the gadgetry that helped make his work easier. "We had two wide-area telephone system lines, one going all over the country, and one going around the South, and I had a tape recorder hooked into the phone and I'd call people up and make recordings. Then my brother, James, would get up at four o'clock in the morning and feed about forty radio stations: 'This is James Bond at SNCC and I've got an actuality for you,'" says Bond, imitating his brother imitating an announcer's authoritative voice.

And, despite his apprehensions about the redneck's propensity for violence, he relished taking occasional swings through the field to see what SNCC workers were accomplishing first-hand. "We went all over the South, whipping down those roads," Bond says, with deep admiration for the young men and women who did that day in and day out, far from their homes and without any real hope of getting sympathetic help should they ever need it. "In 1964, Snick bought twenty Plymouth Savoys and we drilled holes in the backs, put in aerials and stuck in two-way radios. 'This is Zero-one, calling Zero-two; I'm fifty miles from Sunflower and I'm coming in . . .' VARROOM! There were midnight chases, with the cops behind you; we had one guy with a race-driver mentality and he'd get the police behind him and then slam on the brakes and make a moonshiner's turn with his lights out and the police'd be there wondering 'Where is he, where is he?'

"One night, Bob Moses, Jimmy Travis and Randolph Blackwell were leaving Greenwood, Mississippi, and this car pulled up alongside them and actually machined-gunned them, a line of bullet-holes from front to back. Travis, the driver, was shot through the neck." On another occasion, Bond, his wife,

Alice, and his brother, James, were driving to a meeting in a tiny red foreign car and were chased for miles by some local toughs in the same kind of car—who spotted them at a gas station and threatened to kill them—simply because they were niggers with the temerity to be driving the same make of car white folks used.

"The stuff I did," Bond says now about his work with SNCC, "didn't take too much courage, but some of those other guys had *so* much guts."

It did take a kind of courage for a basically shy young man, which Bond was, to stand up in the glare of a press conference and fence with reporters, not all of whom by any means were sympathetic to his cause, or to talk back to the President of the United States. This Bond did when President Kennedy, sending civil rights legislation to the Congress, in June of 1960, urged the Movement to cool down to ease its passage. Said JFK: "Unruly tactics or pressures will not help, and may hinder the effective consideration of these measures."

Speaking for the members of SNCC, many of whom felt that unruly tactics were precisely what would help, Bond fired back, "We cannot, in good conscience, ask American citizens who have been denied their rights for three hundred years to refrain from voicing their demands in any way they choose. We believe the continuation of protests will not hinder the passage of civil rights legislation, but will, in fact, serve to point out the pressing need for it."

The very fact of his light skin made being a militant Negro activist sometimes difficult for Bond; he even had to work hard at being denied service in some segregated establishments. "I remember one time my wife and I went to a movie and some guy asked me what my nationality was," he recalls. Bond told the man that he was an American, and his questioner persisted, demanding to know what his "nationality" was. "I'm American, God damn it," Bond declared, and the reply was, "Hell you are." Bond said, "You mean you want to know what my race is?" The man said, "Yeah," and finally Bond said, "I'm Negro."

"Segregated drive-in movies, can you beat that?" Bond asks, still marveling at the limitless inventiveness of the racist mind.

On another occasion, after comedian Dick Gregory's wife had purchased twenty dollars' worth of stock in a restaurant chain, Julian, his brother, James, and Gregory drove around Atlanta, checking on their investment. "Can't throw me out," Bond would say, "I'm an owner!" But they were thrown out anyway—after Julian produced an I.D. card to convince one hesitant counter manager that he was, in fact, Negro. "Gregory at this time was in his cool period," Bond says, "and he had this beautiful coat, unlike anything I'd ever seen before. It was a coat in which you took off the coat, but the sleeves stayed on . . . the vest was the sleeves. It was a beautiful coat, tight pants, leather overcoat, *green leather* overcoat, must have cost three or four hundred dollars, or so I thought. And this car stopped some place and he had to push the guy out of the way. And the guy tipped Gregory a dime! And he said, 'Thanks a lot!' "

Bond's decision to work at headquarters and his belief in nonviolence, which stemmed in part from his years at the Quaker-run George School, were respected. Although SNCC was shifting steadily toward becoming a black-dominated group, and at the same time losing somewhat at its fringes its commitment to the theme of nonviolence as a means to its goals, there remained within the group a tolerance for a broad variety of beliefs. One of those in SNCC who had chosen a role different from Bond's was John Lewis, a young minister who became SNCC's leader and who was arrested some forty times and savagely beaten four times, getting his skull fractured at Selma and his forehead gashed on the Freedom Rides. "In Snick," Lewis says, "there was the philosophy that each man had to define for himself the role that he would play; and it is to the credit of Julian to have the courage and willingness to remain in Atlanta for a long time in the background of the whole operation, because so many of us in those days were so excited about going out in the field."

Although the members of SNCC felt, in the early days at least, as Lewis puts it, "that Snick and the civil rights movement had the only real integration in the country," and were proud of that fact, antipathy toward whites began to develop on the part of the black rights workers, for some practical reasons as well as common, garden-variety racist reasons. During 1964 and 1965, Lewis recalls, "More and more blacks in Snick, including myself, took the position that the black movement, and Snick in particular, had to be black-controlled, black-led, and black-dominated." At the time, this did not mean, Lewis says, that whites had to get out, but that they did have to move into the back seat and recognize the need of black leadership. The young Turks had come to feel old-line Negro groups like the NAACP and the Urban League were too bound up with white people, too close to their white money supply to have the necessary maneuverability—especially on the ballooning question of the war in Viet Nam.

Young, free and tough, they had come together to *work* together, but in trying to do that, they unwittingly set in motion some powerful internecine forces that would end in the dissolution of SNCC. "When we began," Bond tells his high school audiences nowadays, "we were of the opinion that the only good people were young people, that the only decent thinking, the only progressive thinking, came from young people like ourselves, that the only force for good was young people like ourselves. We thought that anybody over twenty-five was no good at all—that if they were black, they were Uncle Toms, and that, if they were white, they were too conservative to discuss things with. In retrospect," Bond says, "this was good, because it made us an exclusive group, and it caused other young people from other parts of the country to come join us in our work."

United only by their youth and their shared conviction that something had to be done about the conditions and beliefs they so abhorred, it was only natural that the zealots of SNCC would discover the problems of working together were nearly as difficult to unravel as the ones they were assaulting. Huddled together against terrific pressures from the outside—outright hatred from most of the white community and balky suspicion from the black people they were trying to mobilize —the organization began to tremble with rankling tensions. Bond recalls the kinds of pulling and hauling that arose over the massive campaign planned for Mississippi during the summer of 1964:

"The native Southerners, particularly the native Mississippians on the Snick staff, were really concerned that what was going to happen was a lot of bloodletting—and that the bloodletting was going to be aimed at *black* Mississippians, not at those white kids. The closer the time got, the more apprehensive they became and they really wanted to call the whole thing off. Bob Moses, who was the real spiritual leader of Snick, insisted that it had to be done, even if it meant the loss of life, that this would break the back of Mississippi. And he was right—I think it did, it really opened the state up. But these guys were really nervous. They said, 'At the end of the summer, *they* are going to leave, and *we* are still gonna be there. All during the summer, there's gonna be shooting and killing and murder—and it'll be us who's getting killed, and not only us, but local people, non-civil rights people.' "

Bond recalls this dispute over tactics and timing as the first real split in SNCC over whether whites ought to be allowed full participation. "It was resentment based on very pragmatic terms: it caused danger. Then, all during that summer," he says, "a different kind of resentment developed. I mean, you got these girls from Radcliffe, Wellesley, Berkeley, coming down, very articulate, and boys, too, and they'd come into a situation and take it over—not always because they were patronizing, but sometimes simply because they were more skilled. You'd see a Negro girl just learning how to type, who grew up in Greenwood, Mississippi, went to high school there, is just learning how to type on the office typewriter and some chick from Vassar says, 'Here, let me do that—I can do it faster.' And she *does* it, and so this girl says, 'Well, *hell*, I'll never learn how to type if this chick is going to come down here, and by the end of the summer, *she*'ll whip back up to Vassar and I'll still be here, huntin' and peckin'.'"

"So that began to develop and then you'd get these guys, who were much more articulate, who could express themselves better, were just better-educated people, who came from a different culture. And a lot of *that* kind of resentment came. Then," said Bond, "the final thing happened." To the mortification of the black SNCC workers, their white comrades could sometimes get quick results—with certain black people—where they, themselves, had tried and failed. "This had been evident in Snick for a long time. A black civil rights worker would come up to an elderly Negro man, and say, 'We want you to go down and register to vote, sir.' And he'd say, 'Well, no, I don't think I can; I can't do it; you come back and see me next week.' But, you get a young white kid to come up and say, 'Mister Smith, we want you to go register and vote,' and he'd say, 'Oh, yessuh, Cap'n, yessuh, yessuh, be right *down* there,' and it really became people doing the right thing for the wrong reason all over again."

Bond sees these as relatively minor irritants, tiny wedges driven between the white and black members of SNCC, compared to the jagged rift that was left in the organization after the Democratic Convention of 1964. The newly formed Mississippi Freedom Democratic Party, MFDP, in a move not only similar to Bond's own successful effort in Chicago four years afterward, but which helped pave the way for Bond's victory there, had chosen its own slate of delegates and presented itself to the party's credentials committee for seating.

Their claim was that Mississippi's regular delegation did not truly represent all the Democratic votes of Mississippi, and certainly not the state's black Democrats. To prevail at Atlantic City, the Freedom Democratic Party had to persuade eleven members of the credentials committee to sign a minority report supporting their case, thus bringing it out before the convention at large. Understandably enough, such an unseemly public display of strife was the last thing that President Lyndon B. Johnson and his convention managers wanted to see happen in front of the network cameras.

However, so many of the credentials committee members did lean toward the Freedom Democratic Party that Johnson, threatened with an ugly and embarrassing floor fight, pushed the muscle button. One credentials committeeman got a phone call from a high Pentagon official, who spoke softly about the possible loss of a job; another delegate heard California Governor Pat Brown murmur about a judgeship that wouldn't be going her husband's way if she persisted in supporting the Mississippi renegades; Mayor Robert F. Wagner of New York persuaded his Negro secretary to see things his way and withdraw her support from the MFDP. The White House even leaned hard, but unsuccessfully, on Washington lawyer Joe Rauh, veteran liberal and the MFDP's counsel. Finally, when their committee support had been eroded perilously close to the minimum of eleven members, the MFDP people learned the Administration was going to offer them a compromise: two seats at large. That was, Rauh recalls, "like a Russian torture chamber; they get you scared and then offer you a cigarette." The Mississippi Freedom Democratic Party representatives decided to reject the offer, despite warnings that if they failed to accept the compromise Humphrey might lose his chance for the Vice-Presidency.

"That fantastic compromise . . . wasn't a compromise," Bond states with disgust, "it was a sell-out—and for a lot of people that was just the last straw. Political liberals in the party that Snick had always counted on for support, under that kind of pressure, just couldn't stand up to it. They wilted away, and that was the last straw. People said, 'Well, we're not going to get it in politics; you can't count on white people; they'll fink out at the last minute,' and that was it."

Later that same year, Bond, along with John Lewis, Bob Moses, and some others accepted Harry Belafonte's invitation to travel to Africa at his expense. The eerie experience of visiting his racial homeland, cut off from it as he was by generations of time and the severing impact of slavery, had a lingering impact on Bond. "It was really," Bond recalls, "kind of an emotional experience to go to Africa. You say, 'I could have come from here, for all I know, Ghana, Guinea,' and the tragedy is, you will never know, never have any idea." Seeing the events of Atlantic City, so fresh yet in their own minds, as the Africans were seeing them, depicted in window displays of the American information offices, shocked the young activists. "There were all these pictures of Negroes doing things," Bond says with heavy irony; "Negro judges, Negro policemen, and if you didn't know anything about America, like Africans would not, you would think these were really commonplace things. That's the worst kind of deceit."

Returning to Atlanta, Bond went back to his work at SNCC, now and then inserting the phrase, "While I was in Africa . . ." into his conversations with cosmopolitan ease. His family was growing: he and Alice now had two children, Phyllis and young Horace Mann, and his SNCC salary was stretching thin. He had quit the *Inquirer*, the loser in a heated dispute with the paper's management over his sometimes flamboyant layouts and angry because he had not won a promotion from managing editor to editor as he had hoped. SNCC work was his only full-time occupation now, and SNCC work was becoming harder and more complicated almost every day. Oddly, in spite of the disillusionment of Atlantic City, SNCC's own momentum was carrying it, for better or worse, into politics.

Canvassing back roads of the South, trying to draw out the frightened electorate from their tarpaper shacks by their own osmotic example of determined bravery, battering the conscience of the nation, trying to taunt it into enforcing the tenets of its own laws, no longer seemed enough. The Movement for all its drama of confrontation and encounter had been merely an effort to come from minus-something on the scale of democracy, up to parity, a starting point. For those who worked in the Movement, it had been a process of halting discovery, untangling the relatedness of freedom and opportunity and hypocrisy. As the "old ferment" that Jim Bond and others of his generation had struggled to begin now worked in this generation, those seized by it found to their mixed delight and dismay that there was not just one door to be forced open, but many. The issues led one to another as the Movement struggled along—and increased in their complexity, too, making the terms of victory less and less clear. Looking back to the beginnings in the early sixties, Vernon Jordan, director of the Southern Regional Council's Voter Education Project, says now, "The difference is, you could deliver then, and the battle has changed now. The target ain't simple no more; it ain't black and white no more; it's grey. The people thought the Movement was about a hamburger."

No, it wasn't—important as it was to black morale to be able to go in and order the same undercooked mixture of fat, horsemeat, and cornmeal that white people could and be called "Sir" when the order came. Nor was the Movement entirely about the condition of being able to register and vote on election day. Often, especially in the one-party areas of the South, the black man going to cast his ballot found himself merely choosing the lesser between or among evils. SNCC was bound to try to change that situation—which meant that SNCC had to stop standing off on the sidelines of politics sneering at the bhoys and the establishment and the shortcomings of the system and get itself involved, and run candidates, win, lose, or draw. One event that made that entry more likely than it had been was the reapportionment of state legislative districts, aimed at equalizing some of the lopsided pressures that had built up in the statehouses ever since the districts had been gerrymandered to suit the down-country bhoys after Reconstruction. While it threatened to cripple the hicks, reapportionment, made into national law by the Supreme Court decision of 1966, was opening some tantalizing new outlets for political desires in the cities. Julian Bond, like many Southern blacks, lived in the city.

There dwelt in his heart, however, no palpable yearning to run, no desire to govern, no longing for political connivance. He recalls that his thinking then was as follows: "It was obvious there were going to be some black guys elected; people I knew were running; Ben Brown was running; I just said, 'Why not?' I thought it would be good for me. I thought it would be an exercise. See, I didn't think about winning—I thought it would be an exercise; I really thought it would be good for Snick. Snick had never worked in a city. It had worked in a lot of small towns."

Some of his detractors and even some of his less poetic supporters have suggested that Bond's candidacy came about after SNCC's leaders looked long and hard at the troops and picked him as the best-looking, most articulate lamb to be thrown out for the first dance with the statehouse lions. Bond himself remembers that he had a difficult time deciding to run. As the city campaign churned along and the already-declared candidates fumbled through the traditional speeches and rallies, Bond says, "I was just appalled at the sorts of things they campaigned on. I mean, they seemed to have no substantial platforms. They'd say, 'I'm for better schools, better housing, more jobs . . .' And who isn't? Everybody is: Barry Goldwater is, George Wallace is. And I thought you had to have more involvement of people in politics and a lot of Snick people did, too, and they kept saying, 'Why don't you run?' and I said, 'Why should I run?' "

Sure enough, they showed up on his front doorstep, bring-

ing whiffers of offers from the Democrats of support should
he but indicate a willingness, and hints that support might just
be found among the Atlanta GOP, if only Bond would give a
perceptible nod. But he held off, not making up his mind until
a scant few days before the filing deadline, and not without
some coaxing.

The man showing up on the doorstep, bringing compelling
arguments, an engaging personality and the force of old-line
friendship to bear on the reluctant young public relations man,
was skinny Ivanhoe Donaldson, a shrewd and savvy hand at
civil rights work, a polished pool player and a savant of the
Bond mind. He sat one afternoon long afterward in a dim, cool
and quiet Washington restaurant and looked back at the first
race for the State House and said, "To me, it was not a question of Julian suddenly making an entrance into politics when
he made his move. Julian was highly involved and, of course,
he was well-known—his family was well-known in Atlanta,
anyway, and he was a very popular student at Morehouse. If
you examine the history of Snick, and Julian's role inside of
that, you'll notice that Julian was very *key* to a lot of significant things that happened in Atlanta with the student sit-in
movement, the desegregation of public facilities and the question of jobs. Up to about late 1962," said Donaldson, "Snick
was basically a direct-action-oriented organization doing a lot
of voter registration on the side. Well, when you do a lot of
voter registration, you begin to want to maximize *why* people register. People register to be able to run candidates for
office."

Because Bond had worked in the background of a number
of SNCC-sponsored campaigns, running off posters and press
releases for such candidates as Aaron Henry, who ran for the
governorship of Mississippi in the mock election there in
1963, Donaldson said he didn't find Bond's contemplation of
a race in Atlanta a surprise. On the contrary, Donaldson said,
"One would say if you raise certain issues, then the people

who raise those issues and win minimum victories inside those issues should also move forward to represent a more dynamic politics." When the notion of a SNCC candidate making a bid for the newly created seat from the 136th district first occurred to SNCC members, and Bond at first made negative murmurings, Donaldson recalls that it was he who did the persuading. But, Donaldson feels, what spurred Bond to deciding to enter was a wish to oppose a local black minister, the Reverend Howard Creecy, in the primary. "I think Julian very deeply resented Howard Creecy's running for that office. He was the first guy who entered the race and Julian would say to me—we talked a number of times—'Now, here's Howard Creecy, a preacher—now, what has *he* done in Atlanta?' I just think that Julian felt, and people also were pushing him, that *he* represented what was needed in terms of the black community. If we were going to fight for reapportionment, one man, one vote, just to let another abstract politician get in . . . then, that wasn't important. I hate to box Howard Creecy in like that—he's a nice guy personally—but he just didn't appeal politically, he was not where it was at. So, people started encouraging Julian to run."

The exact moment of decision is lost to both Bond's memory and Donaldson's, but it came with finality. Recalls Donaldson, "I had been pushing it to him for almost two weeks, and it almost became a personal campaign of myself. I tried to get Charlie Black to come in there and talk to him and other people, and finally I was sitting in his house one day, and he finally said, 'Okay . . . all right . . . we'll run. Where will we get the money from?' I said, 'Don't worry about that: we gotta campaign!' We sort of drifted into it. I think he wanted to do it, but you know Julian, you've got to drag Julian to something. It's just like the McCarthy campaign; I had to spend three whole hours to get Julian to endorse McCarthy. I got him involved in the Macon convention. Julian didn't want to be involved in that."

Like Donaldson, two other close friends in the Movement—Ben Brown, who himself was running for a House seat, and John Lewis, the leader of SNCC—urged him to become a candidate. Lewis's position was strongly similar to Donaldson's. "I felt," Lewis says, "that in the South, Snick as an organization and the whole Movement had been involved in the whole effort of voter registration, the whole idea of giving people a sense of power, political control of their own destinies, and it was important that in a city like Atlanta, somebody who had been involved in the height of the student movement transfer some of this energy, some of the understanding, to the political arena. I thought it was important. I think it's wrong, in a sense, for the young blacks of the South, or any place, for that matter, to go out and bring about meaningful changes and then let the old-guard leadership take advantages of the changes. It's not enough for Julian or Ben Brown to break down the barriers, to make certain changes, and then let the businessmen types from the black community come in and become the political leaders. I thought the Atlanta community needed Julian and also that his leadership would inspire other people."

Small-town primaries in the South can be ferocious, gut-slitting brawls when the fix isn't in, and the fix emphatically was not in in the 136th legislative district. The area was too small and poor to draw much attention from the monied blacks of Atlanta, and Bond and Creecy were left to slug it out in the May 6 primary election. Borrowing his five-hundred-dollar filing fee from his father, Bond set out to saturate the little district with one idea: elect Julian Bond to the State House of Representatives. Bond's workers set up their headquarters in a wig store on Hunter Street and got to work. Their candidate was without backing from the leadership of the black community; even his old paper, the *Inquirer*, withheld its formal support.

Donaldson would arrive at Bond's house early every morning, make a pretense of an apology to Bond's harassed wife, Alice, and get the candidate out on the street. They tried to reach, literally, every person in the district, leafleting stores, visiting barbershops for brief chats as scissors snipped and clippers hummed. His workers set up tea parties where the ladies of the district could meet Julian Bond; he visited all the saloons and social clubs. "Anywhere we could get a crowd," Donaldson recalls, "Julian was there. And everyone in that community knew Julian Bond's name, and knew Julian."

Bond had short patience with one campaign institution, the mass meeting where candidates appear to make their pitches; at many of them that spring of 1965, in fact, there would be more candidates in line for the podium than there were citizens in the audience. "I decided," Bond says, "that I was getting nowhere that way. I was making speeches to a lot of candidates, but not to many people. So we started to canvass, door-to-door, every house in the district. I just went around, knocking on doors, saying, 'Hello, my name is Julian Bond; I'm running for the state legislature from this district.'"

Frequently, Bond would encounter people who knew appallingly little about how their government was set up, and found himself explaining what a district was and how the legislature worked. Further, he recalls, "I did something nobody had done before—I asked, 'What do you want me to do, if I get to the legislature?'" Many of those faces behind the screendoors just laughed at the beanpole twenty-five-year-old and asked him to do a good job, saying "Kind of young for that, aren't you?" But others saw beyond his youthful appearance and told him their problems, and asked him to try to help them make more money, to protect the rights of working people, to oppose capital punishment. Bond turned around the concern he had tapped, and made it into his platform, had it printed and widely circulated in the district, with two mailings sent to every registered voter. Bond encountered stiff resistance among the few white voters in the district; he found them, by and large, to be poor people, mostly unregistered, and he was frankly afraid of them. "I never went over there, but I sent some white girls over there, Southerners, and one of them almost got arrested for trying to pin a campaign button on a little boy. His father was going to charge her with assault and battery—I've never got any votes from them." One young SNCC worker, a Harvard graduate, Grenville Whitman, who worked with Bond in the press office, later wrote of Bond's campaign strategy, "While his platform might have been considered mildly liberal in New York, in Georgia it was radical. What Julian wanted, even more than a seat in the Georgia legislature, was for people in Atlanta to start talking about their problems—jobs and incomes, housing and residential segregation, education, welfare and health—and to begin to think about solving these problems *politically*."

The people would get together, ten or fifteen in a living room, and Bond would drop by and listen to them, answer their questions. The SNCC people with him would spur questions, and write down the names of the people who had come and then send out letters thanking them the next day. "Look," Ivanhoe Donaldson said, "Julian's longest speech was about *two* minutes; he is still developing his speeches now that he's gotten into this speaking thing, but Julian *used* to have about a two-minute speech. The thing about Julian, and he is best in small groups, is that he didn't speak to people— people spoke to him, and that's what we used to like to foster up as his style. He wasn't trying to sell Julian Bond to the people, he was trying to get people to talk about their problems, the platform, the issues as hand. And he was one of the best people to do it, because his personality helps that. He would speak, and then he would encourage people to talk and they would talk to him, and the guy sitting beside him. And then, when we were finished, I'd get up and say, 'This is what we're about: here we are, we're *all* talking; it's not Julian lecturing you and trying to sell you a bill of goods. The fact of the matter is that, after this meeting, we've probably discovered that everybody in this room has probably talked more than Julian Bond has. He's told you what he's about, and what he'll try, and now we are engaged in a dialogue.' "

Bond ran into some minor difficulties along the way—some of the members of SNCC felt that the organization should campaign dressed the way it worked in the field, in bib overalls and work shirts; Bond disagreed, saying he didn't want to have to overcome resentment about his mode of dress in addition to his other opposition. At home, Alice reminded him that she had *thought* she married a writer, not a politician —a point she would make with increasing frequency in the future. And Dr. Bond, although he lent Julian the filing fee, was deeply disappointed that any son of his should dabble with politics, forsaking the library and the campus to engage in something he, deep down, didn't really think very much of. His mother, on the other hand, took to the campaign like a veteran precinct worker, stopping strangers as she walked to and from her work to plead her son's case, urging them to tell their friends; and she persuaded her husband to help host the small groups she would invite to their home to meet Julian.

Donaldson recalls most vividly that Julian Bond "always used the terminology, '*We*.' It was always 'we this' and 'we that,' and people felt very closely identified at key moments, like the victories. We had a rally right in the community, at Le Chateau, and said, '*We* won.' We created what we felt was the most positive kind of political organization you can build, with a real sense of 'us,' and 'We're going to work together,' and Julian said, 'This is *our* seat.' It was never Julian Bond's seat to Julian. It was always his *district's* seat."

The deskmen in the city rooms of the Atlanta papers had laughed when Bond had brought them his announcement of candidacy; but SNCC's first campaign—and Bond's gamble in trying to include the voters in his campaign as the drafters of his platform—paid off better than two-to-one; he swamped the Reverend Creecy in the primary election by 1,243 votes to Greecy's 522. Bond then swung into the stretch, working just as hard through the general election campaign and won that, too, in a walk, defeating Republican Malcolm Dean, also a black and dean of men at Atlanta University, drawing 2,382 votes, 82 percent of the balloting in his district. Bond on election day, June 16, 1965, was to gloat, "More people voted in my district, proportionately, than voted in any other district in this whole state."

The victory won, Julian and Alice Bond took off for England, on a speaking tour sponsored by a Quaker meeting. Alice, who was pregnant again, disliked the strange food and the damp, chilly weather; Bond, too, was anxious to get home and get to work. Being sworn in as a member of the Georgia Legislature was something he was intending to take special pleasure in: he and some other SNCC workers had been ousted in 1960 when they tried to sit in the white section of the segregated visitors' gallery of the Georgia House. Spying the dark faces peering down from above him, the Speaker had bellowed angrily to the sergeant at arms, "Get those niggers out!" Now Bond was going to be right down there on the floor. Every day.

At home, however, not only in Bond's tiny, ragamuffin district but in all of red-clay Georgia and the U.S. of A. as well, there were certain ions, particles, stirring in the air, and their random, Brownian movements had subtly shifted, responding to some innate magnetic forces. They were converging now, on twin vectors that soon would intersect on . . . Bond's front porch! Right there on that little pitted, parched, blacktopped street!

Although there is a special trip nowadays that includes the Reverend Martin Luther King's old home (Bond now lives four doors away and the buses stop at his door, too), the tour buses laden with sightseers did not venture down such streets in 1965, and thus few whites, even white Atlantans, knew black Atlanta very well. The buses leave, in the mornings and afternoons, from out in front of the soaring new Regency-Hyatt House, from a parking spot on Harris Street in downtown Atlanta across from the Capital City Club, which the busdriver calls "one of our more exclusive clubs." Heading down through the thickening traffic on narrow Peachtree Street, nosing his huge machine between the bright new automobiles and trucks that signal the prosperity here in the town that Henry Grady loved and boosted in his newspaper, the Atlanta *Constitution*, the driver identifies the historic, the dazzling, the living footnotes to an old, old lady of a town—there stands a statue of old Grady ("arthur and statesman," says the driver). Every four years, he says over his crackly loudspeaker, Atlantans faithfully turn out to watch Clark Gable buckle and swash though *Gone With the Wind*, as a tribute to their most famous daughter, Margaret Mitchell. The driver points to the very gas lamp, there on the corner of Alabama and Whitehall, that Miss Mitchell relighted long ago as the "Confederate Light of Eternity," and his tone underlines the bitterness, still keen, that this puny streetlight is "one of the few relics left from Sherman's destruction of Georgia."

As the bus heads on out of town, it is obvious that in many ways the South, at least here, has long recovered from Sherman. Banks flourish, and the old "Underground City," somehow darkly reminiscent of the truckways under the Chicago Loop, is being rebuilt as a new tourist and mercantile center. The driver reminds his passengers that Coca-Cola was invented right here in Atlanta, and they gasp when he points to the gleaming dome of the state capitol building and tells them that $18,000 worth of gold leaf went into achieving that glister. The first stop is the gloomy old Cyclorama Building, in one of Atlanta's swampy red-clay parks. Filing past a tattered Rebel flag, the tourists find themselves inside, surrounded by what is undoubtedly one of the largest cylindrical clichés on earth, a huge painting depicting in gory and gooey detail the Battle of Atlanta. A gum-mashing red-necquette aims her flashlight pointer with the unerring skill of a farmboy pot-shooting squirrels as a recorded male voice intones, over the strains of Dixie: "these devoted lads from Alabama, Tennessee, swarm up the blood-red slopes . . . under the banner of pure white stars and blue bars on a field of blood red . . . Confederate thunderbolts." But, he says, the lads could not prevail, not over this superior force of Federal arms—not a word mentioned of any Yankee bravery. This is, he dolefully reports, the beginning of the end of the Confederacy, this carefully painted landscape, its detailed scenes blending cleverly into the papier-mâché landscape lying in green circularity about the viewing platform. The show goes on, over and over again, interrupted only by the maintenance men moving silently amid the fallen and wounded manikins, freshening up the fake shrubs with dye.

Then the driver puts his bus in gear and heads for another Rebel shrine, Stone Mountain, the Dixie Rushmore, whereon are carved the towering likenesses of Jefferson Davis, Robert E. Lee and Stonewall Jackson in bas-relief. Here a group of disciples of Judge Lynch founded a branch of the Ku Klux Klan and here the tourists may buy little Rebel flags, visit a replica plantation and see, as the driver points out, "those little cabins on our right—those are the actual old slave quarters used by the slaves." The actual old slaves don't live there any more, however—but on the way back to Atlanta, their descendants may be seen out the tinted windows of the bus, a gang of black workmen repairing a cinderblock wall, another black man holding the rod and chain while two white men adjust the transit. Inside the big bus as it cruises across the rolling landscape where the Battle of Atlanta raged long ago, a group of college kids, Californians come to Atlanta to sing at a convention, sing the "Battle Hymn of the Republic," and then swing into "This Land Is My Land." Down the interstate, past a smear of housing developments and low-rent homes, pleasant duplex bungalows on turfed lawns, parenthesized by dreary Negro neighborhoods, the driver heads back into Atlanta, to show the city off the way it prefers to be seen. Neighborhoods of old twenties-dowdy brick and stucco houses with tons of white ornamental iron cemetery furniture in their front yards, on into a section where, the driver marvels, the homes cost upwards of $250,000, until the bus at last reaches a white-columned mausoleum of a mansion set on a broad and sloping lawn, an enormous sand-colored colossus that turns out to be the new governor's mansion. The driver says, in pure Southern, that he chose that route "just to give you an idea of how some of the people around the city live."

These are, in point of fact, the places where those "some of the people" live who run Atlanta, and a good bit of the rest of Georgia, and who are most keenly aware of what goes on over at the Capitol. Their delegated representatives show up for work each day in the building with the gleaming dome, the House and the Senate chambers facing each other under it across an echoing central well. The statehouse abounds in little pinched Southern ladies with wire-tight permanents and serviceable girdles, flouncy and overripe secretaries with mouths like sandsharks' and tough, cigar-chomping men who push their paunches ahead of them down the corridors like housewives jockeying shopping carts at the supermarket. It's a county courthouse to end all county courthouses, granite-floored, oak-paneled, with gilden Corinthian capitals on the squared wall pilasters, and gloomy oil portraits of the pasty-faced old segs who ruled here in days gone by, just as their grandsons do now. There aren't many here who like Yankees, although most are punctiliously polite, and there are occasional hideous little touches here and there, like some moral electric fence, to remind one just exactly where he is—and keep unforgotten where this place has been. The lamp base in the office of the lieutenant governor, for instance, is a montage of Confederate bills—fives, tens, a fifty, a hundred. In the governor's ground-floor office, when Lester Maddox occupied it, the ultra-right-wing *Dan Smoot Report* was stacked on the secretary's desk alongside the equally rabid *Augusta Courier*, published by Georgia's aging kingmaker and *éminence grise*, Roy Harris. Into this anteroom, which alone is four times as big as a sharecropper's cabin, came all manner of Georgians who felt their problems required the personal attention of the $42,500-a-year Governor, and many of them got it. A farmer in bib overalls here to see about a relative's welfare money, even two booted and fringed members of Atlanta's fast-growing hippie community came by on "Little People" day, when Maddox, like some fief-lord of old, consented to see— and maybe even grant them a boon or two—all who came except Yankee newspapermen. Cartridge-belted state troopers moved in and out, inscrutable, their heavy revolvers flapping at their sides. A Negro flunky hustled crates of Coke to the cooler at five P.M.; three or four other flunkies, these white, idled by the telephones which seldom rang, passing the time with exquisite indolence. There was not one sound here of work, absolutely none of the bustle heard ordinarily near an executive center. Here everyone spoke softly, in muted, reverent, drawled whispers, as though in some awesome church, an illusion heightened by the mellow tolling of the carillon across the street.

This dull place, full of cornpone ritual and rigmarole, and the intricate political lacework that so fascinates the state mind, is where Julian Bond wanted to go to work. Those "some folks" might not have found that so surprising, but those other folks, the ones who sent Bond up the hill to the Capitol, were fair baffled. No tour buses rolled past their windows; some 27,000 of them, they lived compressed into their district in a fashion that one former resident, the Reverend Martin Luther King, was to characterize as being "trapped in the squalor of a hideous slum district." That was mere hyperbole, to be loosed by Dr. King in his righteous outrage over the fact that Julian Bond, the man those people had sent up to speak for them, had been rejected as unfit; the 136th legislative district was squalid, for sure, but it was far from hideous. Walt Whitman would have loved its variegated hurly-burly openness. Atlanta downtown after dark could have a cannon shot down its main street after nine P.M. without endangering a soul, but not the West End, not Hunter Street. There the neon blazes and the cars roll past the record shops and the beauty parlors and the bars, all doing business and smiling long after normal closing time downtown.

Back when Bond was first running in 1965, the 136th legislative district was almost 95 percent black, poor black, a tiny little enclave just twenty blocks long, and at its narrowest, two blocks wide. Almost half the able men living there were out of work, nearly 20 percent of the women; the average family income was a miserable $2500 a year. Some lived in old slum alleys that stank of maggots and rotting garbage in the summertime, when rheumy old men sat outside their shacks and too-fat children scrawled in the dusty dirt street. The smell was gone in the wintertime, replaced by the acrid haze of kerosene smoke, and inside, the newspapers stuffed round the window frames did almost nothing to keep out the cold. Some others were better off.

The 136th had two industries located within its confines, a bakery and a broom factory—and one encouraging example of bootstrap black entrepreneurism, Paschal's, a large motel with an outdoor pool, a lively cocktail lounge, a big dining room, a restaurant, and a coffee shop in which more political speculation and intrigue took place every afternoon and evening—and especially Saturday mornings—than in some corridors of the U.S. Capitol.

Nonetheless, Bond could characterize his district as a collage of problems. Schools were old, deteriorating, collapsing; petty crime was rampant; sewerage, streets, lighting, all were in dire need of fixing. There might be a tax base in there somewhere, though, if somehow the pump could only be primed enough to get the people who lived there up to an income level where paying taxes was not the absurdity it sounded like in 1965.

Somehow, though, the notion that the things the district so badly needed could be acquired through the House of Representatives seemed ingenuous to many of Bond's cohorts in SNCC. They had seen many of their projects defeated, John Lewis points out; not only had the Democratic Convention rejected them with a feeble compromise offer of two seats at large to the Mississippi delegation, but the Freedom Democratic Party slate to Congress had been a failure, too. "All these events," Lewis says, "kept moving Snick people farther to the left in forcing people to take the issues seriously." Pressing upon them from another direction was the military draft. The draft was totally against the grain of their belief in nonviolence—nonviolence not only as a clever tool against police batons, but throughout their entire lives. Viet Nam clashed with that, and it also came to be an obscenity to these youngsters because they realized long before most other Americans that the money pouring into the war was money that could have been used to make life better in the United States. Many of those working for SNCC came to see the whole military system as some kind of diabolical plot to exterminate black people and those whites who allied themselves with black people; to them the draft boards were aiming their command invitations directly at the students who were trouble-makers, and once overseas, blacks were a scandalously high-risk group in the field. It all tracked back, they cried, to a white-dominated system; and to many of them, going to work in one of the citadels of that system meant either endless futility or selling out.

Moreover, SNCC's more cautious members felt taking a stand as a group against the war in Viet Nam would risk alienating some of SNCC's financial supporters. "Our staff met in November, 1965," John Lewis says, "and at the meeting, people were prepared and ready to take a strong position on Viet Nam, and they had all sorts of ideas about what should be included in the resolution or any public statement. It was almost a consensus—only one or two people stood out, asking what would happen if we took a position; and some felt very strongly that if Snick as an organization must die, then let it die not because of some so-called lack of support, or funds, but let us die on the basis of principles."

That was the kind of melodramatic rhetoric that the folks at SNCC dealt in every day, and the poignant thing was, they meant it. Take a head-count, draft a position paper, heave it at the Establishment, wherever that was, wait for the old Jeffersonian Democratic process to manifest itself; there was utterly none of the cynical disbelief in almost everything but themselves that hurls the present-day counterparts of SNCC workers into hash jags and against a solid wall of brass-buttoned blue coats on a police line—although that cynicism is the direct lineal descendant of the abortion of that faith in Jefferson.

Providing the final impetus for the issuance of the statement was the murder of a young Negro in Tuskegee a few days before, Samuel Younge, shot down by a white gas-station worker for trying to use the rest room. He was the first SNCC worker to be killed.

So, as the executive committee of SNCC went on with its meeting, SNCC workers Grenville Whitman, Charles Cobb and Bill Mahoney went off to a Hunter Street restaurant, ordered a pitcher of beer, and started drafting SNCC's white paper on Viet Nam. Into it went the thoughts and suggestions of SNCC workers who responded to a questionnaire sent out earlier to field offices, and the manifesto went through many revisions before, at one-thirty P.M. the next day, January 6, 1966, SNCC chairman John Lewis started reading, to a roomful of expectant reporters:

The Student Non-Violent Coordinating Committee has a right and a responsibility to dissent with United States foreign policy on any issue when it sees fit. The Student Non-Violent Coordinating Committee now states its opposition to United States involvement in Viet Nam on these grounds:

We believe the United States government has been deceptive in its claims of concern for the freedom of the Viet Namese people, just as the government has been deceptive in claiming concern for the freedom of colored people in such other countries as the Dominican Republic, the Congo, South Africa, Rhodesia, and in the United States itself.

We, the Student Non-Violent Coordinating Committee, have been involved in the black people's struggle for liberation and self-determination in this country for the past five years. Our work, particularly in the South, has taught us that the United States government has never guaranteed the freedom of oppressed citizens, and is not yet truly determined to end the rule of terrorism and oppression within its own borders.

We ourselves have often been victims of violence and confinement executed by United States government officials. We recall the numerous persons who have been murdered in the South because of their efforts to secure their civil and human rights and whose murderers have been allowed to escape penalty for their crimes.

The murder of Samuel Younge in Tuskegee, Alabama, is no different than the murder of people in Viet Nam, for both Younge and the Viet Namese sought, and are seeking, to secure the rights guaranteed them by law. In each case, the United States government bears a great part of the responsibility for these deaths.

Samuel Younge was murdered because United States law is not being enforced. Viet Namese are murdered because the United States is pursuing an aggressive policy in violation of international law. The United States is no respecter of persons or laws when such persons or laws run counter to its needs and desires.

We recall the indifference, suspicion and outright hostility with which our reports of violence have been met in the past by government officials.

We know that for the most part, elections in this country, in the

North as well as the South, are not free. We have seen that the 1965 Voting Rights Act and the 1964 Civil Rights Act have not yet been implemented with full federal power and sincerity.

We question, then, the ability and even the desire of the United States government to guarantee free elections abroad. We maintain that our country's cry of "preserve freedom in the world" is a hypocritical mask behind which it squashed liberation movements which are not bound, and refuse to be bound, by the expediencies of United States cold war policies.

We are in sympathy with, and support, the men in this country who are unwilling to respond to a military draft which would compel them to contribute their lives to United States aggression in Viet Nam in the name of the "freedom" we find so false in this country.

We recoil with horror at the inconsistency of a supposedly "free" society where responsibility to freedom is equated with the responsibility to lend oneself to military aggression. We take note of the fact that 16 percent of the draftees from this country are Negroes called on to stifle the liberation of Viet Nam, to preserve a "democracy" which does not exist for them at home.

We ask: where is the draft for the freedom fight in the United States?

We, therefore, encourage those Americans who prefer to use their energy in building democratic forms within this country. We believe that work in the civil rights movement is a valid alternative to the draft. We urge all Americans to seek this alternative, knowing full well that it may cost them their lives—as painfully as in Viet Nam.

Words, words, words. Press releases seldom make front page stories, but this time, the reporters with their notebooks and tape recorders and cameras and folded sheets of copy paper hurriedly set about writing their stories, calling their desks and their newsrooms, as the machinery of the press—print and electronic—began to assimilate this break. What the SNCC people had seen as their story, John Lewis's own reason for summoning the press in the first place, was their conviction that civil rights work was every bit as valuable a service to the nation as was going off to shoot the North Viet Namese soldiers they saw as engaged in a civil war. That was, understandably, ho-hum copy for the newspaper guys, who knew the real story here was SNCC's position on the war. The reporters filed stories about SNCC's damning the war and urging what to those "some people" in Atlanta and around the country would sting like treason: resistance. And moreover, knowing the SNCC statement had been in the works, going through the process of refinement in the mysterious workings of the SNCC organization, they had, privately, agreed that the real angle was yet to come. They filed knowing that they would soon be calling their offices back with "sub leads," handling the real top to the SNCC story: newly elected Representative Julian Bond's position. If Bond as a SNCC official disavowed the Lewis statement, then by the immutable laws of daily journalism the reporters had not one but two stories, a war piece and a civil rights piece, with a major figure in the Movement breaking away from his group. But if he endorsed it, why then there would be three stories: Lewis, Bond, and—much more importantly—the flabbergasted reaction from the cemetery-lawn-furniture people when they learned that not only was a black boy going to be commingling with white people in the House, but one who might be considered a treasonous chicken-hearted black boy to boot. A wiser, more political, and more protected man would have deftly sidestepped, would have been simply unavailable for comment for a while, or would have said he needed time to study the implications of this to-some-extent meritorious position taken by a group for whom he had the utmost respect— but from which he had been absent in England for some time and for which, because of his pressing duties in the legislature, he would have even less time, etc. Any third-echelon deskman in the State Department PR office could have fielded the crisis.

But Bond, alas, was off at a YMCA meeting when Lewis

held his press conference, and returned to find a spikeful of telephone messages left by reporters waiting for him. He talked with the first reporter to reach him, Ed Spivia of state-owned radio station WGST, and to some of Spivia's colleagues, with an ingenuous disregard for the political consequences of what he was saying. Thus his response to the questions raised by the SNCC statement came spontaneously as much from his own philosophical disagreement with the nation's defense policies as from his allegiance to SNCC. Spivia, who tape-recorded his conversation with Bond, later produced a copy of his tape for consideration by state authorities and the transcript has entered the public records of the State of Georgia. In its entirety, it reads as follows:

Q. Julian, this is Ed Spivia. I was there at the press conference called by John Lewis . . .

A. Uh, huh.

Q. And Lewis was questioned by newsmen as to whether or not you endorse this release today, and I would like to ask that question to you now. Do you endorse the release made by the SNCC group today?

A. Yes, I do.

Q. Would you say that again, please?

A. I said, "Yes, I do."

Q. Now, could you qualify, Julian, why specifically you do endorse it and what points?

A. Why, I endorse it, first, because I like to think of myself as a pacifist and one who opposes that war and any other war and am anxious to encourage people not to participate in it for any reason that they choose. And secondly, I agree with this statement because of the reasons set forth in it—because I think it is sorta hypocritical for us to maintain that we are fighting for liberty in other places and we are not guaranteeing liberty to citizens inside the continental United States.

Q. Julian, do you feel that you can endorse this statement and effectively set out the duties of your office that you have been elected to?

A. Well, the qualifications for being a legislator in Georgia—that you be over twenty-one years old, be a resident of the State for more than two years and not be a member of the Communist Party, and I meet all of those qualifications.

Q. Julian . . .

A. And, uh, yeah?

Q. I'm not speaking of it in that manner. You have an oath to take come Monday. Will you be able to take this oath with a clear conscience and endorse this statement?

A. What does the oath require? That you uphold the Constitution of Georgia and the Constitution of the United States of America, right?

Q. That's correct.

A. Right. Well, I don't see anything in this statement that conflicts with that.

Q. Now, you started to say, Julian, to start off with, before you were interrupted about the oath, what the oath requires, and why you feel that a . . . if you could just sum all that up in a statement.

A. Well, I said the qualifications—not speaking about the oath —but the qualifications for being a state representative in Georgia require that you be at least twenty-one years old, a two-year, I think, resident of the district from which you are elected, and not be a member of the Communist Party, and I meet all of those qualifications, and consider myself just as qualified as any other member of the Georgia House of Representatives, and just as able, if not more able, to perform my duties as are the other members.

Q. Well, now, of course, according to what you have just given me and I'm sure that's quite correct—that much of it is spelled out. But don't you feel that there are certain, perhaps moral obligations that are implied in taking over such an office as you expect to do, which might be in variance with this view which you've just stated?

A. Well, I think the fact that the United States Government fights a war in Viet Nam, I don't think that I as a second class citizen of the United States have a requirement to support that war. I think my responsibility is to oppose things that I think are wrong if they are in Viet Nam or New York, or Chicago, or Atlanta, or wherever.

Q. Julian, the only thing that's keeping the group that has made this statement from being in treason is the technicality that we aren't at war. If we should become engaged in war and a declaration of war be declared, would you still stand by this statement?

A. Well, I don't know. That puts a different light on it, but one of the many reasons I oppose the war in Viet Nam is because it seems to me that if we are at war and we are at war declared, not by Congress, as wars are supposed to be declared, but war declared by President Johnson, and there seems to me that there is something wrong with that sort of a situation and that is one of the many reasons why I oppose that war.

Q. In other words, you are willing to stand by this as long as it doesn't cost you anything, but if it's going to cost you—you are going to be held in treason—then you can't stand by it?

A. Well, I have to think about it again. I don't know. I don't know if I'm . . . if I . . . you know, if I'm strong enough to place myself in a position where I'd be guilty of treason. Right now, I stand by it, and . . . if it were treasonable by law, I'd have to think about it again.

Q. Well, you were elected by all the people to represent those people. Do you feel that all the folks that voted for you have these same views? Or the majority of them?

A. No, I don't know what the majority of opinion is among my constituents about the war in Viet Nam. I imagine and this is without knowing, I imagine that they oppose it, because I remember being at the bus station in Atlanta and seeing a bus load of draftees getting ready to leave for Fort Benning, I think, and a Negro youngster jumped off and said to the Sergeant who was loading them on the bus, "You didn't want us to go to school with you, you didn't want us to sit at lunch counters with you and now you want us to go overseas and fight and die with you." And this kid wasn't intending to go, but they got him back on the bus and he went, and I think that without knowing, without having taken a poll, that that would be an opinion among a great many people that I represent.

Q. Now, Julian, you don't feel that apparently, from what you stated as other top officials have stated, Governor Sanders among them, who have actually gone over to Viet Nam and talked to all levels of people over there from the top military down unto the lowliest peasant of Viet Nam and also of course to their own fighting men, that if we do not stop Communism there that it is just a question of where will we stop it next, and that eventually, that they would come over and take over this country. This is their avowed aim, and that if they did, I don't think there is very much doubt in many people's minds but not none of us, including yourself, who apparently disagree with our current policy, would be able to voice such an expression of disagreement, and, in addition, to actively advocate avoidance of the draft—this still does not—you don't feel would change your mind in this area?

A. Oh, no. I'm not taking a stand against stopping World Communism, and I'm not taking a stand in favor of the Viet Cong. What I'm saying is that, first, that I don't believe in that war. That particular war. I'm against all war. I'm against that war in particular, and I don't think people ought to participate in it. Because I'm against war, I'm against the draft. I think that other countries in the world get along without a draft—England is one —and I don't see why we couldn't, too.

Q. You don't think this is what would be necessary in order to fight this war in order to stop the Communism from going any further?

A. Well, I'm not convinced that that is really what's going on, but I'm not prepared to argue it. You see, I don't want to say anything about that. I'm not convinced that we are really stopping International Communism. I like—not completely—but I like fairly well, the life I live now. You know, I don't want too many abrupt changes in a direction I don't like, to take place, but I'm not about to justify that war, because it's stopping International Communism, or whatever . . . you know, I just happen to have a basic disagreement with wars for whatever reason they are fought—

Q. Don't you—

A. —fought to stop International Communism, to promote International Communism, or for whatever reason. I oppose the Viet Cong fighting in Viet Nam as much as I oppose the United States fighting in Viet Nam. I happen to live in the United States. If I lived in North Viet Nam, I might not have the same sort of freedom of expression, but it happens that I live here, not there.

Q. Julian, this is Mike [Jones]. Dick [Gray], let me say something to you. I happened to overhear those questions, and I don't think you should use his answers to them. Number one, because Senators and Congressmen who have taken the same oath as he will have to take, only on a much larger scale, have said the Administration is wrong, so I don't see how you can justify asking him questions about that, and I don't think they should be used.

A. Thank you. Well, it is sorta unfair to suggest that it is my opposition to the war . . . my opposition to the war is somehow different from the opposition, say, uh, of Senator Russell, a little while ago—not presently but a little while ago—who said he didn't think American boys should be losing their lives to fight in Viet Nam. You see, and if I'm approaching treason, then perhaps he is, also.

Q. Well, I realize that you wouldn't come out and say that, you know, as long as a newsman is questioning you. You don't want to take the position of being adamantly opposed to questioning, so I thought I'd break in and say that.

A. Thank you.

Mike Jones: Okay.

Dick Gray: Of course, Mike, you realize all those questions weren't mine—so anyway, I do take into consideration and have from the start . . . this wasn't obvious, but I said . . .

The SNCC statement, and especially Bond's endorsement of it—and his embellishment of that position by adding that he admired the courage of draft-card burners—unleashed a wrathful energy that had lain dormant in the body of the state. What happened then has become distilled in the minds of those who took part, and in Bond's own memory. As in some melodramatic motion picture, the reality of what actually *did* happen has been heightened in their retrospection beyond reality. If all the little cerebral film clips they carry so indelibly in their minds could be edited and spliced, then——

At its beginning the narrator of this imaginary documentary would intone that this is the year 1965, that the nation is at undeclared war, and that there are, really, many nations here, each running on its own separate time track as distinct from the others as Rocky Mountain Time is from Eastern Standard. There are here in these United States places where the war means stopping the Reds in Asia before we have to stop them on the banks of the Potomac; places where the war means a red-eyed and tearful old black lumber hostler in a Virginia supply yard, weeping one morning because his son called the night before to say he was leaving for Viet Nam from Benning and couldn't come home to say good-bye.

Bond might as well have been coming from some other world as to come home from England—where opposing this war was a fashionable thing—to a Georgia where it was tantamount to treason. The folk singers in the big cities might be mocking their way through the "Big Muddy," guffawing at Johnson and Rusk and McNamara, but there were folks in Georgia who wouldn't have laughed if somebody had sung "Over There" and to whom "In Flanders Fields" did not sound even the least bit corny.

V

THOUSANDS and thousands of them, swarming down from the White House toward the Ellipse in Washington, and beyond to the Mall, gathered there to make this first massed protest against the war. Surprisingly, they were of all ages, young but many old, many more middle-aged, ordinary people, not bearded trouble-makers, but just ordinary folks come from all over. There was music here, too, as the sun went down on these lofted placards urging, "Stop the Bombings," "Thou Shalt Not Kill," and "Bring the G.I.'s Home Now." Said a black woman from Detroit, resting under a tree near the Ellipse after her all-night bus ride to be there, "I'm here because of my son and all those other sons . . ." Up at the base of the towering shaft of a memorial to a man who had once urged his country to avoid such adventures on far-off shores, Ringo Angerlino, twenty-nine, cradled his guitar against the chill dusk and hammered out a tune, slamming it into the night: "I'm going to let it shine all in the Southland . . . in the White House . . . in Santo Domingo . . . all around the Ku Klux Klan . . . all around the Pentagon I'm going to let it shine. . . ." A big rugged guy sneered, "Whyncha go home,

you sissieswedontlikebeatniksbunchafagsGOHOME!" A prim
suburban housewife told him to pipe down and let Ringo sing.

Somewhere in Viet Nam, the kid from Ohio sat writing
home on soggy paper with ball-point pen. He had played
soldiers when he was very small, and he always wanted to be
a Marine and now there he was: twenty-one, a Pfc.

Dear Mom & Dad,
How's everything going? I'm fair, hot, tired and hungry. We
just came back off operation Dodge City yesterday. We didn't see
any and didn't get any. But they got three of us. A good buddy of
mine got shot in the back. He'll be OK but I don't know if he'll
come back to the grunts or not. I hope he don't. Anyone whose got
a chance to get out of this place should take it.

Rumors are going around about a operation which is supposed
to last three weeks beginning the 30th of this month. I hope not
but everything is pointing to it being true scoop.

I got the package with brownies, stove and donuts. Thank you. I
also got a letter from ***** while we were out on the operation.
I'll write to her as soon as possible. I'm trying to get caught up on
all my letter writing in case we do go out for that three weeks. It'll
be like double-eagle only worse. I don't know what could be worse
except the heat.

On this last operation the heat was terrific. We were on a
semi-dessert type terrain and the white sand that we had to walk on
was like a hot plate and your feet felt like bacon frying looks. I
mean it was hot. We only had a large amount of heat casualties,
but we had them just the same.

As of July 1, I have exactly six months to go. It may be less by
the time December rolls around but at any rate it's still a life time
away as far as I'm concerned. Oh yes my gray hair around the sides
is becoming quite a problem. I may have to die my hair when I
get home.

I got a package of kool aid in a letter Dad sent out on the op. It
was real handy, anything to change the flavor of iodine water. My
body consists of two hundred percent matter, 25% iodine tablets
25% salt tablets 50% C-rations and all this is in a 100% of scummy
rice paddy water. My body will never be the same when I get back.

The young Marine had—just the day before John Lewis read his defiant statement and Julian Bond endorsed it—mailed home his warrant appointing him private first class, and proudly asked that it be framed ("Put the stripes on the safety pins because I still have plenty of time and opportunity to make more rank so don't put them on permanent"). He died a year from the day he joined the Corps, after a Viet Cong grenade exploded near his head at two P.M. while he was "defiantly holding his position." They buried him beneath the sugar maples back home while a trumpeter blew taps and a Marine fired a rifle overhead and his father got a flag folded into a fat triangle to hold and his mother took his heavy serge dress uniform down from where it had hung while he was gone. "He was so proud," she said, "so I should be, too." His big brother, a tough detective, said something different, though. "It's a hell of a note," the detective said, "and for nothing. I don't understand it." They put the letters, from General Westmoreland, from Senator Stephen Young and from President and Mrs. Johnson, in with the drawers full of memorabilia of their son who used to go up in the woods and pan for gold when he was a little kid. Five blocks away, another kid got up at four A.M. and got his gear together, moving quietly around the house so he wouldn't wake up his mother, who stayed in the bedroom so they wouldn't see her cry. His father, waiting to drive him down to the bus depot, tried to tell him how to make it, how *he* made it back in the Second World War—"Don't be nervous about money . . . send a picture of your haircut . . . write every week. . . get in the middle and be quiet. . . ." Over at the rubber-glove factory where they made surgical gloves for combat hospitals, three shifts a day were running them out, and in one of the town's motels two middle-aged women played the piano and the drums in spangled gowns and tinseled tiaras and sang "Pack up your troubles."

The *Journal-Constitution* presses roared into life, the gigantic rollers spinning, the wide heavy paper whistling under the plates, coming out the other end, mysteriously, magically, all folded and cut, thousands and thousands of eight-columned eight-point newspapers, all of them this evening carrying what many Atlantans already knew, having heard it, all about it, as much as they wanted to know.

They had certainly already heard about it in the crisp, modernly furnished living room of Dr. Horace Mann Bond. Julian arrived, just a few hours after he had publicly endorsed the SNCC statement. He and his father talked, both men smoking nervously. Julian's mother listened as her husband said, "Julian, they will never seat you." Julian, she thought, didn't really believe that. But that was because he didn't really know the South, what it could be like. He had lived there only a short time.

The newspapers flopped down in stacks at the end of the line of presses, and the headline on Friday's *Constitution* read, "DEFY DRAFT CALL, SNCC CHIEF URGES." The jump on page twelve was: "SNCC LEADER AND LEGISLATOR BACK DRAFT CARD BURNINGS."

In his Statesboro, Georgia, office, handsome Jones Lane, member of the Georgia House of Representatives, listened in disbelief as the radio newscast told about SNCC's statement and Bond's endorsement. Lane, a commercial and industrial builder, immediately made some phone calls. To Atlanta. To some friends of his. Asking them to start drafting a petition for Bond's expulsion from the Legislature, which was scheduled to convene on Monday morning, four days later. Lane's comrade in the Georgia House, bluff, bulky "Sloppy" Floyd, read the evening paper, put it down after a pause, and he, too, moved toward the telephone. As Floyd put it later, "That was a truly un-American statement and it was real bad for a man to be a public official of the state of Georgia advocating that anybody burn their draft cards to the youth of this nation."

Next morning, at Atlanta's gleaming and bustling airport,

John Lewis, compact and stocky, came down the ramp from the plane which brought him back from a speaking engagement at Hollins College in Virginia. He paused in utter astonishment, staring at the newspaper in the rack. There, in what newspapermen call *Second Coming* type, was the banner on the bulldog edition of the Atlanta *Journal* for Saturday: "LOYALTY CHALLENGE FACES BOND ON VIET MURDER CHARGE SUPPORT." Over at Atlanta's old Henry Grady Hotel, meanwhile, the portly figures of Georgia's legislators were arriving, greeting each other, exchanging family news and then swiftly getting down to the serious business before them: just exactly what to do about this uppity nigger, Bond. Governor Carl Sanders and Lieutenant Governor George T. Smith were worried: somehow this carbuncular wrath must be lanced, but at the same time, Georgia's reputation must not be smirched, its moderate and progressive image kept untarnished. A deal had to be schemed out, sold, consummated. Somehow.

The word got out, to a black member of the House, one of the seven, who, with Bond, were scheduled to be seated there for the first time since Reconstruction, that if . . . look-ahere! "This boy has got to come before the committee, humbly, and recant, and just plain beg a little. We have got to have *something* to hang a hat on. If he will *do* that, it will put the committee on a spot where they'll just have to seat him. . . ."

Meanwhile, forces working along somewhat different lines had already started moving, but not without some difficulties. On a long stretch of Highway 17, cutting south through downstate Georgia, the speeding, Florida-bound cars, their lights on against the mist, were splashing, narrowly missing, Howard Moore, who was vainly trying to jack up his rented car, which had blown a tire. He was not having any success because the jack had no base-plate. Disgustedly, Moore started walking the fifteen miles to the nearest gasoline station. A lawyer, Moore represented SNCC people when they needed it, which was frequently. Moore's day was going to be one of frustration: he eventually got his tire fixed, drove all the way to the court where he was representing comedian Dick Gregory only to find nothing much happen in court that day. When he got back to Atlanta, Moore, who was now even grouchier than he usually is, met Julian Bond, who is his brother-in-law, and learned for the first time of the SNCC statement on the war, and of the interview in which Julian Bond stated his ardent support of draft-card burners. Moore thought about this very quickly and then said: "I think they'll probably kick you out, Julian."

Moore then argued with Bond about what to do next. Bond should, Moore said, sit tight until the Legislature convened Monday morning, making absolutely no further public statements, positively no efforts to explain his endorsement of the SNCC position paper, no modifications of his stand, nothing. And, despite efforts to reach him for amplification, Bond did manage to stay incommunicado—but he was fretting.

The old house in Waveland, Mississippi, on the coast, sat as it had for decades, surrounded by its ramshackle outbuildings, battered by the hurricane that had just passed. Inside it a civil rights group listened to Charles Morgan, Jr., talk. Morgan, in his casual clothing—sport shirt open at the throat, rumpled slacks, wrinkled sport coat—with his thinning hair straying down over his pale forehead, his ample girth slumped in a chair, moving from time to time to lean against the wall or lie on the floor as he speaks, easily dominates the room. Morgan's voice, excited, despite its drawl, energized in its very timbre by the machine-gun workings of his brain, easily cut through any undercurrents of conversation that might briefly oppose it. It is impossible to ignore Charles Morgan. He is alternately bitter, wry, sardonic, knowledgeably shrewd, and he stopped talking only when the phone rang, there in the old house, and the call was for him. The call was from Bob Zellner, a SNCC worker in Atlanta. Morgan looked out at the

gathering Mississippi night, thought of the road along the sea-
wall, and told Zellner he would get back to Atlanta as soon
as he could. The next day Morgan drove to New Orleans,
trying to figure out how he might pull this one out of the fire.

At eight o'clock Saturday night, Bond broke his silence to
show up at the home of State Senator Leroy Johnson. Tall,
lean, elegantly dressed and amply bejeweled as befitting his
position of rising power in Georgia politics, the first Negro
to be elected to the statehouse since Reconstruction, Johnson,
with the governor and the lieutenant governor, thought he
had worked out a way around the outraged legislators who
were planning to bushwhack Bond first thing Monday morning. They sat down, Bond, Ivanhoe Donaldson, Charles Cobb,
James Forman, local attorney Donald L. Hollowell, Dr.
Samuel DuBois Cook of Atlanta University; Howard Moore
arrived late, just back from a quick trip to Washington, angry
at finding that Bond had ignored his advice, and then listened
to Senator Johnson's plan. Suavely, Johnson unfolded the
strategy he worked out in his delicate negotiations with the
state's top officials, who wanted as much as he did to avoid
an unseemly ouster the next morning. It just might work,
Johnson told the tense group gathered in his home, if Bond,
first thing Monday, could get the Speaker of the House to
recognize him before the other members were sworn in. If he
would then rise and speak, and explain himself, introduce himself, turn on his boyish charm, ingratiate himself, let the bhoys
see what an upstanding young, handsome, right-thinking
Negro gentleman the sensation-seeking press had so misrepre-
sented, then, if he could manage to pull that off, why then,
maybe, just maybe, enough votes could swing his way to stave
off his ouster.

"They wouldn't describe their position as being arguers for
modification," Moore remembers of this meeting, "but just for
making a statement, he should make some press statement, he
should have a 'further projection' before the General Assembly met. This meeting was probably something devised by the

white power structure. But my position was that he had a legal right to do it. . . . There are further consequences that Julian had to foresee: He had been active as a student leader, closely identified with a whole generation of protest, and if he retracted or apologized for the statement, he would disappoint or run out on this generation of students and he wouldn't do it and let them down, and if he did, he would lose his own self-respect. Julian *had* to stand by his statement."

The men sat in Leroy Johnson's house far into the night, telling Bond that he must, in some way, beg pardon, must let these angry white men know that he hadn't really meant to say what they thought he had said.

Tell them, Julian, that you had spoken rashly, intemperately, and that they had interpreted it wrongly in their wisdom and that if they just give you another chance, you'll never do it again. Communism, that's it, we've got to say something about Communism. What's Communism got to do with it? Communism—you know what that has to do with it.

As the meeting neared its end, the men worked out a statement, and Bond thought, "They want me to read this to the House. When the moment comes to be sworn in, they want me to say, 'Mister Speaker, I rise on a point of personal privilege,' and to rise, and say, 'There has been some discussion —which is a laugh, it's been all over everywhere—'about me,' and then read that statement. I'm going to read the statement, and they are going to say, 'Ohhh, *that's* what he meant; ohhh, I see; ohhh, *well, that's* not so bad.' "

Bond worked in his father's living room on Sunday with Dr. Bond, trying vainly to come up with a satisfactory statement of his position. Then in Howard Moore's law office later, with Moore and some fellow SNCC members, he went over the points of his position. Then, as he left Moore's office, Bond encountered the Reverend Ralph David Abernathy, assistant to Martin Luther King in the Southern Christian Leadership Conference. Abernathy asked Bond, "What are you going to do?" and Bond said, "I don't know, Reverend Abernathy—some people want me to give in and beg forgiveness and say I was wrong . . . I don't know what I'll do." And Abernathy, looking as he always does, like a plain man, a man long used to working and to people who work, and not at all the way great leaders of movements are supposed to look, said in his deep, slow voice, "Well, just do something you can live with."

And right then and there, outside Howard Moore's law office, Julian Bond made up his mind.

It was arrogance that did it, Bond thinks, "the arrogance of these guys to believe that they had the right to tell me what to say, in effect to tell me what I could and couldn't say, and to question me about something I had said."

That evening, the eve of the opening of the Legislature, Bond took his statement, words so carefully designed to mollify his colleagues in the House, and ran off enough copies of it to send one to everybody on his district mailing list, all those people whose names his workers had garnered during the long spring and summer of campaigning, all the people who had met him at the little tea parties, had asked a question, or come to hear him talk. Bond did this, thinking there must be some people among his constituents who didn't understand what was happening to their legislator, to *their* seat in the House—to themselves—and who deserved to be told. Bond had drawn his line.

Meanwhile, the other side was coalescing, hardening, its position becoming resolute, its strategy blunt, direct and exquisitely practical. Most importantly, it was *sanctioned;* it was okay to do this. The Atlanta spokesman for the FBI announced his office was sending the SNCC statement to the Justice Department in Washington for its decision as to whether any federal law had been broken. Dapper and well-barbered Carl Sanders, the Georgia governor who had described the Committee on Appeal for Human Rights advertisement as having been written in Moscow, told a reporter he thought this SNCC denunciation of the war in Viet Nam was "both inaccurate and intemperate in content." One does not get to be governor of Georgia without knowing just which pedals on the organ to press, and Sanders, with suave certainty, added: "In my judgment, this is the time for all Americans to rally round the flag—not kick it!" One by one, others swung in behind Sanders. Lieutenant Governor Peter Zack Geer stated that the SNCC statement was "a glaring, sad and tragic example of a total lack of patriotism to the United States of America. Wittingly or unwittingly this position exactly suits the Kremlin. Loyal American citizens, white and Negro, will suffer from this far left wing announcement from SNCC and I am sure that loyal Americans, whatever their political persuasion, deplore it to the fullest. It is even more alarming that an elected member of the Georgia House of Representatives would endorse this subversive policy." The headlines were screaming: MURDER IN VIET NAM CHARGE HURLED BY RIGHTS LEADER . . . VIET NAM MURDER . . . REP. BOND'S LOYALTY FACES CHALLENGES . . .

The plan was set: Jones Lane, the Statesboro delegate to the General Assembly, who clearly established the position he occupied by hosting George Wallace in his appearance before the House in 1965, announced he would lead the move to oust Bond come Monday morning. The move was officially sanctioned by "those people": as *Constitution* editor Eugene Patterson wrote in his influential column: "Fulton County Rep. Julian Bond assured his own isolation and ineffectiveness in the Legislature by parroting the Lewis folly."

On the steps of the Georgia statehouse, on Monday, January 10, 1966, Bond, flanked by Morgan and Howard Moore, arrived shortly before ten A.M., timing their appearance carefully because all of Bond's latent fear of the white South had welled up in him and he was now genuinely afraid that one of these vengeful men would assault him. Bearded Jim

Forman, in blue jeans, was with Bond and his lawyers as the men hurried down the corridor to the elevator that lifted them up to the House lobby. There Bond was greeted by Jack Ethridge, the head of the Fulton County delegation. Ethridge, anxious to see the new black House members fit easily into the working of the legislature, had held orientation meetings with them and this morning he feared that all the good will he had tried to establish was going to evaporate.

Charles Morgan, a large yellow legal pad in his lap, was idly taking notes: "9:50—photographers at empty seat of J.B. Gallery filled, few vacant seats, Negroes and whites, SNCC Stokely, the Bonds. 9:57—Gallery filled, some standing, photogs waiting for J.B. 10 A.M.—J.B. arrives, takes seat—camera lights. Gavel five times, 'The hour for convening the . . . all members take their seats . . . all reporters take their seats in the press . . . doorkeeper close the door.' "

The other members of the House were scattered around the well of the big cream-colored chamber, filling it now with the noise of their greetings. The visitor's gallery above was packed. The place quieted as Ethridge then escorted Bond to his desk there in the hot white suffusion of television camera floodlights. Strobes wink as the newspaper photographers snap Bond's drawn, tired face.

The chaplain of the day, an envoy from a quieter world, read from Matthew, the Beatitudes, mentioning the "guidelines of liberty and justice," summoning down into that cockpit of a place divine favor upon "every member of this House," praying loud through the public address system for "a desire to be fair, right, and kind."

Bond stood with his elected colleagues for the prayer, and for a few brief minutes, as the clerk read the Secretary of State's certification of the elected members' victories, it seemed as though the roiling storm around him had vanished. But then the clerk announced the first order of House business. The certified members must now rise for the oath of office.

"I will ask Representative Bond to stand aside, several

challenges having been filed to his right to be seated here," the clerk intoned. Bond was in check now; no more chance for maneuver. Ethridge, sitting on Bond's right, stood; on his left, Representative Charlie Brown got up, too. All around Bond, the other men Georgians sent to Atlanta to run their state were standing, their right arms raised, ready to swear allegiance to the nation, to pledge themselves to uphold the Constitution of the United States.

Bond sat there, his elbows on his desk, his hands clasped, his chin on his thumbs, looking on unbelievingly, numbed, as the 1966 session of the Georgia House of Representatives began without him. Then, clearing off his desk, Bond got up and left the chamber, walking into a milling clot of reporters and photographers who quickly surrounded him as he moved blindly down the corridor. Looking on was Lester Maddox, the little gadfly of a griddle chef, who chirped, with the excited fervor of a fulfilled prophet, "I warned them! I warned them! I warned them that something like this would happen!" Scarcely anyone then paid any attention to Maddox; he was not yet governor of the state but merely a nuisance whom the doorkeepers did their best to bar every day from the lobbies.

Pressed there in the capitol corridor for a statement, for some indication of what his next move would be, to tell the public how it felt to be kicked out, what it was like to be a pariah, Bond started reading from the statement he had mailed out the previous evening to his constituents, insisting once again that he could in all conscience and good faith affirm and uphold his oath of office.

Well, yes, but—some of the reporters wanted to know—and they asked him again and again—was he, as he stood there, was Julian Bond a Communist? Bond repeatedly denied that he was, or that he *is*, and finally, goaded by the absurdity of it, blurted, "I tell you now that I never intend to answer that question again! I will take the oath, but I am putting you on notice now that I am not going to answer that question again!"

Forman, his big Afro haircut bristling above the shoulder straps of his sharecropper overalls, told the reporters that he felt the House action was racist. "If implemented," Forman said curtly, "it would make all previous civil rights legislation pointless. History has to be vindicated—it might even be necessary to have a boycott on Georgia."

Despite the fatigue, the bitter hurt and anger he felt, Bond could still flash some humor; as the reporters clung, hoping to pick up some quote, some aside that would characterize the moment for their deadline coverage, Bond kept moving, and the press conference at last wound up in the governor's press room, where the questions came at him again in staccato volleys:

"Do you still endorse the statement?"

"Yes."

"Do you agree the U.S. is guilty of murder in Viet Nam?"

"I'd rather leave it like that."

"Do you agree with Mr. Forman that this is racist?"

"I can't help believing that," Bond replied. "As I look out in this audience I see a majority of white faces."

"Yes, but seven other Negroes were installed this morning. Don't you feel like you're jeopardizing what they've done?"

"My life has been colored, so to speak, by race. . . ."

While Bond fielded the reporters' questions and Forman fumed nearby, the state's leaders, back inside the House chamber, were working out the protocol they would follow in consummating the Bond affair. The Rules Committee was to be expanded to include two of the newly elected black Representatives; while the full House adjourned until later in the day, the expanded committee would sit in judgment on Bond and hear former Representative Denmark Groover, counsel for the petitioners, argue for Bond's unseating, opposed by defense counselors Howard Moore and Charles Morgan. Bond himself would testify before the committee. Then the committee was to go into executive session and reach its recommendation, report that to the House—and then finally, the House would vote.

As his lawyers huddled, his father nearby, Bond himself, half-dozing, lying on a table, tense and heavily medicated to avert a flare-up of his hives, was hardly able to believe what was happening. There was not much for Moore and Morgan to work out; theirs would be a purely defensive role; they agreed their fulcrum was the issue of freedom of speech, Bond's right to take any position he pleased on the issue of the war or any other question.

It is ironic that they must defend that right in this chamber where so often in the past the segregationist opposition to federal decrees of racial equality had been declared. Ironic, too, that Bond's own philosophy of letting the people of the 136th District dictate his legislative position had run head-on into a similar but more powerful populism. The men opposing him felt that they, too, had a duty to represent their constituents' feelings. Beyond their intent to avenge the white men who had lost their seats in reapportionment, the legislators who wanted Bond out of the House for opposing the war genuinely felt that one of their number had no right, as a public official, to take a stand so deeply against the grain of the majority senti-ment. Basically it was this utter inability to countenance such political heresy that had compelled them to hold the trial that, in just a few minutes, was to begin. How could Morgan and Moore ever hope to persuade their "jury" to dare to consider crossing this chasm, real as any geological fault, that, in a network of cracks and fissures, was dividing not just the Georgia legislature in the beginning of 1966, but the entire country? It was—and is—a chasm, dividing those who believe that the majority ruled—and that in ruling it could silence its opposition—from those who believed with equal fervor that the nation had been born to protect dissent, that its charter document, the Constitution, was founded on the bedrock notion that minorities *must* be protected, who recalled that the country had been settled, in fact, by fugitive minorities. It was *that* chasm that had opened and out of it had come the spawning extremists, the Birchers, the National States Righters, the Citizen Committees, the KKK, the Oswalds (and, later, the extremists of the new left, too—SDS, the Weathermen, the Black Panthers), and so deep was that chasm that Moore and Morgan knew their job that afternoon was all but impossible.

Somehow, from his position out there on the margin, Bond had glimpsed another view of the Viet Nam war, as had his comrades in SNCC, alien to that of the society that then was so enthusiastically sponsoring the war at the expense of so many of its members. Now, in the way that it has of punishing those of its members who have bizarre views, that society was going to punish Bond.

House Speaker George T. Smith, craggy, graying, nervously gaveling the House chamber into silence, repeatedly urged that there be no demonstrations. The audience was mostly white. "We must have order," Smith declared, "and at any instant there is any *dis*order, the gallery in this House will be cleared and nobody will be allowed in this hearing but the press, the news media, the committee and the parties at interest."

These legislators seemed all of a cut: business-suited, with white starched shirts, figured ties, serviceable shoes, presentable haircuts, weathered countryman faces that were tough and impassive. They had picked one of their own to represent them: Denmark Groover, a lawyer who had won a minor niche in the pantheon of Georgia heroes some years before by climbing up the wall of the House chamber and pulling the the clock out of its mounting to prevent the adjournment of one particularly stormy session. Expectantly, they sat at their desks waiting for Groover to begin what they knew was going to be a good show, tingling like kids at the circus in anticipation. Groover told the committee that he represented Jones Lane and the other House members who had signed the two petitions which caused Clerk Ellard to ask Bond to remain seated during the oath-taking, and as the keystone of his case, Groover then read aloud the oath of office:

"I will support the constitution of this state, and of the United States, and on all questions and measures which may come before me, I will so conduct myself as will in my judgment be most conducive to the interest and prosperity of this state."

That was all. Groover's opening statement was over.

It was now the turn of Howard Moore and Charles Morgan to try to puncture the flinty set of the committee, to give the two black members of the committee some ammunition, some position to argue from when the group retired into its executive session to decide on Bond's seat. Both experienced constitutional lawyers, Moore and Morgan, despite the short time they had, had managed to write out a brief, to have it run off and distributed to the committee. In it, they stated Julian Bond had not engaged in treason but, on the contrary, was "a patriotic, dedicated and loyal American citizen." By convening this hearing, they maintained, the House of Georgia was abrogating rights Bond held under a host of constitutional provisions—his right to a trial by jury, his right to due process and equal protection, his right to subpoena witnesses. In making the move to oust him from racial motives, they asserted, the House members had breached his rights under the First, Thirteenth, Fourteenth and Fifteenth Amendments to the United States Constitution.

But aside from the legalisms at stake, Moore and Morgan argued, the plain facts were that plenty of other public figures in U.S. life had spoken out against the war—among them members of the U.S. House and Senate—and moreover, no less a figure than the President, speaking through his press secretary, had admitted his critics' right to oppose his policies. Bond "and all other representatives of the people of the United States have a positive duty to speak on all public questions and issues," declared Moore and Morgan.

This theme of Bond's right and his concurrent duty as a public official to state his position, albeit a minority view and thus on the far side of the chasm, was the theme of Howard Moore's address to the committee—and the theme of the lengthy courtroom jousting that was to follow this hearing. Standing before the committee in the packed House chamber, Moore lined out his client's position:

"The matter that is before you does not relate to any issue of his qualifications as to citizenship, or as to his being a *bona fide* candidate and elected representative—and no issue is before you as to propriety or legality of the election. The issues," Moore said, "which relate and which are before you deal exclusively with—and solely with—his right as a citizen, a *private citizen*, to endorse a statement and to express his views on the policy of the United States, administration of President Johnson, now in office, relating to the conduct and propriety of the war in Viet Nam. It so happens that Mr. Bond's views on this particular issue are different, perhaps, than the views of many people in the State of Georgia and certainly throughout the United States. At least that seems to be the common understanding, and there are no other issues in this petition, or that will be heard before you this afternoon, except the issues relating to Mr. Bond's right to make a state-ment—his right of dissent."

Moore concluded by telling the committee their inquiry was "the worst sort of witch-hunt" and that their "only American duty consistent with your oath" would be to seat Bond.

Groover's turn came around again, now, and he called, as the first witness for the prosecution, Julian Bond. Speaker Smith himself swore the accused to tell the truth, and Groover began his interrogation. Clearly, to the prosecution's way of looking at the case, Moore's claim that Bond had a basic right to say anything he felt like saying was not even worth attack-ing; what Groover was out to have Bond prove for him was that he had in fact uttered those damning, damnable words, had expressed actual admiration for draft-dodgers and that, preposterous as it might have sounded to any right-thinking House member reading about it in the newspapers or hearing about it over the radio, this Snick member Julian Bond not only said those things, but he was going to stand by what he had said.

"Are you the Horace Julian Bond to whom the protest has been filed?" Groover demanded, running Bond through the preliminary jumps. "I will ask you, if you will, please, to examine Exhibit A to Petition A, which is a statement purportedly attributed to the Student Non-Violent Coordinating Committee . . . you obviously are familiar with that statement . . . how long have you been familiar with that statement . . . did you participate in the draft of that statement . . . after having seen that statement, did you make some statement relative to it . . . did you state that you concurred fully in that statement . . . do you still concur fully in that statement . . . do you concur in all portions of that statement . . . without reservations?"

Exquisitely pleasureful as this inquest might have been for Groover and his clients in the legislature, for Bond, and for his friends and family looking on from the crowded visitors' gallery, the hearing was pure anguish. They squirmed as Groover, having got Bond to acknowledge his complicity in SNCC's antiwar statement, now set out to take him through the statement phrase by incriminating phrase, just in case any of the committee members might have missed the point. "Now, I ask you, Mr. Bond, if you concurred in and support the following language: 'We are in sympathy with and support the men in this country who are unwilling to respond to a military draft. . . .'" Do you concur in those words?"

Bond said, "Mr. Groover, I support the statement in its entirety, and I think that one sentence follows another in it, and that one part has a connection to the other, but I agree with that statement."

Over the repeated objections of Bond's attorneys, House Speaker Smith then allowed Groover to inquire into Bond's admiration for draft-card burners, asking him, "Do you admire the courage of persons who burn their draft cards?"

Up in the gallery, Alice Bond could scarcely stop herself from screaming out. Bond's father sat dumbfounded with new admiration for his son. "I get mad when I get under pressure," Dr. Bond says, "and I was sitting up there getting furiouser and furiouser, but he kept his cool. I didn't know he had it in him, this self-possession. I didn't know he had it in him when they had that kangaroo court."

Bond, answering Groover, said, "I admire people who take an action, and I admire people who feel strongly enough about their convictions to take an action like *that*, knowing the consequences they will face, and that was my original statement when asked that question."

Groover was not going to let that barb pass, so he asked again, "Do you still adhere to that statement?"

"Yes," Bond said, "I do."

In proper courtroom style, Groover then said, "Let me see if I have your statement correct—that you admire people who are willing to take the consequences, to stand up for their principles, is that substantially what you said?"

Bond admitted that it was, and Groover asked him: "And does that admiration of such people go to taking such a stand —when such a stand is in violation of a valid law of the United States?"

Bond had been answering that question for four days now and he said levelly, "I have never suggested or counseled or advocated that any one other person burn their draft card. In fact, I have mine in my pocket and will produce it if you wish. I do not advocate that people should break laws. What I simply tried to say was that I admired the courage of someone who could act on his convictions, knowing that he faces pretty stiff consequences."

Like many political conversations, this one seemed to be in code, a courtly verbal semaphore, following the tacitly understood protocols: in spite of his relentless effort to expose the full depths of Julian Bond's perfidy, Groover was in fact giving him an opportunity to recant, to modify his stand, to disown the SNCC position; and Bond, in telling of his admiration for the courage of draft resisters, was in effect telling the prosecution lawyer and the committee what his own sense of honor would not permit him to say in so many words, that much as he wanted to join the legislature—if he were *really* a fire-breathing treasonous anarchist, would he submit to this inquest?—his sense of honor and personal integrity would not permit him to back and fill, to grovel. They could take it or leave it—but if they did not take it, they would have a fight on their hands.

Groover had just one more witness, radio newsman Ed Spivia; despite the objections of Howard Moore and Charles Morgan, who insisted Spivia had breached federal regulations in tape-recording his interview with Bond without a "beeper" on the line to remind Bond of the fact that he was being taped, Speaker Smith allowed Groover to play a transcription of Spivia's interview. Groover then rested his case, confident that nothing the defense could say in claiming Bond's right to say what he had said would diminish now the impact of those recorded words—or the legislature's angry hunger for vengeance.

Speaker Smith rejected Howard Moore's move to dismiss the unseating petitions on the grounds the prosecution hadn't proved they had any merit, and Moore then called a succession of character witnesses. One after the other, the Reverend Howard Creecy, who had opposed Bond in the Democratic primary, Malcolm Dean, his opponent in the general election, State Senator Horace Ward, State Senator Leroy Johnson, all Negroes and all men of upright standing in Atlanta, urged the House committee to seat Bond. The young SNCC worker,

Johnson told the legislators, "is only twenty-five years old. This is his first political venture and he is bound to be misunderstood. Mr. Bond's effectiveness has been greatly damaged in this legislative body and he has undergone, I am sure, many unpleasant experiences. In my judgment, this man has suffered and has been punished to such a degree that it would do this august body little or no honor to deny him his elective seat." Not only out of compassion for youth should the House stifle its wrath, urged Johnson, but it should beware of a stampede "into performing an act today which may be an albatross around our neck for the next decade."

As the House committee settled back then to listen to some old-fashioned jury-rail-thumping summations, Groover said he would answer questions during part of the time he was allowed for his conclusion. Representative William Alexander, a lawyer, a partner of Howard Moore, and one of the Negroes elected to that session of the legislature, then rose, and despite the considerable political risk to himself, confronted Groover head-on with what seemed to Bond's side the key question: "Do you contend that a member of this body must conform to the prevailing views of any political body?"

Groover reached into the Southern conservative's catechism for his answer: "In no way must a member of this body conform to the political views of any body at any time, but he must, if he is to take an oath, conform to the laws that are on the books, and not advocate or condone their violation—nor approve of others who advocate and condone their violation."

Alexander intruded on this by inquiring, "Can you state whether or not you are aware of any official of the United States Government who has issued any statement to the effect that any member of this House or member-elect has violated any state law?"

Violation of any laws or not, the very idea that any federal official should be meddling in the affairs of the Georgia House was a loathsomely absurd idea to Denmark Groover. "This

House of Representatives of the State of Georgia," he said, "is the judge of members, of the qualifications of its members, and I don't care what any member of the Congress of the United States, including the President, has to say on the subject. *This* is the body that is called on to judge that."

Uncowed by the prosecutor's passion, Alexander asked him if he could recall any previous instances of comment by Georgia officials about federal affairs.

Groover readily admitted, "Yes, sir, a heap of us has criticized President Johnson, and a heap of people criticized Senator Goldwater. There has been a lot of statements made about a lot of people, but I am not aware of a member of this body . . . actively advocating the giving of aid and comfort to the enemies of the United States of America."

That, Alexander quietly reminded Groover, was just a matter of his opinion.

When Groover had finished, Charles Morgan got up to talk to the legislature's special committee on the ouster of Bond. These men certainly knew *of* Morgan, if they didn't know him personally. It had been Morgan who raised all that hell in Birmingham after the black children were killed in the Sunday school bombing there, standing up one day, a white man and a lawyer, to say that, no, it had not been the black people who had bombed the school to arouse sympathy for their movement, and while it may have been extremists who did the actual bombing, it had in larger fact been the entire city of Birmingham that was responsible for the deaths that morning. Morgan had been standing up like that most of his adult life. He knew George Wallace as a young man back in the University of Alabama law school, but he, Morgan, was peculiar. He stood up to try and calm things down when they started talking about admitting Negroes to the university, and he stood up for civil rights workers in trouble the way he was now standing up for Bond.

"Mr. Bond," Morgan told them, "has a right to speak,

and that is purely and simply all that this case is about." If Bond had committed treason, Morgan said, then the thing to do with him was to haul him up before a court of law—which, he reminded them implicitly, this particular assembly didn't happen to be—and try him for treason. "And," he said, "if a member of this body desires to swear out a warrant for Mr. Bond's arrest, then surely that should be done. But that is not what this is all about."

No, Morgan said, the thing that this remarkable hearing was about "is the right of every Georgian and every man to speak *for* segregation or *against* it; *for* the war in Viet Nam, or *against* it, for whatever he desires." What they ought to do this afternoon, Morgan advised them, was "demonstrate to yourselves, demonstrate to the world abroad that there is freedom here in Georgia. Demonstrate to the people what Americans are supposed to be fighting for, demonstrate that we can really exercise those rights here."

Morgan's exhortation fell like a stone in a puddle. He had made no converts.

Denmark Groover got one last shot at sealing the committee up tight; he thereupon launched into the argument that the prosecution would adhere to until the very end of its legal pursuit of Bond months later. "If Julian," Groover said, lapsing into that refusal of the old South to call a black man mister except in sarcasm, "as a private citizen stood upon the streets of the city of Atlanta and said, 'I sympathize with and support the men in this country who are . . . unwilling to respond to a military draft which would compel them to contribute their lives to the United States' aggression in Viet Nam,' then he would have that right, and would be subject only to such sanctions as the United States government saw fit to impose.

"But that is not the issue. If you as a private citizen stood upon the streets and said, 'I will fight to the death,' or, 'Blood will run in the streets,' or, 'No, not one,' and advocated defiance of a federal edict of a federal court applying to you, in a case duly brought against you, or in a federal statute, then you, too, would be subject only to such sanctions as the federal government and those courts might impose."

But what the committee had to consider, Groover told them, was another question entirely, since Julian Bond was an elected official. The House could not try Bond for treason, but it could and must decide "whether or not he in fact subscribes to the Constitution of the United States, which specifically prohibits the giving of aid and comfort to our enemies." Bond, Groover asserted, had given such aid and comfort. Having done so, he then had barred himself from sincerely swearing allegiance to the country, and obviously could not take the oath of office. "Is a man qualified to sit in this House," Groover asked, "who has to think about whether he would commit treason under a given circumstance?"

It was a good question, apparently.

The committee members went into closed session, asking no more statements of Bond despite an invitation from Speaker Smith to do so if they wished, and debated his fate for several hours before returning their decision, on a split vote, to recommend against seating Bond.

The full House then heard impassioned arguments for and against adopting the committee's recommendations. Some of the newly elected blacks urged their colleagues to consider the implications of their decision for Georgia's national image, and to seat Bond, but it was Representative Robert C. Pafford, a white legislator of the 97th District, who struck what was to be the victorious theme of the evening:

"The events of the past now sadden us. We find ourselves now involved in a problem which challenges the dignity of the House, in which we sit, for there is blood that runs down the trenches in a far-off land, that causes tears to run down mothers' cheeks whose sons have perished, to run down widows' and children's faces whose husbands and fathers made the supreme sacrifice for a freedom that we all enjoy. And yet there are those in this land that love not country more than self, and advocate doctrines that ring at the very heart of our nation itself.

"Usually these creatures are far, far away from this land of beautiful rivers, great cities, pine forests, fresh air and pleasant living known as Georgia—but now we find not only our state, our counties, but the Legislature itself has been invaded by one whose 'Snicking' pursues not freedom for us but victory for our enemies.

"But, ladies and gentlemen of this House, the issue that whether he be with us or not is not what plagues me most—but what tears at my soul is that his chair was emptied by a court edict which threatens to tear at the very heart of this nation as founded by our forefathers, for many great and noble Georgians, whose service in this hall has bettered our state and led it to unprecedented heights of prosperity and advancement, are gone."

The old departed bhoys, Pafford declared, were God-fearing and law-abiding fellows, noble and distinguished statesmen no less, and, worst of all, these stalwarts were not only ousted by reapportionment, but the court reapportionment decision had "shoved in their stead—that this state might see darkness instead of light—the infamous Mr. Bond."

Just one more legislator spoke, a man who accused SNCC of hoking the whole thing up, press conference, Bond's endorsement and all, just to regain some of its fading notoriety and thus fill its empty coffers once again with contributions. Then the matter of Julian Bond's membership in the Georgia House of Delegates was put to a vote.

Solicitously, Sloppy Floyd, who with Jones Lane had led the early stages of the move to unseat Bond, asked Speaker Smith to get the reporters into the press box, clear the floor of wives, kinfolk, cousins and Senators, and invoke Rule 200, barring members from voting for absent colleagues. Then, the sworn members of the Georgia House reached up to the little toggle switches on their desks and cast their votes on the voting machine. The red and green lights on the big tally boards up on the walls flickered and clicked like some enormous pinball machine; "the ayes 184; the nays are 12."

Just as though this were the end of any legislative day, the House then went into its traditional adjournment procedure. "All in favor of the gentleman's motion that this House now adjourn until 10 o'clock tomorrow morning, say 'aye.'" The members shouted a chorus of "YES!" "All opposed, say, 'No.'" There was a louder chorus of "NO!" "The ayes seem to have it, and the ayes do have it . . ." and Speaker Smith ran around the front of the rostrum, bowed three times and ran out of the chamber.

Julian Bond stared at the tally board through a blur of tears.

Bond went home that evening and found there, ironically, a present from a relative: it was a tiny American flag on a silver pedestal, intended for his desk in the legislature. "I was not angry," he says now, "in the sense that if somebody hits you, you get angry at them for having done it. I just felt this terrible wrong had been done, to me personally, and to the people who had elected me, to people who had helped me in my campaign and all along. I was just *incredulous*. I didn't believe it. I didn't believe it would happen. I'd never been in a situation like that before and just could not believe that those fellows, these men, were actually going to put me out of the legislature. I just could not . . . it was unbelievable to me. I had not thought about not being in the legislature. I mean, it was just a matter of course—I was going to go up there and *legislate*. As it began to build, I *never* thought—until the vote was taken—that they would unseat me. My mother told me later that I was terribly naïve not to have thought that, but I never thought they'd do it, I just couldn't believe they'd do it. I was tense; I was nervous. I'd broken out in hives all over my body, taken my little nerve pills . . . terrible."

Overcome by bitterness, Bond considered dropping the fight to regain his seat, but was quickly talked out of that by, among others, his father, who convinced him of the importance of trying again, this time in the courts.

As Howard Moore and Charles Morgan pondered over their strategy, they lighted upon a provision of the U.S. Code that seemed promising. Under it, a special three-judge court could be convened to hear Bond's case against the state of Georgia. The two lawyers began their preparations. Meanwhile, the Reverend Martin Luther King cut short a trip to California to return to Atlanta, threatening "creative" demonstrations to protest the House's treatment of Bond. "It is incumbent upon me today," he rumbled upon his arrival, "to express my indignation for the state legislature's unconscionable refusal Monday to seat Representative-elect Bond." Not only would he lead the Southern Christian Leadership Conference in a demonstration march, King declared, but if that didn't work, then the organization would consider invoking a national economic boycott against Georgia-made products. King told a press conference that he saw Bond's ouster as an alarming indication of a drift toward an America "where dissent is equated with disloyalty." He reminded his listeners of President Kennedy's grim warning that "war will exist until the distant day when the conscientious objector enjoys the same reputation and prestige that the warrior does today." Many of the same legislators who had cast their votes against Bond in the House were, King said, "the very persons who have consistently defied the law of the land through their irresponsible acts and statements." There had not been, King recalled, a move to unseat any of those Georgia legislators who in 1954 had called so loudly in defiance to urge evasion and circumvention of the Supreme Court order to desegregate Southern schools.

Outside Georgia the editorial writers were at last aroused to full voice, declaring sonorously, as did the liberal *Washington*

Post, for instance, that not only had the Georgia House flaunted the principle of representative government, "it has doubtless made a martyr of a foolish young man who had discredited himself as a potential legislator. By attempting to muzzle a critic," the *Post* said, "the House has committed a more serious offense than the one it sought to condemn." The editors of the *Wall Street Journal*, admitting that to them Bond was "a noisy civil rights activist and Viet Nam pacifist, most of whose views strike us as puerile and repugnant," nonetheless condemned the House for, the *Journal* said cautiously, appearing to be "misusing their authority to accomplish a narrow end." Syndicated cartoonist Herb Block of the *Washington Post*, depicted a giant redneck labeled "Georgia Legislature" hustling a harried-looking young Negro out the front door, with the caption: "Equal rights doesn't mean you can be as foolish as we are." The Scripps-Howard chain's now-defunct New York *World-Telegram* told its afternoon readers that while Bond was "about as wrong as anybody could be," the House nonetheless "is even more wrong in denying him the House seat to which he was elected." Liberal columnist James Wechsler, with his customary perception, wrote in the *New York Post* that the House action had come "at a time when the Defense Department was revealing that Negroes comprised a disproportionately large percentage of our fighting forces because so few of them could claim college or other special deferments." Bond's ouster, Wechsler surmised, was another example of the fine hand of "The Committee to Reduce America to Absurdity," and a cameo illustration of how denigration of minority rights so often passes for majority rule, all the worse in that instance because to those Negroes fighting in Viet Nam "we sent news that Georgia's legislature was exhibiting its dedication to the cause of freedom by exiling a lonely Negro dissenter. . . ."

In Atlanta, *Constitution* editor Eugene Patterson saw the booting of Bond as an act performed by men too angry to think straight. He said, however, that the legislators had "probably voted the sentiment of the people. No recent issue has brought such a demand for action on Georgia legislators. Families with sons in Viet Nam called them up and made it plain that they wanted Julian Bond's hide." Patterson, to dramatize the enraged thrust of the House, quoted Stephen Vincent Benét's poem, "John Brown's Body," which told of Wainscott Bristol, "who, under overwhelming attack, stepped alone from his cover and dropped his hat, while his pistols cracked with a single crack, cried:

> 'Here we go on the red dog's back!
> High, low, jack and the goddam game.
> And then the answering volley came. . . .'

"Goaded beyond even wanting to calculate its folly," Patterson wrote, "the House bid high, low, jack and the game and jumped with a splendid Southern flourish right into the other side's trap." This trap Patterson took to be a bid by SNCC for a renascence of national attention upon itself. Based as it was on no clear law, Patterson wrote, "the House action probably can't even survive a simple test in court."

Readying their own answering volley, Howard Moore and Charles Morgan were nearly set to try such a test. Joining Bond as co-plaintiffs against the state of Georgia were two residents of his district, Mrs. Arel Keyes and the Reverend Martin Luther King, who entered their own emotional brief; in part it stated: "Had a member of the Ku Klux Klan, or the John Birch Society or the White Citizens Councils spoken against federal policy, he would have been cheered. Had Julian Bond failed to exercise rights guaranteed by the Constitution . . . had he recanted, begged or crawled, he might have been seated. These things he would not do. No free man should. No free man would." Bond's own brief underlined the historic precedent for dissent, citing William Lloyd Garrison's burning of a copy of the Constitution, Lincoln's opposition to war with Mexico, and General Billy Mitchell's defiance of the military. "History," Bond told the court in his appeal, "vindicated them." But the issue before this specially convened federal tribunal was not dissent; the three judges had to determine instead whether in fact the Georgia constitution had been properly applied by the Georgia House in barring Bond, and whether in its application the state constitution had run counter to the United States Constitution—thus violating the Fourteenth Amendment.

The hearing began at one P.M., January 28, 1966, before Judges Elbert P. Tuttle, Griffin B. Bell and Lewis Morgan—who was not related to Bond's attorney. The arguments eventually were to fill a transcript nearly half an inch thick, more than 30,000 words. The elements were plain: Georgia Attorney General Arthur K. Bolton as the counsel for the defendants, Sloppy Floyd, Jones Lane and the other capital officials under attack by Bond, merely cited the degree of U.S. involvement in Viet Nam; Bond's lawyers claimed his right of free speech. Where Bolton said, "Bond was denied his seat because what he said, we believe, was not only a violation of the law itself, but he also encouraged and tried to induce others to violate the law," Morgan and Moore came back again and again with the claim that Bond was shielded from house sanctions by his right to speak his mind.

In the end, as he had known he would, Bond lost in the federal court, too. In a split vote, Judges Bell and Morgan, after a week or so of deliberation, agreed that the House, whether wisely or not, was within its own legal purview in ousting Bond and they said "the judgment of this court is not to be substituted for that of the House." Bond had a right to criticize national policy, the two judges asserted, but he had no such right to endorse a statement such as SNCC's, which they characterized as "a call alien to the concept of the pluralistic society which makes this nation." Judge Tuttle alone found that Bond should not have been denied his seat, and he based his decision on the fact that Bond had been, he said, "disqualified on account of conduct not enumerated in the Georgia Constitution. . . ."

Judge Tuttle's two colleagues on the bench had based their conclusion on Bond's endorsement of that call to action. They said bluntly that "the call to action, and this is what we find to be a rational basis for the decision which denied Mr. Bond his seat, is that language which states that SNCC supports those men in this country who are unwilling to respond to a military draft." All of Howard Moore's eloquence in support of the First Amendment, which, he had argued, shielded Bond from the ouster, had been overwhelmed in the minds of the two federal judges by the force of Attorney General Bolton's litany of U.S. involvement in the war.

Bond faced another election, one intended to pick a successor to himself, but one that he meant to win and keep on winning until he was allowed to occupy the seat he felt was rightly his; Howard Moore and Charles Morgan went back to their law offices, to draft new appeals—to the Supreme Court of the United States. And the world outside, which at first had reacted to Bond's ouster with scarcely more than a shrug, was mounting an outcry of indignation that merely hardened Bond's Georgia opponents deeper and deeper into their positions.

The Julian Bond who not long before was excoriated as the worst kind of zealot, and only faintly defended on the grounds of principle alone, was now suddenly the object of that process of lionization that sometimes happens in America: he became a cause. Vice-President Hubert Humphrey, asked about Bond on network television by some reporters, said he wanted to forewarn every American "that one of the most precious freedoms we have is the right to be different." Twenty-three United States Congressmen immediately fired off a telegram to Georgia's Governor Sanders, telling him that "the right of every American stands in jeopardy if the action of the Georgia House is not reversed." Then the beautiful people stepped in, taking out an advertisement that occupied almost a full page of the *New York Times* asking, "Will you join the defenders of Bond's right to dissent?" Among the signers were writer-comic Woody Allen, actor-singer-activist Harry Belafonte, Joseph Heller, author of *Catch-22*, Dr. Benjamin Spock, pediatrician turned antiwar leader, and Dagmar Wilson, a women's rights activist and a leader in antiwar efforts. They snubbed Georgia's pols altogether and asked sympathizers to send telegrams directly to President Lyndon Johnson himself on behalf of Bond. Three Republican Senators and five Congressmen issued a joint statement in support of Bond—despite their equally mutual abhorrence of his views on the war. The young legislator found himself invited to a luncheon at the United Nations, hosted by the ambassadors from fifteen black nations, and seated among Martin Luther King, Belafonte, James Forman, and veteran rights strategist Bayard Rustin. That same day, one of the most beautiful people of them all, the mayor of New York, John Vliet Lindsay, who does not greet just everybody who comes to his city, greeted Bond, and greeted him most warmly indeed, telling the young Georgia pariah, "If I were still in the private practice of law, I would be pleased to take on the case and argue it."

With that sometimes baffling and persnickety way he has of going his own route, Bond—amid all this warm embracement as a martyred young black politician cruelly handled by those rednecks down South—suddenly and perversely, it seemed to his supporters, made a decision that was to cast his every move into doubt and suspicion. He retained as his counsel before the Supreme Court two controversial left-wing New York law-yers, Leonard Boudin and Victor Rabinowitz. His brother-in-law, Howard Moore, remained in the case, but in a private capacity and no longer as a representative of the American Civil Liberties Union, as he had been before the Georgia

House and the special federal court. The ACLU, upon learning of the entry of Boudin and Rabinowitz, withdrew from the Bond case, issuing a statement as it did so that the organization would remain as *amicus curiae*, friend of the court, but not as a representative of Bond. "The introduction of attorneys not affiliated with the ACLU creates a conflict," the ACLU statement said, "with this practice of primary responsibility by ACLU counsel." Asked to comment further, Charles Morgan snapped, "The statement speaks for itself." Bond, out campaigning in the special election, told an inquiring newsman that he thought the ACLU withdrawal was "just another white man's trick."

Digging elsewhere, the press soon discovered that Bond's new attorneys were as shocking—to Georgia sensibilities—as the views of the man they were defending. The reaction in Georgia was swift and electric: BOND LAWYERS PAID $40,000 BY CUBA was the headline on a page-one story in the *Journal* when the paper's Washington correspondent, Margaret Shannon, unearthed records indicating that Rabinowitz and Boudin were registered agents of the Castro government and for the tiny African nationlet of Kenya. *Constitution* reporter Bill Shipp discovered that Boudin and Rabinowitz belonged to the National Lawyers Guild and the Emergency Civil Liberties Committee, both of which groups had been fingered as Communist fronts by Congressional committees. Bond had known full well of his lawyers' connections with both the ECLC, the NLG, and foreign governments, but felt, Shipp said, that his new lawyers, with Moore, would afford him the "best legal counsel available."

Bond's understandable interest in top-drawer legal talent aside, the press saw this shift as a clue that the case—and Bond, too—was turning in a sinister direction. "It represents," said the *Constitution* editorial, "ACLU's refusal to be used for a political cause not germane to the case. It is also a warning that the Bond case is about to follow the classic pattern of a captured cause. The appeal to the U.S. Supreme Court will be turned into a vehicle for fulminations against U.S. policy in Viet Nam; there probably will be fund-raising campaigns and rounds of public appearances.

"As for Mr. Bond," the paper growled, "it is growing increasingly difficult to attribute his poor judgment to naïveté. Whatever other purpose his continued flirtation with the far left may serve, it does not serve his constituency well. If he is ever seated, he will be isolated and ineffective. And the whole civil rights movement suffers by this grafting on of spurious issues."

Bond today explains the change in lawyers by saying that Rabinowitz, whom he already knew through Rabinowitz's daughter, Joni, a one-time SNCC worker, called him to volunteer his legal assistance in the appeal to the Supreme Court. "I said yes." But at the time, old ties of friendship went unmentioned. Bond simply told inquirers that "just because a lawyer represents a murderer doesn't make a lawyer a murderer," and let the people draw their own conclusions.

Working in his large office at the Forsyth Street headquarters of the ACLU, or sprawled in his living room in suburban Atlanta with his lawbooks and papers scattered on a card table around him, Charles Morgan readied his *amicus curiae* brief to the Supreme Court. In one bitter passage, Morgan said, "Under the terms of the Georgia constitutional provisions as construed and applied below, a conscientious person who aspires to be a legislator must play a type of Russian roulette. He must speculate about the controversiality of every statement and the intentions of his fellow legislators. If he guesses wrong, he loses his political life." The nine justices of the Supreme Court must reinstate Bond, Morgan urged them, so that "the nation can once again be instructed that transgression upon the rights of unfettered speech will not be tolerated."

Boudin, Rabinowitz and Moore, at the same time, were drafting their own appeal to the Supreme Court, and in it, they struck at the heart of the state of Georgia's position. The opinion of the federal court, they said, "does not challenge the constitutional right of SNCC to make the statement. Rather, it emphasizes the fact that Mr. Bond 'was more than a private citizen; he was an officer and employe of SNCC and was about to become a member of the House of Representatives of Georgia.' The court below was of the opinion that an elected member of the House was entitled to less constitutional protection than the average citizen. Underlying the opinion is," Bond's attorneys pointed out, "the unarticulated view that Mr. Bond's elected position imposed upon him the obligation to support 'national policy' or to be restrained in his criticism of it.

"This," they said, "is a conception of second class citizenship for a legislator, totally without support in logic or in the constitutional history of legislative bodies. It is completely inconsistent with the duty which the office itself imposes upon the incumbent to engage in a continuing dialogue on public affairs with his constituents."

Georgia Attorney General Arthur Bolton, in defending Sloppy Floyd and the other officials against Bond, maintained eloquently that there had been ample legal justification for Bond's ouster. But at the same time, Bolton, in his lawyer's language, portrayed Bond as a man entrapped by the web of Southern political sense. More than politics, that sense is a highly moral, deeply ingrained way of looking at one's town, one's state, one's nation, and one's self. Religious, conservative, ancestor-worshiping, choosing unmindfully more often to look not ahead but to the past, Southerners have always been fond of calling themselves Populists, always quick to declare where their allegiance lies in the nation-old debate over whether government exists to guard minorities or to enforce the will of the majority. America is, their leaders say from bunting-hung rostrums, a nation of laws and not of men—and always there is the sly, shared, ineffable understanding of just precisely whom it is—*which* men—that those laws serve, which side of that deep and jagged chasm rending the national soul they stand upon.

"The purpose of the constitutional provision and principles involved in the case at bar," Bolton told the nine justices in his brief, "is to insure the right of the people to self-government. This concept of self-government is the unique feature of our political system. The function of the courts should be to support and uphold this concept.

"Our Constitution creates a fundamental distinction between the people and their political servants. The citizens have the right and the duty to speak freely on public issues, and to criticize those entrusted with public duty." But on the other hand, Bolton said, "The representatives of the people, including state legislators, are required to support the fundamental law which provides for self-government.

"The people must have the power and authority to take proper measures safeguarding the public service from disloyal conduct, else their liberties cannot long endure."

Bond, Bolton said, was "a servant of the people." As such, then, he was required to meet certain qualifications. The House found that he did not meet them. This power to determine the worthiness of its members, Bolton said, "at least in the absence of some extraordinary and gross abuse which clearly and unambiguously violates a federally protected right (e.g., a clear showing of a purposeful and systematic exclusion on the ground of race, color or religion, or the showing of a continued pattern of some other abuse of which no possible remedy appears, such as a malapportioned legislature) should be preserved."

Bond, Bolton said, lacked the ability to support and uphold the United States Constitution—and just in case, in ousting him for endorsing the SNCC statement, the House might have trampled on Bond's First Amendment rights, Bolton cited a

1950 Supreme Court decision which stated, "Obviously the framers of the Constitution thought that the execution of an affirmation of minimal loyalty to the government was worth the price of whatever deprivation of individual freedom of conscience was involved." Bond therefore had gone beyond First Amendment protection, Bolton contended, and in doing so had called down upon himself constitutionally required sanctions. He had no rights as a citizen-critic because, Bolton said, "by virtue of his candidacy and election he became the servant of the citizenry."

The state's brief might have been an epitaph for a view of government, of society, that simply did not contain within it the spring of progress, the germ of enlightenment. Leaders were thereby muffled, stifled, limited to mere response, their initiative forbidden.

The Supreme Court, of course, saw through all this persiflage immediately, and its verdict came down surprisingly soon after the oral arguments were given.

Standing before the high bench in the huge marble room, its somber atmosphere softened not at all by the crimson drapes and warm umber hues of its deep-stained wooden chairs, Leonard Boudin listened as Justice Abe Fortas asked him, "Suppose an elected official advocated overthrow of the government of Georgia by force and the institution of a military dictatorship?"

"As a matter of principle," Boudin replied, "he still could not be excluded. He has an absolute right to speak, subject of course, to criminal action. Freedom of franchise is involved here, as well as freedom of speech."

Boudin invoked the memories of Hamilton and Madison as he maintained before the Supreme Court that barring an elected official from his chair is against the grain of American history, that our founders had agreed a legislature should abjure passing on the men their constituents sent to legislate.

"I refer to the Wilkes case," he said, in which John Wilkes, barred from Commons for seditious libel in his attacks on George III in 1768, had his ouster expunged by the House in 1782 because his exclusion was "subversive of the rights of the whole body of electors. . . ."

"Suppose," asked Justice Black, "he stated that he was opposed to federal anti-discrimination laws? Any difference?"

Boudin replied, "No, it's the same case."

"You're taking the position that a person can say what he wants," Black said. "Then we reach the question whether the oath can penalize?"

"The Georgia legislature has taken action," Boudin said. "Mr. Bond has done nothing. The fact that a governor-elect took action to deprive citizens of rights would not bar him from being seated. The Georgia oath is merely a solemnification; it is not something by which we can judge conduct or speech. The oath can't be used to exclude."

"You come back to the proposition," Black said, "that you can't restrain speech as a qualification for office."

Justice White interjected: "Or statements subsequent to election."

Boudin said, "Yes."

"Or actions?" asked White.

"That would be a different problem," Boudin said. "There is no question of expulsion here."

Later in the hearing, Justice Black asked Attorney General Bolton, "So you have very nominal qualifications in Georgia. Is there any qualification at all involved?"

"Support of the Constitution," Bolton responded.

"You don't suppose that means that a man will never express an opinion hostile to national policy?" Justice Black inquired.

"No," Bolton said, "but it is necessary to support the Constitution."

"But members of legislatures everywhere do express themselves, and vigorously," Black said. "So that's no bar."

"But the legislature can hear him," Bolton said.

"You mean, can hear his views?" inquired Chief Justice Warren, somewhat puzzled.

"The legislature," Bolton said, "in an Article VI hearing, can hear any relevant evidence."

"The question," Justice White said, "is what being 'bound to support' means. Suppose he advocated amendment of the Constitution—I take it you would think that was all right. So a man can disagree with others and still be protected? You concede that Bond can state his views, but if he said, 'I will not obey the Constitution,' that's different?"

"Yes," answered Bolton.

"And you say that's what he did? He advocated law-breaking?"

"Yes."

Chief Justice Warren asked, "Where do you find that?"

Whereupon, Bolton read the taped interview, including the portion in which Julian Bond expressed his admiration of draft-card burners. Bond stated he carried his card—and would gladly show it, and denied he advocated burning draft cards.

"Is that all you rely on?" Justice Brennan asked. "Is that it?"

Justice Potter Stewart asked, somewhat increduously, "Are you telling us that there is a requirement to support a 'war' that Congress hasn't even declared? You're differentiating legislators from other people?"

Said Attorney General Bolton: "Yes."

Stewart rejoined: "There is no obligation on anyone to support Viet Nam, is there?"

Bolton admitted there was not.

Chief Justice Warren then said, "But you tell us that he can't be seated."

"The legislature had a rational basis," Bolton replied. "We are not concerned with whether another forum would have judged differently."

"Can't we also determine whether the House had a *right* to

judge him?" inquired Chief Justice Warren. "What authority they had?"

Bolton came back with the answer that "the House is the sole judge of qualifications. And upholding the Constitution is a qualification."

Then Justice Black asked, "Even if they impose an unconstitutional qualification?"

Bolton admitted, "Of course, that's no good."

Chief Justice Warren asked Bolton, "Would that give us jurisdiction to determine the propriety of the rejection?"

When Warren asked where the dividing line was between the court having jurisdiction and having none, Bolton answered, "Whether Constitutional rights were violated." And the ordeal was almost over.

Delivered by Chief Justice Warren for the entire Court, the unanimous decision quickly reviewed the entire case from Bond's election, through the issuance of the SNCC statement, the House hearing and ouster and the District Court decisions. Warren wrote:

We are not persuaded by the State's attempt to distinguish, for the purposes of our jurisdiction, between an exclusion alleged to be on racial grounds and one alleged to violate the First Amendment. The basis for the argued distinction is that, in this case, Bond's disqualification was grounded on a constitutional standard—the requirement of taking an oath to support the Constitution. But Bond's contention is that this standard was utilized to infringe his First Amendment rights, and we cannot distinguish, for purposes of our assumption of jurisdiction, between a disqualification under an unconstitutional standard and a disqualification which, although under color of a proper standard, is alleged to violate the First Amendment.

We do not quarrel with the State's contention that the oath provisions of the United States and Georgia Constitutions do not violate the First Amendment. But this requirement does not authorize a majority of state legislators to test the sincerity with which another duly elected legislator can swear to uphold the Constitution. Such a power could be utilized to restrict the right of legislators to dissent from national or state policy or that of a majority of their colleagues under the guise of judging their loyalty to the Constitution. Certainly there can be no question but that the First Amendment protects expressions in opposition to national foreign policy in Viet Nam and to the Selective Service system. The State does not contend otherwise. But it argues that Bond went beyond expressions of opposition, and counseled violations of the Selective Service laws, and that advocating violation of federal law demonstrates a lack of support for the Constitution. The State declines to argue that Bond's statement would violate any law if made by a private citizen, but it does argue that even though such a citizen might be protected by his First Amendment rights, the State may nonetheless apply a stricter standard to legislators. We do not agree.

The state of Georgia, the Supreme Court acknowledged, did indeed have the right to insist on having its legislators—if not all its citizens—swear to support the Constitution.

The opinion continued:

But this difference in treatment does not support the exclusion of Bond, for while the State has an interest in requiring its legislators to swear to a belief in constitutional processes of government, surely the oath gives it no interest in limiting its legislators' capacity to discuss their views of local or national policy. The manifest function of the First Amendment in a representative government requires that legislators be given the widest latitude to express their views on issues of policy. The central commitment of the First Amendment as summarized in the opinion of the Court in *New York Times v. Sullivan* is that "debate on public issues should be uninhibited, robust and wide-open." We think the rationale of the *New York Times* case disposes of the claim that Bond's statements fell outside the range of constitutional protection. Just as erroneous statements must be protected to give freedom of expression the breathing space it needs to survive, so statements criticizing public policy and the implementation of it must be similarly protected. The State argues that the *New York Times* principle should not be extended to statements by a legislator because the policy of encouraging free debate about governmental operations only applies to the citizen-critic of his government. We find no support for this distinction in the *New York Times* case or in any other decision of this Court. The interest of the public in hearing all sides of a public issue is hardly advanced by extending more protection to citizen-critics than to legislators. Legislators have an obligation to take positions on controversial political questions so that their constituents can be fully informed by them, and be better able to assess their qualifications for office; also so they may be represented in governmental debates by the person they have elected to represent them. We therefore hold that the disqualification of Bond from membership in the Georgia House because of his statements violated Bond's right of free expression under the First Amendment.

The metallic voice of the public-address system called out his name as Bond waited in the Indianapolis airport for his flight to Atlanta. As he listened to the voice on the telephone, his face registered ecstatic surprise. A radio newsman on the other end of the line told him about the Supreme Court decision, asking him for a comment, and Bond, happily, gave him the quotes he needed for his next show. "I was surprised," Bond says now, "surprised because I didn't think it would be unanimous." He added, "What the Supreme Court set up was a precedent—in the future, no legislature will ever be able to do this kind of thing again." But, really, there was no way of expressing that suffusing joy in words that radio could carry. "I mean," says Bond, "I really felt happy—happy, as we used to say, as a sissy in Boys Town. The court ruling 'made it up to me,' financially—I got all my money back, my $2,000 pay that I missed. It vindicated me; it really set the record straight. But nothing . . ." He pauses, trying to express the bitterness he felt toward these men who tried so hard to bar him from the House, and finally Bond says, "I didn't *really* feel vindicated until the summer in Chicago." (Bond was referring to his victory over Georgia's Democratic regulars at the 1968 party convention.) "Some of the people who voted to get me out of the legislature were in that delegation in Chicago; I can't remember their names, but that was sweet vindication . . . sweet, sweet vindication."

The public-address system paged Bond again and again as the nation's press sought his reaction to the court's decision, and when at last the plane arrived in Atlanta, Bond found a battery of television cameras awaiting him, a forest of microphones at the end of the ramp. "And I was just as happy as I could be. But . . . I wasn't happy. It wasn't my accomplishment that the Supreme Court had ruled; what happened in Chicago was *partly* my accomplishment—I directly had some influence over that; I had little or none over the Supreme Court."

Almost a year of litigation had followed Bond's ouster on January 10, 1966, before the Supreme Court handed down its decision on December 5, 1966, drawing Bond's attention away from the affairs of the Student Non-Violent Coordinating Committee and leaving him little time for working there. The organization by the time he was clear of the courts was scarcely the same one he had helped start. Always at best a loosely knit coalition of ferociously independent individualists, SNCC was suffering severe internal upheavals and strains, exacerbated all the more as contributors who had sustained its field operations in the past now sent their money elsewhere; they were either disturbed by the organization's increasing militance and its growing unwillingness to allow participation by whites, or, feeling the goals of the group had largely been accomplished by the passage of civil rights legislation and that antiwar efforts were now more urgent, they contributed instead to that cause.

Within SNCC, many of the members were losing interest themselves. Some of them had finished college, and wanted to start getting settled. Others—radicalized by their experiences in the field and disillusioned about the effectiveness of non-violence and the likelihood of ever accomplishing their goals within the system—wanted to launch a direct thrust at the social barriers confronting Southern Negroes. Bond's mother later observed that at this stage the "gangsters" were taking over. One of SNCC's most influential members, Robert Parris Moses, who had directed the massive summer campaign in Mississippi during 1964, quit the organization abruptly and dramatically at its annual meeting in Atlanta in 1965. During the conference (at which SNCC had decided to formulate the stand on Viet Nam that was to cause Bond so much trouble) Moses decided something that not very many people and certainly few leaders ever decide: that he did not want to go on being himself any more. It was complicated, but many of his friends, Bond among them, thought they understood. A young Negro who had studied graduate mathematics at Harvard and then taught at a private preparatory school in New York, Moses had at first aroused considerable suspicion among the young SNCC workers when he appeared in Atlanta in the early 1960's. With his obvious intelligence, his articulateness, his strange story of forsaking a career in education because he wanted to work in the Movement, Moses impressed them as some preposterous fraud. "At first," says Bond, "we thought he was a Communist." Before very long, however, Moses had not only won the confidence of the young people of SNCC, he had become one of their most revered leaders. "If he had asked people to jump out of a window for him—not that Bob ever would," Bond says, "there would have been a line forming at the window in no time." That kind of esteem and awe weighed heavily on Moses, as did the burden of leadership itself, and he began to feel deeply that it was one of the very things wrong with SNCC.

At the 1965 meeting, recalls Grenville Whitman, Moses walked out during a dispute over some issue, "and then, about an hour later, he came back. He seemed to have been drinking, but he was not drunk. And he started saying he was going to change his name, that he just didn't want to be known as Bob Moses anymore—everybody would look to him for advice. The point he was trying to make was that Snick was saying, 'We're the Movement,' and Moses was saying, 'The longer you sit here in this church and argue, the more the Movement is passing you by.' And," Whitman says, "Moses was saying, 'You're setting yourself up in a leadership role and you shouldn't do that.' He felt always very strongly that people looked to him for leadership, and so, sort of symbolically, he changed his name, and he said, 'I'm not Bob Moses anymore—I'm somebody else.' And he walked out—it was a stunning thing."

Moses today is rumored to be in Africa, but none of his old friends really knows where he is; but they do think that they know the real reason he changed his name—to Bob Parris—and walked out of SNCC forever, and it was only partly that he was weary of leadership. There was another, more ominous reason, foreshadowing the eventual disintegration of the civil rights movement as Bond had known it. Moses was becoming increasingly persuaded that whites and blacks simply could not work together as they had in the early days of the Movement, and had come to believe instead that blacks had to work among themselves, within organizations of their own making to achieve their own goals. Friends like Bond recall hearing how Moses at last approached, one by one, his white friends, shook hands, and told them he would never again speak to another white man. Perhaps the story is apocryphal.

By the time of the next annual SNCC meeting, outside Nashville in May, 1966, that tension had become nearly unbearable for both blacks and whites in SNCC. For the first two or three days, the conference occupied itself with far-roaming, free-wheeling discussion of SNCC's relations with other rights groups, especially with the Reverend Martin

Luther King's Southern Christian Leadership Conference, its position in relation to the U.S. government, and its policy regarding its own white members. Back and forth, the SNCC membership chewed over their views of their future, the war, and the need that some of them saw now for new leadership, new blood. Some of them, who had worked in a project in black Atlanta's Vine City ghetto, came forth with a "black manifesto," strongly urging that SNCC drop its official commitment to nonviolence and become a sort of guerrilla force, changing its name at the same time—and barring whites from membership.

The atmosphere was clearly one of dissatisfaction with the old regime—John Lewis, chairman, and James Forman, executive secretary—who were being eyed with disdain as hopelessly old-fashioned and too moderate for the kind of militance the membership was moving toward. The group opened its balloting for officers on Friday evening around eleven, and the voting continued on through the smoky night until finally, about three o'clock Saturday morning, Lewis emerged still the chairman, winner by a large vote. Then, as the group started to vote on candidates for the executive committee, the proceedings were interrupted by a member who challenged Lewis's victory as illegal, kicking off a renewed and this time more heated debate. Friends turned on old comrades, and bitter tears were shed. Around 6:30 A.M., SNCC voted Stokely Carmichael, who had worked to launch the Black Panther Party in Lowndes County, Alabama, its new chairman. Announced Carmichael in a SNCC statement to the press, "Snick is going to intensify its efforts in the area of independent politics. Our experience organizing in the hard-core racist areas of this country has been one of inaction on the part of the federal government. We will struggle as we have in the past for human rights and join with those around the world who know the same oppression that we know, and the same deception on the part of the so-called United States government in its claims of concern for democracy." Asking blacks to join the Democratic Party, Carmichael said, in explaining why independent political efforts—such as his own in "bloody Lowndes," where several civil rights workers had been killed and wounded—were essential, "is like asking Jews to join the Nazi Party."

Carmichael's brand of civil rights work was too raw for many of the whites in SNCC, and they promptly quit; a great many of the group's blacks soon followed, including John Lewis, who resigned on July 22, 1966, and Julian Bond, who resigned in early September. For both men the decision to leave the organization they had built and watched come apart was a painful one. Lewis felt SNCC had ceased to exist as a group and had become instead a clique of personalities, and he advised Bond to leave for the same reasons. The organization by the time they left was broke and barely alive; Carmichael's strident outcries were steadily offending its few remaining supporters, and to draw new ones he reached further and further toward tactics the old SNCC would never have countenanced.

While other cities erupted in racial violence, Atlanta managed to survive 1966 without incident until early September; then police shot a suspected car thief and there on the scene, Stokely Carmichael yelled, "We're tired of these racist police killing our people—we're going to be back at four o'clock and tear this place up!" By the time police had quelled the five hundred Negroes who exploded in anger at the shooting despite Mayor Ivan Allen's plea for them to go home, seventy-three people had been injured and sixteen arrested—including Stokely Carmichael, charged with inciting the riot and held in $10,000 bond.

In the wake of the riot, Bond resigned from SNCC, telling a reporter he was doing so because "there are things I want to do and Snick is doing some things I don't want to do. But primarily it's because I'm twenty-six years old now and it's time to find out if there's *anything* I can do." Now, Bond looks back and says the main reason he resigned was that he didn't feel right about accepting a salary—$85 a week—from an organization he hadn't had time to work for.

To support his family, Bond tried to replace his SNCC salary with income from speeches and articles. His lecture fees in those days ran around $200, which left him little profit after his travel expenses; he usually did not ask a fee for a speech in Atlanta, but when one small church offered him $5, he took it because he needed it. Leisurely evenings of listening to jazz and writing down the poetry it evoked in him were rare now —he had to turn out his words for cash money. One of the articles he wrote for *Ramparts* magazine dealt with his unseating and in it he anonymously voiced his apprehension of what was in store for him when the legislature convened in January for its 1967 session. Under the byline of "our Georgia correspondent," Bond wrote:

> Rising to argue against being expelled from the Georgia House of Representatives, a Negro man compared the pleas for justice made by his fellow Negro legislators to "slaves begging under the lash."
>
> "You may expel, Gentlemen," he continued, "but I firmly believe that one day you will repent it. The black man cannot protect a country if the country doesn't protect him; and if tomorrow a war should arise, I would not raise a musket to defend the country where my manhood is denied. I will say this much to the colored men of Georgia. Never lift a finger in defense of Georgia, unless Georgia acknowledges that you are men, and invests you with the rights pertaining to manhood."

The speech Bond quoted was uttered by another Georgia Negro ninety-eight years before his own experience at the hands of angry white legislators. All that white Georgians had learned in the intervening years, Bond wrote, was that race must not be "an open factor in excluding a dissident member." Tracing the brief history of his own exclusion, Bond wrote that he foresaw no trouble in being sworn in when the House convened—but said that he expected difficulties immediately afterward. "There are members of the House who will never speak to him, some who will vote against any measure he sponsors, and some who will refuse to serve on committees with him," wrote *Ramparts'* Georgia correspondent.

The legislature did nothing to prove Bond wrong when he presented himself on opening day, 1967. Although he came now armed with the Supreme Court decision, and despite the fact that he had resigned from the Student Non-Violent Coordinating Committee, he still had maintained his ties with the Movement and had even taken steps himself to keep up with its adventures into new radical directions. In mid-1966 he had helped found the National Conference for New Politics, aimed at raising money to back antiwar candidates in upcoming Congressional elections and a presidential candidate "committed to peace in Viet Nam." Politicians have long memories, and Bond's new forays were not only cause for alarm in themselves in Georgia, but they kept bright and alive the memory of his suspicious behavior in the past. Thus, no one was less surprised than Bond himself when some members walked out as he entered the House chamber. To underline the reluctance with which they were admitting him, the men who managed the protocol of the House decided that—rather than swear the oath of office in mass, as they had when Bond was requested to remain in his seat while the others stood together—this time the legislators would stand in small groups, their hands on separate Bibles, to swear their fealty to state and nation.

"I don't want nothing to do with him," Sloppy Floyd told reporters as he conspicuously exited, and many of his colleagues obviously didn't, either. Amplifying his reasons for leaving, Floyd said, "I don't want to be associated with any individual like him. He's a liability to everything he touches, and he reaches the height of stupidity when he acts like we are going to treat him like any other member of this body."

Floyd said he was shocked and amazed by the Supreme Court's decision, and added that he, personally, did not feel that Bond was any more entitled to sit in the same House with him because of the ruling than he had been the previous January. Jones Lane, another of the instigators of the move to oust Bond, his anger as unabated by the decision and the passage of time as Floyd's, said, "It does seem a shame that the highest court of this land would decree that the laws of a sovereign state and the welfare of its people may be determined in part by a person who openly and flagrantly gives aid and comfort to our nation's enemy."

Outside Georgia, the reaction to Bond's victory in the court was scarcely more enthusiastic; editorials in the *Washington Post* and the *Christian Science Monitor* lauded the court's defense of free speech, but scored Bond as an advocate of an unacceptable and offensive philosophy; *The New York Times* observed that the court had written a "new chapter in the constant battle for man's right to think and speak as his conscience dictates." In a separate story, the *Times* claimed to be able to perceive a curious kind of nonmoving motion by Bond, stating, "the young man is no longer at the far left edge of the militant civil rights movement. That position has been commandeered by the Black Power people and thus, without moving a step, Mr. Bond has become more respectable." Bond, of course, never had been at the far left edge of the Movement, and if he had suddenly become the darling of a certain kind of Yankee negrophile civil rights devotee, that by no means made him more respectable in Georgia or the Georgia legislature.

Like so many other things the Supreme Court had lately stuffed down the white South's throat, or thought it had, Bond would be tolerated, but just barely. "If this is the law of the land," said Governor Carl Sanders, hearing of Bond's triumph in the Supreme Court, "I will abide by it and I believe the people of Georgia will, too."

Outwardly at least, Bond gave no public indication of his

awareneses of the still-smoldering resentment against him. "I don't think most members of the House care at this point whether I'm here or not," he told reporters on opening day, 1967, "and that's the attitude I want them to have." He was there not to please the other members of the House, Bond said, but "to push the little button for those people" over in his legislative district.

VI

IF, says one of the unwritten maxims of American politics, you want to *git* along, why, then, you just got to *go* along. Now, Julian Bond not being a man who by the very nature of his being was good at going along, and not being a man with whom very many of his colleagues in Georgia politics could or would risk being seen going along *with*, it just followed with mathematical and inexorable logical certainty that he was not going to get along very far. And, Q.E.D., he did not. Not in Georgia, anyway. All of his platform promises, the dream of a minimum wage, of an effort against capital punishment, of the demolition of anti-union right-to-work laws, lay fallow, as Bond went the first three terms of his tenure in office without once rising to speak for them, without once standing to ask a question, without once introducing a legislative bill requiring the action and approval of his fellow members. This was strange behavior indeed for a young man who believed that, rather than try to destroy the governmental system (as so many of his contemporaries seemed to believe was the way to attain their goals), black people should work within it, and who had gone so far and fought so hard for his right to perform the work that he had been elected to do. Passing strange, indeed.

Was his dilemma that, as Charles Morgan, who has remained his friend in spite of his shift of attorneys before the Supreme Court, puts it, Bond is a liberal in a legislature so far right that within it, "Adolf Hitler would be considered a middle-of-the-roader"? Or was it, really, that because of his youth, his inexperience and his basically poetical, abstract cast of mind, he was just incapable of the kind of practical thinking necessary in a legislator? Bond himself admits to certain serious shortcomings as a legislator, but insists that in spite of them and in spite of the isolating opprobrium in which he is held in the House, he is an effective representative for the people of his district. If he seems an anomalous sort of representative to emerge from the impoverished, poorly educated populace of that district, he is certainly no more so than, say, Adam Clayton Powell (one of Bond's heroes) has been for the ghetto-dwellers of Manhattan. And, undoubtedly, one of the elements of the charm he has for his constituents is his very pariahhood among the white men in the capital. Certainly he moves about in a low-voltage, easy-going manner that does nothing to bespeak a gap in age or background between him and his people; and he feels this very closeness works both to his and their advantage: not only can he stay in touch with them, but they can keep an eye on him at the same time, see that he wears no extravagant clothes, no costly jewelry, drives an ordinary low-priced car, lived until recently in a home just as run-down, tiny and crowded as their own, does his share of taking the children to school, carrying the washing to the laundromat, doing his share of the baby-sitting while his wife shops—and yet, at the same time, there he is on television, there he is in the newspapers!

"I try never to do anything that is a misapplication of trust," Bond says, as he sets out to explain his political style, talking over a cup of coffee in Paschal's restaurant. "You see, it's very easy for me. Much easier for me, say, than for an alderman in Chicago, because I represent many fewer people. If I walk from Paschal's, I'm going to see a good percentage of my electorate, on a sunny day. If I walk down Hunter Street, I see another good percentage. People can see me, talk to me, feel me, call me . . . well, they can't call me up on the telephone after I get my answering service." (To shield his family life from some of the interruptions fame has inevitably brought, Bond found an Atlanta answering service with no Southern accent to handle his phone calls, but still has to change his unlisted number frequently to maintain privacy.)

Whatever doubts about his value to his constituents his colleagues may have about Bond—and they have plenty—Bond himself is self-assured about his standing with his people. "I'm not going to get beat, that's one thing I know. I'm not going to get beaten in this stuff," he can say, having been re-elected twice to his seat after the House ousted him and then twice again in regular elections—the third and fourth times with no opposition. "And you know why? It's not because I've been on TV so many times and it's not because I make a lot of speeches. It's because, for this district, *I'm a good representative.*" Bond says this matter-of-factly, with faint exasperation, with the annoyance of a man defending himself against what he feels to be unjust insinuations, and somehow it comes out not sounding offensive at all, but refreshingly vigorous in this man who seems so often languidly unconcerned with the details of his job. "It's because people know they can call me up and come see me and I'll go to bat for them. Sounds like a lot of bullshit, but it's true. I'm a damn good representative from that point of view—I'm not very good down there in the Capitol."

Bond's view of the value he renders the people who vote for him is as hard-headedly practical as that of any pork-barreling, log-rolling Southern Congressman trying to wig-wag another airplane factory into his district. "Now," he says, "look at me in the legislature. I'm not getting any bills passed, and that's frustrating, but I am providing a service for my constituents that they might not get from another guy. They have their complaints, and they call me up and I try to take care of them. I can see something being *done*." The tangibility of politics, it turns out, is what appeals to him most, is what keeps telling him that blacks have to keep plugging away at getting into the system. He scoffs at the notion of someday becoming a mayor. "I can drive down a street that used to be muddy and now it's been paved—because *I* made a complaint. Or, I can go down another street, where they used to have purse-snatchers, and now it's police-patrolled. I can *see* what I'm doing—what can Lindsay see? Rioting—even that's not something he's done, it's something he's stopped other people from doing. What will he be able to say at the end of his four years, what will he point to? I can point to little sidewalks . . . maybe in fifty years, they'll call it the 'Julian Bond Memorial Sidewalk.' "

While Bond can freewheel on these purely local problems that require only the approval of the other members of his county's delegation to the House, no one is more aware of or more bitter about the frustrations he has encountered in the legislature on broader legislative aims, such as the very agenda he used as his first campaign platform, which would require the approval of the whole House and considerable lobbying over on the Senate side to achieve passage. He has abandoned the idea of working for a $1.60-minimum-wage bill with his name attached to it; "I don't think," he says, "that with my pushing it, it will get anywhere. But other people have picked it up." Likewise, Bond says, others in the House have seized upon anti-capital-punishment legislation and a bill to hold city elections by wards, notions that were initially his own. "So," he says with small satisfaction, "I've really been a kind of starter; I've built things; I've put out ideas that other people have picked up on."

The palpable dislike that some of his colleagues in the House have for him is just one reason Bond shies away from giving them a chance to hoot and guffaw at legislative proposals;

another and perhaps more basic reason is that it is genuinely difficult for him to formulate legislation, to see problems, beyond the pothole scale, in terms of their cures in law and statute. His lack of the legal training which so many of his colleagues have is apparent as he speaks of the problems that afflict his constituents. Bond is keenly astute in defining them, movingly articulate in making concrete the abstract situation, but his speeches are woefully lacking in hard solutions.

Compressing his thoughts on what ought to be done into the dry legalese of political solutions, is, Bond says, "a problem for me. Now, I know what all the problems are, but how you can correct them with legislation. . . See, these other guys are lawyers. Let me tell you the big difference," he says, "Bill Alexander may see in his mind that slum housing is a problem, and can go to a code and look it up and find out what the law is on it, and what needs to be done to change it. He *knows*, see. Now, I get copies of the code in the mail; we all get copies of all the Georgia laws. I give them to my brother-in-law—he's a lawyer, he needs them. I don't need them—I don't understand them. It's like Greek to me, really, how to change the laws." Thus the genesis of Bondian legislation is apt to be a somewhat casual process, in spite of the deep concern he feels for the underlying problems.

Bond, for example, had long been distressed by the shoddy housing occupied by many of his constituents and which their absentee landlords simply refused to repair or improve. The answer eluded him until one day he was in Pittsburgh to make a speech and noticed an article in a newspaper telling about a rent-withholding plan in effect there. He clipped the story, sent it back to his secretary, asking her to get a copy of the Pennsylvania law. When it arrived, Bond took it to the legislative counsel to the Georgia House and asked him to draft a similar measure in three versions, one state-wide, another county-wide, and the other affecting just the city of Atlanta. But even that last measure—which was the one Bond chose to try to get passed because it would require approval only by his county's delegation—failed, because, his critics say, Bond did not work hard enough at getting his colleagues from Fulton county to support it.

Some other Bond ideas never seem to get much beyond the talking stage, such as his counterproposal answering President Richard Nixon's "black capitalism." Bond dubbed his scheme "community socialism," which to him meant mass local ownership of business enterprises within a community, and he had some specific ideas for projects in his own neighborhood. "Take the house across the street," he said one day as he sat in his tiny front-porch office. "It's got a basement in it the size of this room and somebody, I guess the owner of the house, has divided that basement into six rooms, and they share a common toilet. If I report it to the health department, they'll all be evicted. Where will they go? They're all living in filth now, but they'd be living *nowhere* then. They probably couldn't pay to live in a house this size, although some of them could certainly use a house this size. They don't have any capital themselves and what they need is, for those who are able to work, a job that's going to pay them enough so they can move into something decent."

But more than just a job, these poor people, Bond said, "also need somebody to develop some low-cost, low-income housing that's not cheap and shoddy. Get an architect with some imagination to build something decent, and not lump it all together. We'd have a block of public housing here and a couple of houses there, and they could make it look like some place in Connecticut." The owners of such a project would be not the government nor a cartel of private individuals but sharcholders living in the community, their venture financed by high-risk government loans.

More than just housing, Bond can see community socialism developing, right there in West End Atlanta, an urban business center, in which the men who run the small neighborhood

156 · JULIAN BOND

grocery stores, the local ministers, the dentists, chiropodists, podiatrists, beauty-parlor operators, all join together, "all together as one base for a development, a real complex," Bond says, "with housing, schools, a shopping center. And the difference between this and what people usually put up is that the profit from these things would not go to these guys, these individuals." The profits arising out of rent, Bond says, would then be invested into more enterprises. But, although he has urged community businessmen to form such a group, Bond has been unable to "get anybody to take step one. Great talkers they are, they talk a great game."

Two things get in the way of Bond's pursuit of the role of impresario of his area's development, he says. One is the lack of time and a support staff to handle the detail work, the research and the drafting of rough legislative proposals, and the other is a hangover from the days of the civil rights movement. "If we get the staff I'm thinking of," he says, "all of us, all the Negro legislators, are really going to be in much better shape. Up to now, we have faced several handicaps that are not connected to our race. One is that the capital is located in our home town and that means that, for example, Bill Alexander, who is a lawyer, tries to practice law and be in the legislature at the same time, while these other guys just take a leave from their law practice during the legislative session. It also means that my constituents, Alexander's constituents, can come see us any time they want to, and that really is a disadvantage. While these other guys can devote their full day if they wish to legislative problems, we have to meet constituents, take kids on tours, really time-consuming stuff. And then, our home lives intrude on our legislative days, more than with these other guys, who live in hotels, spend enormous amounts of money and are able to be much more serious about the job than we are."

The hangover from the days of the Movement, Bond says, is the fact that none of the black representatives had ever held public office before, and many of them had developed a kind of tunnel vision that was focused clearly on the issues of Negro rights but little else. Also, concern with racial oppression has developed in him and many of his black colleagues, Bond feels, a kind of stimulus-response pattern that in itself does little to generate new ideas and approaches to his district's problems.

"We're always reacting," Bond says. "The first couple of years we were up there we were usually reacting to something somebody else did and we're still doing it now. We ought to be acting. But the reason we don't act is that we don't have the time to sit down and think and plan about the things we want to do. That's the story of a large part of the civil rights movement—they were always reacting. A policeman will beat someone up and *then* you get angry about police brutality. Someone's refused a job, and *then* you get angry about job discrimination. The Movement has suffered from not having aggressive programs; it has always had defensive programs.

"I'm not," Bond says, "a very good legislator; I don't pay as much attention to what's going on there as I ought to. But I'm a lot better than some, I *will* say. Some of them are drunk all the time. I have to learn to be more aggressive. For instance, I've never spoken in the well of the House, except the day I was put out. I've never asked anybody a question on a bill. I have two troubles; one is that I'm not serious enough to study all the bills that come before me, and very few people are, but I ought to take more time to do it. Another thing is that I'm really *so* busy, involved in so many different other things. I need an aide, a guy who works for me. I've got all these other commitments in the city, these little groups I belong to . . ."

Bond, in fact, belongs to enough clubs and organizations to fill up several of those signs one sees entering little Southern towns, but some of those he belongs to would never appear in such company as the Lions, Rotary and Optimist. Bond served on the governing council of the library documentation project for the Martin Luther King Memorial Center. He is on the board of directors of the Southern Conference Education Fund, the delta ministry project of the National Council of Churches, the Robert Kennedy Memorial Fund, the Center for Community Change, the Highlander Research and Education Center, the National Sharecropper's Fund, the Southern Regional Council, the NAACP Legal Defense and Education Fund, Inc., the New Democratic Coalition and the Voter Education Project, and he is a research associate of the Voter Education Project, a visiting fellow of the Metropolitan Applied Research Center in New York City, an honorary trustee of the Institute of Applied Politics, and a member of the board of the Urban Coalition. In addition, he lends his name and energies from time to time to a whole host of ephemeral groups which arise to meet current needs, run full-page newspaper advertisements soliciting funds for some cause or other and then disappear, and he takes smirking delight in having masters of ceremonies, as they tick off the above list of associations from the biography his office sends out in advance, come to the initials I.P.F.U. and the honorary fraternity, Southern Correspondents Reporting Racial Equality Wars. The former stands for International Pig Fuckers Union, an imaginary group dating from Bond's teenage days, and the acronym of the latter is SCRREW. Even his duties at most of the real groups are largely ceremonial and his chores as a member of the Education, the Insurance, and the State Institutions and Properties Committees in the House are scarcely more demanding.

As might be expected, this concatenation of outside activity, coupled with Bond's own self-admitted lack of interest in mastering the intricacies of political intercourse in the House and his consequent singular lack of success there, all have caused some of his colleagues to be somewhat harsh in their appraisal of him. Some, of course, would have been so regardless of what Julian Bond had done, and, in fact, their prejudicial harshness may to some degree be responsible for that paralysis Bond seems to feel. But some of his friends, too, are equally impressed by his lethargy and his failure to try and diminish the onus left upon him by the ousting in 1967.

His friend Charles Morgan, a shrewd observer of Southern politics, says Bond will find his political life difficult for some time to come, "because Julian represents to a number of folks that hate symbol, because he has been right on all the issues and most Southerners are wrong. You know, there's an old saying about white Southerners, that they hate niggers and love war, and when you get one poor fellow who's against war and black, too, then he is in real trouble. And he consequently represents to a great number of them about the most radical thing they've ever seen."

That Morgan is right is underlined by the tendency of friends as well as enemies to use words like "poison" and "anathema" and "infamous" when they talk about Bond's political currency in Georgia. Oddly, his fame outside the state does little to change that, and instead merely goads his critics into more intense anger as they see the press doting on this man. One high-ranking state official, refusing to discuss Bond for direct quotation because "it would ruin me politically," said flatly: "Politically, Bond is death in this state. And the Negroes know that. You can't win a statewide race with Bond." Creating that situation, he said, was the fact that "first, the segregation issue is still a touch-and-go issue in the South, and second, *that*, plus the fact he did make the statement he made supporting the draft-card burners and the statement he made that he wouldnt't take up arms to defend his country, his family, his children. If he had been a white man, he probably could have got away with it. But they tied the two of them into one package and beat you to death with it. The terrible part of it is, we had got so far with the Negroes. But Senator Johnson, they nearly beat him to death."

State Senator Leroy Johnson, who worked so hard to try to

save Bond from the humiliation of an ouster, is today matter-of-fact in describing Bond's position in the legislature. The bull with the red horns, Johnson calls Bond, a scapegoat. "If they want to be against anything," Johnson says, "they connect it with Julian Bond." This, says Johnson, is a change from the old days, when the most handy, absorbent and versatile scapegoat a Southern pol could want was the nearest nigger. "Now," says Johnson coolly, "rarely will you hear the word *nigger* used on the floor of the General Assembly of Georgia, either in the House or in the Senate. Now, instead of using the word *nigger*, they use *Julian Bond*, and it creates the same type of resistance, the same type of waving of the red flag." This, of course, Johnson admits, might change in time, but he says, "I don't think he's put forth any effort to say to the House, 'Now, look, let bygones be bygones; I'm a member of this body and I want to be effective and pass some legislation.' I don't think he's done that and I can understand why— I think he might look upon himself as kind of the conscience of the legislature, kind of a prodder."

Just how Bond manages the role of superego to the Georgia representatives and senators, or gadfly, or both, without once opening his mouth during their sessions is, Johnson says, a neat trick accomplished by making little end-runs through public forums, through the media "and by maintaining a very visible figure." Glamorous as that seems, Johnson is far from sanguine about Bond's future. "In Georgia politics," he says, "Bond's chances of going further or going into any other area do not seem to be too bright because in this game, you know, you got to be effective in the circle itself. Negro politicians will either have to get into the arena of politics and play the game the way it's played, and try to change it from within, or they'll have to get out of it and leave it to somebody else to do it."

Johnson—who works from the effectively simple philosophical principle that if you are sufficiently powerful to stop legislation that other people want passed from passing, then

they will listen to you and help you pass *your* legislation—
thinks that in the end, Bond must decide what it is he wants to
do when he grows up. Says Johnson, "Julian is fine, but he is
aloof. You have to approach him to get to know him, and you
have to pursue him to get to know him. In politics, as you
very well know, you cannot be aloof—you've got to get in the
arena, and you've got to spread yourself out and make yourself
felt." Bond did not get his housing bill through, Johnson said,
because he didn't push it. He paused meaningfully and added:
"Nobody can be more interested in your legislation than you."

Is Bond really that much of a "bull with the red horns"?
Has not the wrath of the men who kicked him out in 1966
abated with the passage of years—years in which the whole
national attitude toward the war changed? Have not these
men, too, tempered their judgment of Viet Nam and civil rights
workers? "No sir," says Jones Lane, "not one iota." To hear
Lane tell it, the House is still exercising that censure they
voted against Bond in 1966. "He could propose anything and
it'd never get any place, no sir. His attitude is what caused him
to have this image in the House." Lane and others like him in
the legislature believe that, at bottom, what Bond is really
seeking is not the humdrum and drudging accomplishments by
which men in statehouses all over the country reckon their
careers, but, as Jones Lane puts it, "I think his primary aim is
he likes publicity, and that's the only thing I've ever regretted
about this whole thing, is that it took a nothing and tried to
make a something out of him in the eyes of this nation."

Just suppose now, that Jones Lane were not a well-off white
contractor in Statesboro, but a black man from the Atlanta
ghetto with the kind of record to live with that Bond has in
the eyes of his fellow legislators—what would he imagine himself doing by way of getting out of that fix? "Well," says
Lane, "if he really wanted to represent them, and not to be
a-runnin' and to be a representative, to hold some prestigious
office, the first thing I would do is, I would do everything in

the world I could to get some constructive things for my people in my district. That's the first thing I'd be doing, first thing I would have *been* doing. He has not done that . . . whether he has done one thing or not, it's beyond me to say."

Sloppy Floyd, too, shares this view, and says, "Only people what held him in good faith or have anything to do with him are just a few individuals and the only reason they have is, they're afraid not to—they live in the same district, the same area he does. He is not effective whatsoever; I think he's just a waste of time to the people of his district. I don't know of anything he's done. In fact, he spends more time out of the House chamber than it looks like to me he does on the floor. It looks like to me that his people ought to make him stay in the House chamber. He went all the way to the Supreme Court to get the seat and he ought to stay here and tend to his duty. He ought to be here, tending to his business, instead of running around all over the country making speeches at five hundred and fifty, seven hundred and fifty dollars a speech. I noticed he made a speech that he would encourage combat veterans, Negro combat veterans, to use their combat weapons against the American white—now, that's a shame and a disgrace for a public official to state that." Floyd, like Lane, speaks with the ringing clang of finality: he has made up his mind about Bond, and nothing that Bond is ever likely to do is ever likely to change Floyd's mind. "I don't think he can do any good, and I may have to eat my words, but I hope I don't. I have a son and two grown daughters, but if my son ever made the statements Julian Bond's made, I'd rather see him dead."

Black men have lived hard up against this kind of rancor all their lives in the South; diffused as it sometimes is by the courtly language and the flourishing manners, it nonetheless can be grabbed and hacked through, and no one does it with more dispatch than Lonnie King, the college football player who persuaded Bond to join him in beginning the student movement at Morehouse. "Julian is anathema to the white power structure in the legislature," King says. "They may be a little envious of the fact that Julian is internationally known. They find that difficult to quite fathom, you know . . . here *they* are, all of them supposed to be superior to black folks and here's a black guy sittin' up there and every time they look around, here's some international or national press coming to see him. I think, as a result, there's a lot of resentment on their part—it has hampered, to an extent, Julian's effectiveness. You see, if they listened to Julian Bond, Julian Bond has the mind to put together the kind of legislative program that would help this whole state—he's got ideas, he can think—but he just happens to be black, which is a waste of manpower and brainpower in Georgia, because Georgia—God *damn*, man, we *need* some brains!" King thinks Bond is the brightest politician in the city of Atlanta. He also thinks Bond will never be able to rid himself of the stigma of his unseating or the views that led to the ouster.

"No," he says. "You understand that the Southern white man, particularly the country Southern white man, has always had as one of his greatest fears the unleashin' of black power—the unleashin' of that black slave he's been oppressin' for so many years. In his mind, you know, Julian Bond is superior to him, and if he opens up the door and lets Julian Bond come through, Julian Bond is going to set all of them in the back seat and the only way they stay in the front seat is by keeping him out. You know—if you're going to control him, then freeze him out. It's as simple as that."

State Senator Leroy Johnson, a colleague, a would-be adviser in that time of crisis in 1966, and to some extent a rival, as a Negro politician vying with Bond for the leadership position in a city boiling with politics; sworn political enemies Jones Lane and Sloppy Floyd, both near-caricatures of die-hard resistance to Bond in the House; Lonnie King, old buddy, business colleague with Bond in a consulting firm they have tried to start to advise businesses on how to deal with the emerging problems of minorities on the payroll—all these men know what they are talking about, but all are close, probably too close, too involved.

One man who knows Bond, and sits next to him in the Georgia House, seems able to speak of him with amiable dispassion. He is Gerald Horton, an earnest, articulate, Harvard-educated young white man who now earns his living as a consultant on urban affairs in Southern communities. At Harvard, Horton was an editor on the *Advocate*, the college's once elite literary magazine, a member of the Signet Society, the school's exclusive literary fraternity, and thus he shares with Bond a kinship in their love of books and language. Horton sees the future of the Democratic party in Georgia, in long-term Kentucky-windage scale, as lying in the hands of legislators around their own age, vastly different men by dint of background from the "landed Bourbons" who have controlled it in the past. "Julian could not be much of a force at this time in the House or in pulling together that kind of a group," Horton says, "because close association with Julian for most guys is anathema." Linkage to Bond is hazardous not only because of the lingering memory of the '66 ouster, but because the men in the statehouse keep hearing of Bond, Horton says, "that what he is really doing on his speaking tours is going around kicking the shit out of the South."

Horton says he thinks Bond's real future does not lie in the Georgia House of Representatives, nor even necessarily within the confines of politics, and that one of the genuinely unfortunate aspects of his experience in the legislature is how sharply his future has been curtailed by events there. "By being Julian Bond, there may be a lot of things that he may want to do—and that he is intellectually and technically capable of doing—that he won't get to do because he *is* Julian Bond." Horton cited as an example his own consulting firm. "You've got to remember some terrible things about a guy like Julian. Right now, for instance, we're looking for three new guys for our firm, and Julian knows I would never think about having him in the firm—and that's the kind of thing that's sort of hard. He knows that I think the world of him, but, see, I could not have, as an associate, Julian Bond. It's something that's unthinkable because it would just gut my business. And, you know, that's got to be hard on a guy."

Horton has known Bond ever since the early days of the Committee on Appeal for Human Rights, when Horton was a director of economic research for the Atlanta Chamber of Commerce, and thinks he can detect a certain wistful regret in Bond that his life has been so one-dimensional. "I think one of the things about Julian—it really is sort of sad and it's sad about all the young guys out of the civil rights movement— Julian would like to be more of a substantive character than he is. Just making speeches, you know, that isn't *all* of Julian Bond. We were talking about it; it's the difference between working and not working. Julian doesn't *work*, and he's smart enough and creative enough and substantive enough as a human being to recognize that no matter how much money you make out of it, to go around and just make this speech night after night, is not a constructive kind of, creative kind of, activity. But that's true of a lot of guys who were in the Movement—it's very hard for many of them to find a profession. Very few of them come out to *do* anything."

Scarred personally as Horton thinks Bond was by his unseating ("It must have been a terribly traumatic thing, coming over for your first day, your mother and father are here and you've bought a new suit and you're all buttoned up and got on your watch-chain and all and they don't want you and they get up and they curse you and revile you . . .") and circumscribed by that, Bond's first chore might best be reexamining why he is in politics. "I think the thing that would determine a lot about Julian is what he does as a person—not as a politician, but what *he does*. You know," Horton says, "Julian used to call himself a writer; now, if he were to go back to writing, and I'm not talking about just polemics, but writing, and get published, he might be able to better identify for himself who he is."

It is Horton's suspicion that Bond upon doing so would discover that he is unlike these men in the House, and doesn't, really, belong there. "Most of them," Horton says, "regard themselves as professional men who are members of the legislature, and that's historically true of the South. Money doesn't mean a thing. It's the prominence of it. You practice law in Fitzgerald, Georgia, say, and you're there nine months of the year and then three months of the year you're up in Atlanta. And in your office, next to your diploma from the University of Georgia Law School, there's this great prestigious thing that says you're a Representative, and that's a big thing in your county."

There is, however, no such genteel separation between the public and the private lives of Julian Bond; they tend to blur indistinguishably together in a pell-mell maelstrom whose vortex is inevitably right there on his front porch, or a few steps inward, in his cluttered office. And, if he ever yearns to become a writer again, as his wife wistfully hopes he would, he manages to conceal it well, doggedly plugging away instead at the now-routine business of making speeches, attending political meetings and trying to broaden the base he knows he must build if politics is to be his future. Philosophy and not just pragmatics demands an organization:

"I'm really very antipersonality," Bond says. "I think what is really the bad thing about my having been elected four times is that I've done it without having an organization. What I would like to do first in my district is build an organization and the second thing I want to do, if I can find the machinery through which to do it, is to help other Negroes in the South build political organizations—I think that is just crucial."

Toward that end, Bond has in fact cruised through a good bit of the South, and not merely shaking hands and getting acquainted, he has interviewed several score black political candidates, winners and losers, and produced a booklet about their experiences for the Southern Regional Council. The need to consolidate the growing black electorate in Atlanta constantly nags at him, too, and he devotes a large number of the evenings he is in town to attending meetings of the myriad neighborhood political and civic organizations that abound in the city. Often it is in these little groups that the political savvy and energy, which he represses within the chamber of the House, manifest themselves.

One such group that Bond was especially interested in fostering was the Young Men on the Go, a loose-knit fraternity of young Negro professionals in Atlanta. At one of their evening meetings, Bond and the other black legislators present came under heavy fire from one of the members who accused them of being "just involved in a lot of pseudo-bullshit issues that have nothing to do with the black masses . . . and just sitting around doing nothing!"

Bond rose to answer, visibly stung, and reeled off a rapid-fire rebuttal, saying the problems he and the other black House members had come to grips with were indeed vital. Had it not been for their efforts against capital punishment, Bond said, "people would be going into the chamber every day." His seatmate, Ben Brown, was working hard on legislation to improve the teaching of black history, Bond said, "so we can give these children some knowledge of where they came from." Legislation to win tenure for black teachers, he said, was crucially important in certain downstate areas, where black teachers, lacking tenure, were traditionally among the first fired. And, in the course of the same tempestuous meeting, punctuated by catcalls and bottles rapping on metal folding chairs and men constantly moving to the bar and back to the meeting, Bond overcame considerable opposition to ram a whole new set of by-laws into effect, razzle-dazzling it past his opponents with a virtuoso display of parliamentary wizardry. As he shouldered his way to the bar, one of the members laughed and said over the smoky din, "That Julian, he's pretty slick!"

Just as he went from door to door as a candidate and explained the process of the legislature to his constituents in the alleys and on the back porches of his district, so today he goes from platform to platform, explaining the larger political process, and he is as much missionary of the political system as he is advocate within it for them in the House. He stands before one tiny gathering, in a dimly lighted, linoleum-floored common room of a housing project, and berates them for the scant voter turnout: "There are," he says sternly, "fourteen thousand people old enough to vote in this district, and there are only seven thousand voters. It's obvious that only half of the eligible voters are registered—I can't imagine why." He pauses and looks around the little group of embarrassed middle-aged black people, and then says, "It just struck me that part of the reason is, they can't read and they are ashamed to go down to the voting center and register to vote." He reminds these people, gently, to go and tell their neighbors that "since the voting rights bill has been passed, they don't have to be able to read and write to be eligible to vote." This is just a wee, small pep talk; nothing momentous will be accomplished here tonight; it is vastly different from some of the glittering arenas in which Bond has appeared, but to him this is one of the most important places he can spend this evening, because it is in places like this that the flame of political awareness just might be sparked off.

"Let me tell you just a little bit about the importance and necessity of having a strong political organization in this area," he says in his low voice. "I have been able to get some things done because I am a Representative. Not because I am Julian Bond, but because I am a Representative."

These people here tonight live in this low-rent housing project, and they are worried about security in their neighborhood

—and there is no consciousness among them of the irony in their worry, of the sad irony in the fact that poor people, too, worry about crime in the streets. They have listened tonight to housing authority policemen talk about auxiliary cops for the area. So the people listen keenly as Bond tells them, "I went to Alderman ———, and he assigned a policeman to stop purse-snatching in the university area. He didn't do that because he likes me, but because I am in a position of power and I decide how much money he makes. If each of us tries to do things by himself, we are not going to get much done," Bond tells his audience. "It's like trying to move a great big rock. But if fifteen or twenty or thirty of us get together, then we will do it easily." There are exactly twenty-eight people listening to him.

Then he says, this man who has heard the entire amphitheater in Chicago resonate to his chanted name, and who has told sophisticated audiences in hotel ballrooms in Manhattan that politics must be the business of who gets how much of what from whom, that "I hope we try to build this organization a little bigger, a little tighter."

Next came the questions, not snaky little Gov 124 seminar questions, but plain questions, like who picks the poll workers and how come the lights are so dim over the voting machines that old folks have trouble seeing (I'll speak to Rep. ——— about that," Bond says), and how come the precinct boundaries are so hard to find out ("I've sent a map of the new boundaries out to the names on my mailing list," Bond says, offering to send out some more) and then he launches into a little defense of the legislature, in the guise of an invitation for them all to come down any time, saying, "Some people go down there and sit in the gallery and look down and see representatives sitting down there drinking Coca-Cola and eating boiled peanuts and they think we're loafing—but really, we're working very hard!" There are some indulgent chuckles at this shameless persiflage.

They ask him what it was like in Chicago, and he modestly tells them, "It was very exciting—I don't think anybody who went up there with us had been through anything like it before and I don't think anybody would want to go through it again." They ask him about the chances of electing a black man mayor of Atlanta, and Bond reminds them that Negroes in the city are only thirty-five percent of the electorate, "because we're not registered the way we should be," and they laugh when he mentions the wooing they are soon to get by white candidates: "I remember the summer Ivan Allen ran for mayor; I almost *lived* on those chicken dinners they had up and down Hunter Street."

The meeting is breaking up now, and the elderly man who is chairman of this group pledges their support to Bond in the next election "if he is alive and chooses to run," and then the elderly man says, in words grim as clanking iron, "This is a time for guts and backbone and enough guts in your craw; if you're babies, better put you to bed early, for this is a time when if you out in public, better bare your breast and open your coat to be shot at."

That's the way it sounded in the colored district of Atlanta, Georgia, Julian Bond's district, now called the 111th, in 1969. Nobody thought the elderly man was kidding.

VII

OUT in public, the old man said. Julian Bond got out there, irrevocably, the once-private man melding with the politician to become something more than either of them had separately been, by going to Chicago. The one had existed in a quiet world of books and ideas and poetry; but the private man had found less and less time to be private, as the demands of the Movement and the people it was trying to help became more insistently pressing. Then, in Chicago in the summer of 1968, in a kind of transmuting process that many other men have yearned to experience, Julian Bond was seized by the invisible force-field of national attention, and changed forever.

It is hard to get men to talk about what it is like up there in that stratosphere of popular acclaim. Men in sports feel something like it and, without even examining what it is that compels them to strain their aging bodies against the iron demands of the game, seldom can bring themselves to abandon the thrill. Robin Roberts late one night was bashfully fiddling with some scrambled eggs and ham in a Boston hotel dining room. He had just beaten the Yankees, who had unceremoniously traded him to Baltimore after buying him from the Phillies. In Boston, this legendary man who had blazed an unexcelled career as a fast-ball pitcher said, "You see, being a regular starting pitcher in the major leagues is something I'd still like to be." Robin Roberts was well onto being a middle-aged man when he said that, and any man who has tasted the thrill of the crowd could understand. An old heavyweight, now a second who holds a towel and a bottle of salts for contenders, said, when somebody asked him what he missed most about being a contender himself, "The people yelling, 'Hi, Champ!' "

That kind of talk makes Bond uneasy; he tries hard not to let the thrill he experienced in Chicago touch him, change him, but being merely human, it has. Ideally, of course, any account of the so-far brief life of Julian Bond should contain a stirring portrayal of just exactly how it was that young Julian, at the age of twenty-eight, capped his meteoric rise against overwhelming odds of race and ideology by leading his faithful little band of insurgents to their—and his own— triumph in Chicago. As luck—but more than luck, the nature and character of Julian Bond—would have it, Chicago didn't happen in quite that way.

Political conventions are ordinarily thought of as the places and the occasions where and when the major candidates of a party, having spent their exhausting springs and frantic early summers courting the primary election voters, go to woo the party's delegates. Having panned the streams for traces of support, the candidates now start combing the canyon walls for lodes, heading ever upward toward the wellsprings of those streams, hoping to find there the bonanza that will land them in the White House. Anachronistic, frenetic, chaotic, conventions are—it has become fashionable to say—nonetheless essential to the functioning of our form of democracy.

There is, of course, another, more pragmatic view, which says that these quadrennial gatherings of HO-gauge Machiavellis are in fact bazaars. To them, from all over the country, come the cottage-industrialists with their wares, to sell and trade. One such delegation came to Chicago not to be romanced by the candidates at all, but to press their own special suit upon them, to try by main force of remonstrance and charm to pry their way into the convention itself. The candidates, the other delegates, the milling hordes outside, even the folks watching the whole shebang back home with a can of beer and a bowl of popcorn and a tally sheet, all were fair game for the suasion. The delegation mounting this all-stops-out campaign of its own just to get in the door of the Amphitheater was led by Julian Bond.

The Georgia situation was similar to that posed by Mississippi in 1964 when the Freedom Democratic Party confronted Lyndon Johnson's Democrats in full public view with their embarrassing claims on a right to party suffrage; the way, in fact, had been paved by the Mississippi Freedom Democratic Party in 1964 for the assault by Bond's group in Chicago in 1968 (and at least one Bond supporter likened him to Fannie Lou Hamer, the doughty figurehead of the Mississippians at Atlantic City).

Successful politicians, whatever they are like in their living rooms—a quality the best go to enormous lengths to conceal —usually turn out to have in themselves a deeply resonant symbolic quality, a protean capacity to reflect back whatever wavelengths of lightbeams are shone onto them, a marvelously absorbent concavity that can accept the troubling issues of the time and somehow transmit them back out mellowed by humane concern. If they are *really* good, these men become symbolical of the issues and come to embody the very spirit of the times in their initials: there was LBJ and JFK and HST and FDR—and Ike—and all those great societies and new frontiers, eras straddled by these identifiable figures larger than mere people. Hubert Horatio Humphrey was one of them, could have become HHH, in fact was well along toward doing just that—until he was almost blotted out and blurred by the glare and heat emanating from his incandescent boss. Meanwhile, Richard Nixon, out there alone on his missions and

tours and visits and appearances in behalf of selected candidates, Nixon, in spite of his loser's image and his loser's track
record and his negligible legislative history, Nixon stayed, or
rather, *became* as Eisenhower aged and faded, an individual
figure in his own right. People, ripe for a change from big
Lincolns and beer cans and elusive coon-skins in Viet Nam,
just might have plunged for HHH—if they could have made
him out from the babble of hysterical words and ballet-
dancing to the old choreographer from Texas. He came, after
all, within just a whisker of the White House; the blur did
make the difference.

While Mayor Richard J. Daley yelled "Get that mother-
fucking Jew out of here!" at United States Senator Abraham
Ribicoff of Connecticut, who was at the moment nominating
his colleague, Senator George McGovern of South Dakota,
as President of the United States, and while Daley's street-
cleaners were out with their big sweeper trucks washing the
blood and pocketbooks and shoes and gas-induced tears off
Michigan Avenue in front of the delegates' hotels, Hubert
Horatio Humphrey was kissing his wife's image on his television set.

That's just the way it was out there, and as a result only
three figures emerged strongly from Chicago: Richard Daley,
George McGovern and Julian Bond. Daley was absurdly
powerful, a force, hardly a personality any more at all, but
something almost beyond accounting. While others might
fret over the war and the poor and blacks, Daley fumed about
people sleeping in Chicago parks. Daley stood for clean streets
and parade permits and all the other rigmarole that city halls
delight in fooling around with. McGovern was hot on Viet
Nam and hunger and poverty and youth and he wept as he
looked down from his fourth-floor window in the Blackstone
Hotel and he broke down again as he cursed into the telephone
to Ribicoff when the Senator from Connecticut called the
Senator from South Dakota to tell him how it was there on

the convention floor. McGovern had been saying the night before that, no, he didn't think having all those cops and all that barbed wire on the jeeps like big four-wheeled cheese-slicers was overreacting by Daley. But now McGovern was saying words like *son of a bitch*, words that he very seldom let himself use and he was wising up to what Daley was all about and what Chicago was all about. But it was too late.

Some people learned long in advance, on the streets, up against Daley's cops, what the convention was going to be like. One sculptress in Chicago, Ruth Migdal, for example, gave over part of her North Side basement studio, where she ordinarily assembles huge wooden collages, to her friends in the Peace Movement to use as a makeshift bandage-rolling and splint-making factory. Yet, even knowing what they knew, they came to downtown Chicago, poured into its lakefront parks, moved in a torrent down Michigan Avenue, lingering there as a reproachful and haunting ghost of a nagging con-science. They couldn't get near the Amphitheater. Reporters went to the Amphitheater like correspondents going to the front. Cops stopped the cab two blocks from the big barn of a building. Identification cards were shown. The electro-magnetic Amphitheater cards, dated and color-coded, had to be shown. Only then was the car allowed past the checkpoint. Nearer the Amphitheater, the car was stopped again, this time under a flood of streetlights like magnesium flares, twenty cops or so to each intersection, lounging against the barri-cades. You flashed the ID cards again and walked the rest of the way to the Amphitheater—across a gray square as empty as a movie set when the shooting is over. At the building, you went in through a narrow slit of a door, one person at a time, and immediately you had to slide your electromagnetic pass into a box that unlocked the turnstile. People who lived in the neighborhood of the Amphitheater came and went with special resident passes like patients in some gigantic asylum.

Being neither resident freeholders or visiting press, the

shadow delegation which had come to Chicago could not move, really, very much at all beyond the confines of the parks along the lake. There was, to be sure, the same right to petition for redress of grievances accorded them by virtue of the Constitution as was enjoyed by everybody else in Chicago —on paper—but it didn't work out that way. It came down to not having the right permits. No tickee, no washee. The cops learned a lesson on the Wednesday night that Hubert Humphrey was nominated the Democratic Party's candidate for President of the United States. The clobbering they gave the kids out on the street in front of the hotels at Michigan Avenue and Balbo, in all its revolting horror, had been entirely too public. The next evening, when the protesters decided to try to walk to the Amphitheater itself, the cops laid a neat ambush, letting the demonstrators walk south on Michigan as far as Eighteenth Street, and then, without much benefit of television or press coverage, sprang their trap. Lobbing tear-gas canisters at the crowd's feet, the cheese-slicer Jeeps rolled forward, slowly, firing gas, then moving again, until the crowd broke, scattering down alleys, pushing over fences, driven on by a rain of gas and railing billy-clubs in a blind panic of weeping fear.

Nobody who saw it, who went through it, could ever really believe in this country again. Some blacks, who had by and large avoided this scene, laughed privately and bitterly, saying they were glad that at last Whitey had got a tangy mouthful of the kind of bile the cops had been feeding the ghettos all these years. Some conservatives said the kids got only what they had wanted to get—what, in fact, they had deserved. Some said it was just Chicago, just Daley, just a police riot. But in their hearts the blacks knew that, if it could happen to Whitey, then there was no hope for Blacky; the conservatives eventually were to realize that the kids were their kids, or, rather, had *been* their kids and were no longer. And it became unmistakably clear that it was not just Daley, and not just Chicago, but that Daley had been acting for Johnson, and that Chicago was, lock, stock and barrel, what America was now, a place of savagery and trodden law, a line drawn through it as unmistakable as Michigan Avenue, the cops and the troops on one side, on the other only some funky garbage fires and the friendship and camaraderie of embattlement.

That, of course, didn't bother Chicago, any more than, really, it bothered Johnson or Humphrey. Chicago was used to embattlement, so used to it that it had forgotten all about it. Cops went out, four to a cruiser, when it snowed hard on freezing winter nights, and prowled the city waiting for it to happen. It always did. The kids hit the liquor stores, the TV stores, the radio repair shops. The cops parked the car, locked it, then ran, guns drawn, across the snow, firing into the starless night. The kids stopped. The cops marched them into the looted shop, whapping the last kid across the back of the skull with the barrel of a .38 Special just for emphasis, and the names and ages and addresses were taken, the wagon was called, and the cops then went back to the cruiser, unlocked it, squeezed in, and waited for the radio again. Embattlement was something they lived with, white cops and black cops, without even thinking about it.

Embattlement: an unmarked cruiser, a green Chevrolet, pulls up in front of a beauty parlor on Sixty-first Street off Stony Island in South Side Chicago. This is Blackstone Ranger territory. Any Devil's Disciples caught around here are dead. That's all. Inside, three or four Rangers sit, their arms folded in a gristly horseshoe of biceps and tendons and knuckles and scars across chest. Their conked heads are shoved up inside hair driers. One of them at the window chuckles, "Here's the Green Hornet." One of the cops gets out to talk with some of the Rangers lounging on the sidewalk outside the beauty parlor. He wants them to get inside. At the same time, his policeman companion, still at the wheel, watches the street narrowly. One Ranger nudges a friend, nodding at the driver.

They see that, casually, inconspicuously, the cop's right hand, half-under his jacket, is holding his .38 Special revolver. This is broad daylight on a main street in South Side Chicago. The cops are working on some very heavy charges against the top Rangers: murder counts. The Rangers own this territory; these "hoods" are theirs. When they get together, several thousand strong, just to show their colors, as they sometimes do, the cop cars turn off their Mars lights and haul out of the hoods until things calm down. But that seldom happened and things, on the surface at least, usually *were* calm. Calm as far as downtown Chicago knew, anyway. But, then, how much downtown Chicago actually ever knew is really questionable. "The Mayor's office," said one knowledgeable Chicagoan, "has a pipe into it from every group in town—the Irish, the Italians, the Poles, the Jews, everybody. Except for one group. Except for the blacks."

So, it just might have surprised Chicago Mayor Richard Daley to hear what the Rangers were talking about—not that they had any bearing on this convention in any direct way. But what they said, as they motored through the dark streets and alleys of South Side Chicago, talking about how they felt about the draft, about the city, about the nation, was a distillation of how the protesters uptown felt, those feelings boiled down to their elemental hardness. We don't exist, they said, with laughter rippling through the night, so why should we worry about the draft board? Nobody knows we're alive, most of us, or where to find us if they do. The city? Taxes? The money they made, off their hustles, their whores, their own prostitution, that money was absolutely tax-free; the money they would get, from the foundations lined up for little earnest presentations in the big church in Woodlawn that served as Ranger headquarters, that money would go to themselves, to their people, to get cars out of impounding yards, to pay light bills, wives, girl friends, grocery bills, that was for them, got by themselves for themselves. The nation? What nation? The only nation they knew or cared anything about was their own nation, the Blackstone Nation they called it, Mighty B! Mighty Blackstone Nation!

That was a caricature, of course, or, if you will, a psychotic delusion; but that was the way it was in the South Side in the months before the convention. These young black toughs had as little in common with Julian Bond as they did with Richard Daley, but Bond *knew* about them, and Daley didn't, and that was the difference.

But, then, you didn't need to have talked with Gene Hairston, handsome, restless, accused murderer of a president of the Rangers, or to Sylvester Hutchins, one of Hairston's top sidekicks, who said that what it would take to fix up the ghetto would be dump truck after dump truck full of peace powder and money, to know how it was in Chicago. All you had to do was look out the window of the car on the way from the airport and see the Army trucks, the cheese-slicer jeeps, and know that if this was still America then there sure as hell was something gone badly wrong with it.

How bad, Bond knew, and he had been brooding about it all that summer. The radio woke people up one morning with the news that Bobby Kennedy was dying now, shot by some crazy punk in a hotel kitchen. Bond had liked Bobby. Martin Luther King had been a friend of his parents, and had talked with him about philosophy, had marched for him when he lost his seat; and although like a lot of other youngsters in the Movement, Bond had chuckled sometimes at King, and called him "De Lawd," Bond admired King. He had admired him enough to write a little couplet about him, lifting a line from another hero, Ray Charles:

> Look at that gal shake that thing—
> We can't all be Martin Luther King . . .

Bond liked to recite that couplet to audiences, especially white audiences, delighting in the puzzled frowns, the straining toward meaning that he saw out there over the rostrums he spoke from; to him the meaning was simple: live and let live. Now, King was dead, murdered, too. In the summer of 1968, barely recovered himself from the rough ride through the courts to an uneasy seat in the Georgia legislature, badly shaken by the murders of two friends, Bond lay up in Atlanta and pondered what to do—if anything at all. Things outside were fractured, shapeless, chaotic; Atlanta was warm and quiet, lazy, solid. He had been dabbling in the campaigns, and rippling rumors had gone around—Bond was for Bobby; that was over. Bond was for Humphrey; that wasn't true. Bond was for Senator Eugene McCarthy of Minnesota; Bond wasn't sure, hadn't given the matter much thought. They had certain surface similarities, the Senator and the state legislator. Poets, introspective, Delphic, moody, attuned to a vague stirring they felt out there. Against the war, populist. Against Johnson. One a Roman Catholic, the other areligious; one a white man, an Irisher, the other black, entwined with the Deep South: they seemed an unlikely combination.

But, again, the forces that were stirring, against the war, against Johnson, for McCarthy, for getting politics out of the back rooms and into the hands of the people, against Humphrey and against a rubber-stamp convention, these forces swirled and eddied and one little tributary crossed Julian Bond's front steps in the unlikely form of dark-haired, intense young Charles Negaro of Connecticut, a McCarthy volunteer.

In his dabblings, Bond had got involved in a rump group of Georgia Democrats, one of those *ad hoc* coalitions of soreheads that adorn American grass-roots politics, arising like mushrooms in the dew to attack a city council bent on zoning in more gasoline stations, a health department that looks the other way when its commissioner owns slum housing. Their cause won or lost, they ordinarily shrivel and die. But this group had not died. It had its beginnings during the circus of an election the Georgians threw for governor in 1966. Lester Maddox had won the Democratic primary runoff, facing Howard "Bo" Callaway, a textile manufacturer, in the general election. Disgruntled Democrats launched a write-in campaign behind former governor Ellis Arnall. They did not succeed, but their organization did develop enough muscle from its standing start to throw the gubernatorial election into the Georgia General Assembly, which elected the feisty little diner chef governor of the state. Moreover, the surprising strength of the group convinced its leaders that it was worth keeping alive, a weapon worth honing against the day when it might be used to strike again against the Georgia power assemblage. With Atlanta labor leader E. T. "Al" Kehrer, southern director of the A.F.L.-C.I.O. civil rights department, as its head, the group announced that it would henceforth be known as the Democratic Party Forum. With Kehrer on its board was Julian Bond.

For about a year, the Forum quietly went about its business —which was scarcely headline material—trying to fire up the folks to press for a more democratic Democratic party in Georgia. But then, in December of 1967, Lester Maddox himself provided the little group with just the sort of goad it needed to flourish. Anybody who supported the national ticket, Maddox said, was either stupid, a fool, a coward or a traitor. This diagnosis was leveled in particular at Maddox's lieutenant governor, George T. Smith, who had suggested, in an address before a gathering of Democratic women, that Georgians, and Georgia Democrats especially, ought to support the party's nominee in 1968. Regardless of Maddox's intended target, the members of the Democratic Forum saw this intemperate remark as just the kind of self-incrimination they thought would give them a sound basis for striking at Maddox in the national ring. "We decided," recalls Al Kehrer, "that this would be a basis for challenging the Maddox delegation—the delegation being hand-picked by the governor."

The Forum went through the usual who-struck-John of all such efforts, holding meetings, and drafting letters and having lunches—and throughout most of these early tactical-planning sessions, Julian Bond played a minor role. He came to the luncheon on June 29, 1968, at which the Forum announced it was going to challenge the Maddox delegation to the Chicago convention. "But," Kehrer recalls, "he did not participate in the meeting other than being there." The Forum had first tried to impress its views upon the Georgia Democratic Party, writing a letter to James Gray, the party chairman, declaring its intentions of challenging at Chicago the delegates selected by Maddox, requesting time before the party's executive committee in which to discuss broader representation among them. But Gray—and the party—ignored these upstarts. (Ironically, Kehrer noted later, "if Gray had followed the broad outlines of what we had suggested, he would have been home clear at Chicago. We hit the major issues: the number of Negroes, the method of selection, the abandonment of the unit rule . . .") Turned down flat by the men who controlled the Democratic party in the state, the Forum's leaders then decided to hold their own convention, elect a slate of delegates, and, just as the Mississippi Freedom Democratic Party had done in 1964, send them on to the convention, there to challenge the official party delegation before the convention's credentials committee.

Insurgent moves like the Forum's were putting Hubert Humphrey in a tough spot. The man who had ruptured the 1948 Democratic convention, splintering off the Southern Democrats into a Dixiecrat faction, was himself, in 1968, in the same desperate need of holding together all the support he could garner. Humphrey's political fate had been cast in doubt in 1964 when the Mississippi challengers were told to back off if they wanted Humphrey on the ticket. In 1968 a similar kind of pressure, this time tacit, existed: civil-rights-oriented efforts to gain seats in the convention could cost Humphrey the support he might otherwise get from delegates like those appointed by Lester Maddox. Atlanta attorney Al Horn, counsel to the Forum and one of its challenging delegates, observed after the convention, "Fantastic as it seems to anyone who remembers the 1948 National Convention, Hubert Humphrey was in 1968 the Democratic candidate most acceptable (or rather, least unacceptable) to the 'South' —undoubtedly due to a little Johnson armtwisting and to murmured remembrances of the many military bases and other federal goodies showered on the South. But the 'South' that accepted Humphrey was in part the South challenged by the Forum and similar groups."

Therefore, although Humphrey had sent a telegram of congratulations to the Forum applauding its birth, he and his workers ignored their challenge effort, declining to send spokesmen to the rump convention which the Forum decided to hold at Macon, Georgia, for the selection of a protest delegation. This the Humphrey camp did in spite of the implorings of the Humphrey supporters in the Forum; the reasoning, no doubt, was that the labor people like Kehrer would hold the Forum delegation firmly in line behind Humphrey whereas the candidate had nothing to gain by giving the dissidents diplomatic recognition and would risk offending the regular delegation by sending representatives to Macon.

The reasoning was politically sound, as far as it went, but it did not go far enough to reckon with the McCarthy forces, represented in Georgia by Charles Negaro, a young Connecticut lawyer who had ventured south to try to cultivate support for his candidate among the Georgia regular delegates. Failing that, but learning of the Forum's protest convention, he excitedly reported back to McCarthy headquarters that in Macon there just might be a marvelous little secret weapon for the McCarthy cause, a nearly finished Trojan horse just waiting to be seized and occupied, greased up and ridden into the convention. The only obstacles Negaro saw blocking his hopes were the hesitance of the McCarthy headquarters staff about plunging manpower and money into an uncertain effort —and the determination of Al Kehrer and the others on the Democratic Forum who wanted to see their delegation leave for Chicago allied with Hubert Humphrey, or at least uncommitted. But if Eugene McCarthy himself could be told of the delightful possibilities inherent in the Georgia challenge, the great potential there for making mischief with Hubert Humphrey's vaunted image as a friend of the liberal cause would be irresistible. Then, if enough money were made available to Charles Negaro to make an all-out bid to seize that challenge for McCarthy, why, Al Kehrer and the other Humphrey men on the Forum could do very little to hold their delegation for the Vice-President.

To people standing on the beach, tides appear to rise without cause, and to many in Georgia, it just seemed as though the tide came in, floated off Julian Bond's little bark to national fame, and swamped Al Kehrer's visions of a renegade Democratic group loyal to the national ticket. Tides, of course, don't merely occur without cause, but instead respond to the passage overhead of the moon, and so did the tide in Georgia respond to the gravitational tug of a passing body, that of Eugene McCarthy; and when McCarthy had set in the political heavens, the tide receded, leaving Bond to row for himself. But that did not happen immediately and while it lasted the surf was fine indeed.

The success of the McCarthy cause had been flamboyant enough in the primaries, but to make any showing at all in Chicago, his strategy depended on the daring hope of chipping away at delegate strength, on making an historic breach in the traditional unit rule that bound maverick delegates to vote solidly with their fellow delegates. Until Charles Negaro went south to Georgia and sniffed out the Democratic Forum and sensed the potential it held for McCarthy, the Senator's advisers had been banking on making big gains in the scraps within the Texas and Alabama delegations. An end-run, chancy kind of gambit, but these were desperate times. The people in politics, especially Democratic politics, were willing to try almost anything to keep their causes alive. Many of the young men and women who had allied themselves with Robert Kennedy went to Chicago to work for George McGovern. Not because of any innate whorishness of politics, but because they genuinely believed that the young man they had themselves so deeply admired would not have wanted them to abdicate, to concede, but would have wanted them to play out their commitment. Desperate? Pierre Salinger actually telephoned the Rockefeller family and made what in any other times would have been a totally preposterous proposal.

"The night the Republican convention nominated Richard Nixon," Salinger said later, "I was so God damned depressed by that whole thing and by the prospect of having Hubert Humphrey as the nominee that I called Nelson Rockefeller. I didn't get Nelson, but I got his cousin, a good friend of mine, and I said, 'What would you think of the idea of Nelson Rockefeller becoming a Democrat? If he does, I'll try to put together a draft for him and get him nominated by the Democratic convention for President!'

"Aldrich said, 'That's a God damned good idea; let me talk to Nelson about it.' And, the next morning about noon, Aldrich called back and said, 'First, I want you to know Nelson Rockefeller is very grateful to you. That call, coming at the time it did, did a lot for his morale. They had a three-hour meeting on it this morning and finally they decided the hell with it. They can't do it; there's no way to do it; they don't think it can be done.' "

Undaunted by the official Rockefeller rebuff (and perhaps remembering that the New York Governor had been known to change his mind on political matters) Salinger asked Jesse Unruh what he thought of the idea of drafting Nelson Rockefeller for the Democratic nomination. Unruh told him,

Salinger says, " 'I can't do that, because I'm a regular in the party, but I don't see any reason why you shouldn't.' "

But then George McGovern declared himself in the race and doughty Pierre had a more orthodox cause to embrace. But the fact that he could even entertain such schemes illustrates the desperation of liberal Democrats on the eve of the convention, a desperation which could make the notion of wooing McCarthy support away from Deep-South delegations like the one led by Georgia's Lester Maddox seem almost possible. So Charles Negaro took a leave from the law firm where he worked and went south, to Atlanta.

It didn't take Negaro very long to discover that the Maddox delegation was impervious to his blandishments, the very name Eugene McCarthy—and the appearance of the youthful Negaro and his even younger assistants—no doubt personifying for those delegates the precise reasons that the candidacies of Lester Maddox and George Wallace held the charms they did.

The dissidents within the Democratic Forum and the Forum's upcoming convention in Macon, Georgia, however, did look like promising targets for McCarthy scouting. Negaro was indeed delighted at what he quickly learned: that, although Al Kehrer was an ardent Humphrey supporter, as was the Reverend John Morris of the Voter Education Project, who was working with Kehrer in setting up the convention, the Humphrey camp was ignoring the Forum's repeated invitations to send emissaries to the Macon meeting. With all the excitement of a field geologist who has found a promising oil pool, Negaro notified McCarthy's Washington headquarters of his discovery, and waited, eagerly, for the go-ahead to start developing it.

The word was not long in coming. Gene McCarthy hurried out to Logan airport the morning of July 26 to catch a Washington flight; he had spoken the evening before at Fenway Park; with him was Washington lawyer Joe Rauh, who told McCarthy in the plane about Negaro's enthusiastic reports from Georgia. "Gene," Rauh recalls, "loved it, and before the day was up, everything was in motion." The basic appeal, of course, was that in Georgia the McCarthy forces could underwrite a McCarthy-Humphrey confrontation that would not only highlight the candidates' differences over Viet Nam policy but that would also serve to diminish what some critics felt was Humphrey's edge over McCarthy in domestic attitudes. By linking Humphrey with arch-segregationist Maddox—and posters were being made up of an old news-photo showing the two arm in arm—the McCarthy workers could, they felt, slide past their champion's track-record in civil rights, which by comparison with Humphrey's was rather slight, and obscure the fact that beyond a vaguely concerned posture, McCarthy had nothing really substantial with which to oppose the Johnson Administration's domestic accomplishments. To a large degree, in fact, it was in that very vagueness that a good deal of the McCarthy appeal lay, in the tacit insinuation that if only McCarthy were elected, then the programs would take care of themselves, that once the terrible caul of the war in Viet Nam were removed from the people some innate popular wisdom would assert itself, the programs would just percolate upward from their needful mass, and once more the nation would enjoy proprietary control over itself. But first McCarthy had to get elected, and before that, nominated, and to do that, his troops were going to have to bust Chicago wide open. Georgia looked like a good opening wedge. Charles Negaro was to get, McCarthy and Rauh decided, "whatever he needed in the way of help." Julian Bond did not occur to them until later.

Not that Bond had been ignored by the McCarthy forces, or by Negaro; far from it. But their efforts had been to enlist his endorsement for the purposes of suasion on a national basis. Negaro, failing in his attempts to lure delegates out of the Maddox fold, had been in touch with Bond almost from his arrival in Georgia, had made it a point to consult with him, just as he had with other Negro leaders in Atlanta, as part of his alternative campaign to rouse popular support in Georgia for Senator McCarthy. Negaro had tried to convince Bond that, with Bobby Kennedy dead, McCarthy offered the best hope of the kind of Democratic candidacy he wanted to work for. Bond was not easy to convince.

"I think one thing about Julian that summer," Negaro says, "was there was a tremendous reluctance on his part to step forward. There was a feeling in Atlanta, 'Where is Julian Bond?' The guy had risen to be the epitome of being a leader of the community, and then, all of a sudden, he wasn't a leader anymore. I think you could ask, 'How was he supposed to lead?' I mean, I don't think he knew."

How much Negaro himself, as a white Yankee outsider, *really* knew is problematic, although he, to be sure, came to feel a concerned friendship for Bond and some of the other Georgians who eventually went to Chicago as challenging contenders for the seats held by Lester Maddox's hand-picked slate of delegates. Joe Rauh, too, feels a fondness for Bond that goes beyond the mere cordiality of transitory political alliance. Nonetheless, the concern of Negaro and the other McCarthy forces for Bond's cast of mind in the summer of 1968 had nothing, essentially, to do with his welfare, but rather with their own. As to his willingness or lack of it to assume some kind of leadership role in Atlanta, to begin to make some move to pick up the mantle dropped by the fallen Martin Luther King, all that sounds nice, but Julian Bond would have been nearly as useful to the McCarthy people stuffed and mounted as on a white horse. Their main problem wasn't his character, but simply getting him to consent to back their man, first, and second, they soon realized, getting him to attend the Macon convention. Once he was physically there, they reasoned, their sheer force of numbers—a relatively easy thing to achieve, in view of the fact that Hubert Humphrey's people were staying away in droves—could carry Bond into the chairmanship of

the convention—if he didn't fight too hard against it. Mc-
Carthy's men didn't want Bond for any quality of generalship,
for any political acumen, for, in fact, he had so far demonstrated none; they sought Bond's endorsement, and his minimal
acquiescence in their cause, simply for his symbolic quality, his
trademark value, to wave like a flag. *Julian Bond* would be on
their side; *Lester Maddox* would be on *Hubert Humphrey's*.
In the hysterical atmosphere of the summer of 1968, such was
the political logic. It made sense. But Bond wasn't buying it.

Failing to persuade Bond by himself, Negaro turned to
others for help; one was Ivanhoe Donaldson, the energetic
young Negro who had talked Bond into running for the
Georgia House a few years before. Around mid-July, a fort-
night or so before the Macon convention, Donaldson arranged
to arrive in Atlanta and drop in on his old buddy of sit-in days.
"I mean," says Donaldson, "I wasn't interested in McCarthy,
per se, you know—it was the issues. I decided I had to do
something in the campaign, so I did what I can do best. I know
a lot of young black cats who have political prestige and who
run political organizations.

"I went down and Julian wasn't doing anything—and didn't
want to do anything. He worked with Kennedy. Kennedy had
been assassinated. Julian had a lot of attachment to Senator
Kennedy and McCarthy's cold turkey. You really got to
believe to work for McCarthy. I mean, I did. You got to think
an issue is so blasted important that you go out and do that.
McCarthy's a whole other story.

"I went down there because of Charlie Negaro. I went
down to see what they were doing. I talked to Charlie, and
said, 'Well, where's Charles Sherrod, Hosea Williams?' I
named people all over the state. These guys weren't interested
in talking to Charles Negaro. 'He's a carpetbagger,' they said.
'He's from New York; he hasn't tied any Georgia people into
his campaign. . . .' "

Next, Donaldson says, "I went to see Julian, and said, 'Well, hey, man, whatcha doing? You involved in the Macon thing?'

"Julian says, 'No.'

"I say, 'You not going to be a delegate?'

"He says, 'No, I don't think so, man.'

"I say, 'Come on, Julian, be serious! Look—Kennedy is *dead*. We still got a lot of country and a lot of issues to deal with, and we just can't sit back and loaf the rest of the summer. You know, decisions are going to be made, and the question is, are you going to participate in them—or are you just going to let them happen by default?'

"So," Donaldson says, "we had a few words, and he got revved up. I said, 'I don't want your support for McCarthy.' At that point, I said, 'What's important is that we have a good delegation on the issues out of the Macon convention.'

"I called John Lewis, and I talked John into going down there and the rest started to roll. They're old Snick people."

Donaldson gave Bond a day to think about his urgent pleadings—while he himself went off to Jackson, Mississippi, with Joe Rauh and Michigan Congressman John Conyers, to consult with Mississippi's insurgent Democrats, who themselves were getting cranked up for their own trip to the Chicago convention. Back in Atlanta the next morning, Donaldson said to Bond: "I'm not going to talk to you about endorsing McCarthy—but I think you ought to make some public appearances on the question of this war *now*. You don't have to campaign for McCarthy, but you *got* to campaign for Humpty-Dumpty up there." Vehemently anti-Humphrey, Donaldson kept hammering at Bond until at last Bond agreed to speak on the same platform with McCarthy on the war, and went on tour with him through Ohio. A week or so before the Macon convention, to Negaro's enormous relief, Bond endorsed Eugene McCarthy for President of the United States. But he still had not agreed to attend the Macon convention.

Meanwhile, Negaro was doing his best to flood the state with pro-McCarthy material, some of it thinly disguised as urgings to attend the Macon convention. McCarthy himself had visited Georgia briefly in July, and Negaro and his troops managed to have several thousand people, mostly young students, out at the airport to greet him. Following that, they scoured the state for McCarthy supporters, congressional district by congressional district, realizing that attendance from many of them was going to be sparse—and that, since representation on the convention caucuses would be by congressional district—they could seize control of much of the challenging delegation with relatively few people if they could just turn out the McCarthy voters. All in all, Negaro reckons, he spent about $8000 of McCarthy money in getting set for the convention: a half-hour television show took about $2500 in Atlanta; another in Macon cost about $1000. Radio spots, newspaper ads, and charter buses to carry the faithful to Macon accounted for the remainder.

"What we did," Negaro admits cheerfully, "we stuffed the convention, quite frankly. We simply got there first with the most. It was a very exciting thing: we spent some money and we advertised. We really put in a concerted effort to get people to come out to the convention. John Morris puts it in terms of our teaching the people of Georgia a lesson about conventions—he thought you called a convention, you got a handful of people to come out and they all then decide to do what the people who called the convention wanted to do—which was to be an independent nonpartisan delegation.

"To which," Negaro says, "we just said: 'Bullshit, it's going to be a McCarthy delegation.' We also, I think fairly legitimately, felt that it was the best thing for the delegation, because McCarthy people would not sell out."

History, of course, was to prove that McCarthy people would, in fact, sell out, just as McCarthy was to sell out himself at Chicago—not to any crass and demeaning compromise settlement of their suit, for none such was possible; but both McCarthy and his miserably depressed followers sold out, in the end, to their own pride, to their own arrogance, to their own galling sanctimony. But for some mere convention seats, no, McCarthy people would not sell out.

The wonder of August in Georgia in 1968 was the expectation that there might even come a chance to whore it a bit, that a challenge delegation would even get propositioned in Chicago, that Johnsonian town where so many places and so many notions were officially off-limits, not the least of them the heretical idea that the Democratic Party wasn't entirely democratic. Mississippi would get a good play there, because too much fuss had been made over the shoddy treatment it got in Atlantic City in '64 for it to go ignored this time around. But Alabama, Georgia, Texas, the other challenge states—if *all* those challenges were to be aired, listened to, perhaps deliberated over, a major chunk of the Southern wing of the Democratic party would be under attack, some mighty good men would be put on the defensive, some good men who were finding it awfully hard to explain to the boys down at the hardware and at the courthouse just why it was they were thinking of working for that no-account, Hubert Humphrey, instead of a good ol' bhoy like George Wallace.

That kind of thing could lead to a repeat performance of 1948, to a whole new Civil War inside the Democratic Party, and anybody out in front in it was bound to come away with some bad cuts and bruises. The problem facing Julian Bond, on the eve of the Macon convention, was whether, in fact, he really did want to become involved, to chance another drawn-out political fight so soon after the Supreme Court decision. The whole notion of challenging the Maddox delegation, assembled as it was by the obnoxious little man who had become governor and by his rival-turned-ally, James Gray, the Democratic party chairman, seemed hopelessly Quixotic. But the gamble, long though the odds were, offered some enormous stakes if it could be won: nationally, a victory in Chicago might crack open a flood-tide on the convention floor for McCarthy. Even if it did not do that, a victory for the Georgia challengers in Chicago would certainly signal the beginning of the end for boss politics, for the kind of hand-picked rubber-stamp delegations the Maddox regulars typified. And locally, in Georgia politics, a victory in Chicago would infuse the Democratic Forum with the kind of self-confidence and muscle that might sustain it in the future, making of it precisely the kind of grass-roots political entity that Bond felt was where the Movement should be working nowadays. In the end, the arguments, and the arguers, were overwhelming. After hearing Negaro, Donaldson, and his old comrade John Lewis out, Bond decided to go to Macon; he drove down that Saturday morning, August 10, 1968, with John Lewis.

The men largely responsible for mounting the convention —who did not include Bond—had more or less agreed among themselves that their challenge delegation would be dominated by Humphrey supporters, with a token representation of McCarthy fans aboard. They had attempted to broaden their base beyond the core of three hundred and fifty or so dues-paying Forum members, and selected Macon as the convention site because it would be more accessible to more people around the state than Atlanta, in spite of the fair certainty of getting a bigger turnout in Atlanta. *Their* challenging issue, as they saw it, was to be primarily the questionable loyalty to the Democratic party on the parts of Maddox and Gray. But it was with a gnawing sense of helplessness and growing wrath that they watched the McCarthy group seep in. "We became aware," Kehrer says, "that the McCarthy people were moving in on us, but there wasn't much that could be done. And, in terms of what the state leadership for McCarthy had pledged —that it would be essentially a nonpartisan effort aimed at the challenge of the Maddox delegation—we didn't anticipate that it was going to become a McCarthy take-over . . . until the day before the convention." Then, Kehrer recalls bitterly, "the advertising took an interesting shift: they ran a series of ads around the state, saying, 'Come to Macon and elect Eugene McCarthy President of the United States,' and 'Support the Georgia Challenge' was a much smaller line of text in the thing."

That there was a McCarthy scheme at all only began to dawn on Kehrer the week before the convention, when he was visited in his Atlanta office by Negaro and McCarthy's national youth coordinator, Sam Brown, who wanted to discuss splitting up the delegates. "They didn't get very far with that," Kehrer says. But on the eve of the convention, in the Dempsey Hotel in Macon, Kehrer learned that he and his hopes for a Humphrey-oriented delegation were in big trouble. Down from Washington was Joe Rauh, in response to the Forum's invitation to McCarthy headquarters to have a representative on hand (the Humphrey camp to Kehrer's vast discomfort had sent no one) and along with Rauh had come another top McCarthy staffer, Kurt Gans. While Kehrer was becoming increasingly apprehensive about the outcome of the Humphrey hopes in Georgia, the McCarthy cadre in Macon were themselves uncertain of their own strength there, and were anxiously discussing their strategy for the next morning. Kehrer, angry when his wife was ousted by Negaro from one of the McCarthy plotting sessions, ran into Rauh and Gans in the Dempsey lobby and the heated confrontation became a wrangling argument as it shifted to a room upstairs where, for the next four hours, Rauh and Kehrer haggled over what kind of convention this was going to be.

During the session, Rauh listened as Kehrer declared the Georgia delegation was going to be a Humphrey delegation— and that, unless it *were* a Humphrey delegation, it would not stand a chance of being seated by the Chicago convention's credentials committee because the Humphrey forces would control that committee. Rauh's answer was blunt: first, the Georgia challengers would be going to Chicago as a McCarthy delegation because the McCarthy group was going to have the votes the next day to make it such, and second, the challengers would not get seated unless they *could* embarrass the Vice-President through a row over Maddox and McCarthy support. Privately, the McCarthy group decided to dump Kehrer if he remained obdurate; but such a move, they knew, would shatter the fragilely knit Forum and make them appear to have wrecked the Macon convention. In return for pledges from the Reverend John Morris and Ben Brown, Bond's seat-mate in the Georgia House, that Kehrer would chair the convention fairly, the McCarthy leaders agreed not to mount a move to remove Kehrer as convention chairman.

The convention-eve meeting broke up with nothing settled, after hours of heated debate over whether Rauh would be the man to present the Georgia challengers' case to the credentials committee; over whether the McCarthy group could examine the convention rules, which Kehrer insisted they could not. The spat resumed the next morning, however, when the McCarthy group hung copies of a photograph showing Hubert Humphrey with his arm around Governor Maddox in the convention room, and Forum officials demanded that delegates to the convention remove their McCarthy hats in obedience to a rule barring candidate paraphernalia from the floor—and take down the offending photographs.

Bond and Lewis arrived amid this jangle of fervor and acrimony, and joined the six hundred or so other delegates, about half of whom were black, to listen to Al Kehrer gavel the convention to order. After some quick speeches, applause for Joe Rauh as McCarthy's envoy, and an embarrassed admission that the Humphrey camp had sent none, the convention fractured into its district caucuses. There, the McCarthy organizers were certain, they would capture the delegation. Typical was the Fifth Congressional District caucus, where both Julian Bond and Ben Brown were nominated for the chairmanship. "That," Bond recalls, "was the first Humphrey-McCarthy contest. Ben Brown was a Humphrey man. I defeated him rather soundly. That was an indication of where the votes were, and from then on, it was just a straight push on through. From then on, we had it."

As the other caucuses reported McCarthy-dominated delegate lists, and his defeat seemed more and more certain, Kehrer's anger grew, until finally, when the convention resumed its general session, he announced his resignation as chairman, and stalked out of the room. Kehrer's departure from the hall, however, did not mean that he was abandoning the effort to keep the Georgia challenge true to Humphrey; what it did mean, to the considerable dismay of the McCarthy workers, was that their job in Chicago was going to be considerably more complicated than it might otherwise have been. And, finally, it was to mean that the Democratic Forum would not become the forceful and independent political guerrilla cadre in Georgia that Bond had hoped it would.

But the delegates gathered in the Dempsey Hotel had more immediate crises before them: they needed a new chairman, and they had to decide what to do about the brief, stating the merits of the Georgia challenge, which had already been mailed off to the credentials committee. The brief that was on its way to Chicago stressed the questionable party loyalty of Governor Maddox and of Gray, the Democratic party chairman; the McCarthy people wanted to come in hard not on that so much—because McCarthy's own party loyalty was in some doubt—but upon the issue of Negro representation in Georgia Democratic party affairs and in the Maddox delegation.

Lonnie King, who had gone down to Macon to watch the convention, says that after Kehrer abandoned the chair, "Charlie Black and I looked around, and there was just chaos. Where there's chaos, the politician moves right in. Charlie nominated Ben Brown, and while he was on his way up to the podium, some labor guy grabbed his coat-tail and he went up and declined. So we started working on Julian, and Charlie nominated him—and then he did the same thing. Then Joe

Rauh came over, and some white girls, and they said, 'Oh, please, Julian, you've *got* to do it!' Now, you *never* ask Julian to *please* do anything—he'll just fold his arms and sit back and refuse. So, we decided to take it into caucus and we did it there . . . Julian's not too good in strategy. When the action gets fast, Julian just clams up. He knows what's going on, but he just clams up. People say he's so cool and all, but he just clams up. Here, black people had come from all over Georgia to this hotel where you couldn't even drink in the bar downstairs. Julian was saying it was all over, and I said, 'Just change the issue, from loyalty to black representation!' "

Not only had Lonnie King nominated Bond for chairman, but Al Horn, the Atlanta lawyer who became the counsel to the challenge delegation, did, too. Bond, however, continued to insist he did not want to chair the convention—*or* to lead it to Chicago, to the vast exasperation of the McCarthy lieutenants who now saw him as all but crucial to their efforts. From the moment he and Lewis had arrived at the convention, one McCarthy aide or another had been urging him to indicate he would accept the chairmanship of the delegation and he had continued to decline, saying the job would entail too much work. But, after the Reverend James Hooten of Savannah had been nominated to chair the convention, and had accepted, and the elected delegates to Chicago then went into a separate session to elect *their* leader, Bond at last relented, and agreed to share that chairmanship with Hooten. The job as he saw it would be a fairly simple and undemanding one—a quick trip to Chicago to appear before the credentials committee—and most likely an unsuccessful one.

Ten days later, having prepared a new brief and sent it off to supplant the earlier one entered by the Kehrer group, the leaders of the Georgia challenge delegation caught an early morning plane to Chicago; that afternoon, at the office of Chicago lawyer Alton Harris, they readied themselves for their presentation the next day before the committee, cramming like so many college students boning up for final exams.

Chicago in August is as unpleasant as Chicago at any other time of year only hotter, dirtier and smellier; and when they arrived, Bond and the others had no intentions of staying any longer than their business demanded. Bond, Al Horn and Ben Brown checked into a $3-a-night YMCA near the Loop, their rooms tiny cubicles containing just beds and dressers—in contrast to the suite the Reverend John Morris had somehow managed to come by at the Hilton, the hotel where the Vice-President would stay the following week and where the credentials committee was meeting.

That evening, buoyantly confident that they were ready to counter any arguments from the Maddox regulars and field whatever questions the credentials committee might throw at them next day, the Bond delegates got a jarring surprise. Al Kehrer, along with six fellow Humphrey supporters who were as unhappy as he was about the outcome at Macon, had arrived in Chicago to mount a flank attack, intending to appear before the credentials committee in what Kehrer candidly admitted later was a "plague on both houses" move. Learning of this, some of the challenge delegation set up a meeting aimed at reconciliation, and Bond and Negaro cut short a conference with singer Harry Belafonte and Detroit Congressman John Conyers to rush back to the Hilton to attend the parley. Before he met with Kehrer, however, Bond placed a telephone call to Vice-President Humphrey. When Humphrey returned the call, Bond asked him to intercede with Kehrer, lest the entire challenge be scuttled in the credentials committee hearings by the appearance of a lack of solidarity—and the inevitable confusion over who really represented the will of the Forum's members that would surely arise —if Kehrer persisted. Humphrey responded with a question, asking Bond what had happened to his earlier support of one Hubert Horatio Humphrey. The Vice-President reminded the young legislator that he had been among the first to support Bond's right to be seated in the Georgia House in 1966.

"That was 1966, Mr. Vice-President," Bond told him, "this is 1968." That report of his support, Bond told the Vice-President, had been a misunderstanding and now some high-level assistance was really crucially urgent. Humphrey asked for the details, got them, and said he would look into what he could do. Then the challengers held their own strategy conference, one of the last Negaro or any outsider was permitted to sit in on—they were achieving a group identity beyond being merely a McCarthy campaign device, and Bond was picking up the job of being their leader. What, they wondered, did Kehrer really expect to achieve by coming to Chicago? Some of them saw his arrival as mere spite; others saw it as a last-ditch move to salvage some success for labor in Georgia before the convention began.

Kehrer's real purpose, it became clear soon after the meeting began, was to attempt to avert a blow-up over the Georgia seats that might damage Humphrey. He would, he proposed to Bond and the other Forum delegates, not press his counter-claim on the Georgia seats if they in turn would agree to abide by the credentials committee decision and not carry their case to the floor of the convention if that decision did not please them. "Oh, you should have heard the screams of outrage," Kehrer recalls, "that I should dare even suggest such a thing! I became even more convinced than ever that they were really part of the McCarthy operation."

On the other hand, Negaro says, "This was where we knew that he had sold out—there was no reason to present that kind of argument unless you were being pressured by national union people or national Democrats, because that was like saying, 'We'll go half way and then we'll kick in.'" Divided over which brief should carry the challenge to the credentials committee, and adamant about a floor fight, the former allies parted angrily for the evening, braced for a clash in the committee's hearing room the next day.

Before it took up Georgia's case on the afternoon of August

21, 1968, the credentials committee heard the challengers from Texas, who were protesting the seating of the delegation led by Governor John Connolly, a close friend of Lyndon Johnson. Watching the proceedings from the observers' seats—so as to be close to the challenge table when the Georgia case came up—were Bond and his fellow plaintiffs. Unless they were right there on the sidelines, and ready to move when the Texas argument was over, Joe Rauh had warned them, they might get elbowed out by Kehrer and his group, who were scheduled to be heard first. Rauh's arguments with the committee, headed by Governor Richard Hughes of New Jersey, won the Bond group the starting position, however. As they presented their case, and noted the reactions of the committee, they began to sense for the first time that they actually had a real chance of success.

Bond began his statement to the committee by telling them they were about to hear of racial exclusion throughout the Democratic party in Georgia as well as in the method of selection used to pick the regular delegation. That situation, he said, was in direct conflict with the official party call, the summons to the 1968 convention, which had stated—largely as a result of the embarrassment in 1964 over the Mississippi challenge—that a state party had to assure that *all* voters would be eligible to take part in all party affairs. But, Bond said, in Georgia, where blacks were twenty-three percent of the registered voters, and faithful Democrats as well, having given the Democratic ticket ninety-four percent of their votes in 1964, they themselves had been given only the merest token representation in party leadership. The two-hundred-man state executive committee had only five Negroes on it; of the one hundred members picked by party chairman Gray, just one was a Negro; Georgia's one hundred fifty-nine counties had their Democratic party affairs overseen by some three thousand executive committee members, but of them all, only fifty were black and those fifty blacks lived in just four of the one hundred fifty-nine counties. Citing the Maddox delegation's defending brief, Bond told the committee, "The Maddox delegation has mentioned that there are eleven Negro members, all Democrats, in the Georgia House and Senate—they neglect to mention, however, that these eleven represent only four point three percent of the make-up of the Georgia legislature, and come from only three counties of the one hundred fifty-nine. If you seat the Maddox hand-picked delegation, the black voters of Georgia will be represented here at this convention by two point oh one [2.01] percent of Georgia's delegate votes. How can this be considered, in the year 1968, as anything but tokenism?"

Following Bond, Al Horn reminded the credentials committee that Maddox and Gray had been Goldwater Democrats in 1964 and now couldn't be trusted to put the Party's nominees on the ballot in November, if their delegation were unseated by the convention. The Reverend Morris then spoke, calling the question before the committee, "whether the racist barons of the Old South shall be allowed to speak for the people of Georgia or whether the people themselves shall have a say in this initial part of the process by which the President of the United States is chosen." Georgia, Morris said, had enjoyed a renascent progress as racial demogoguery faded; but now, "with a resurgent Dixiecrat racialism having come to the fore, our progress hangs in the balance. . . ."

The regulars answered by dismissing the Macon convention as a ragtag assemblage of just a few hundred persons, in which "the local rump group was out-flanked and out-maneuvered by a nationally directed organization." Far from being a segregated machine, they maintained, their state party organization was a showcase of fundamental democracy and one-man-one-vote participatory grass-roots politics. As for the aspersions cast upon their leaders' loyalty, the regulars declared: "Historically and traditionally, the regular delegates to the national convention from the Democratic party of Georgia have supported the nominees of the national convention, and it is expected that this tradition of loyalty will be honored."

Kehrer's statement to the credentials committee, in the end, did nothing either to alarm the regulars or cripple the challengers. Without a slate of delegates to oppose the Forum group or the regulars, Kehrer merely attacked Maddox in what had by then become the routine fashion, and loosed some criticism at the Forum delegation for the way they had seized the convention. After a short recess for dinner, the credentials committee hearing on the Georgia challenge was over. Governor Maddox himself, the challengers felt, had given them considerable assistance by daring the credentials committee to unseat his delegation and by referring to Governor Hughes as a raving Socialist. "With him on the other side," Al Horn mused later, "we hardly needed allies."

Their original plan had been to return to Atlanta after making their pitch to the credentials committee, but, Bond recalls, they discovered that the credentials committee members were not unwilling to stand in hallways and chat, would make themselves available for dates for drinks, or for coffee, and so, since the Reverend Morris had his room booked at the Hilton anyway, Bond says, the delegation decided "we might as well stay on another day, at least, and do a little politicking." The committee was to meet in closed executive session the next day, Thursday, but as compromise feelers probed back and forth between the challenge delegation and the committee, the meeting was set back again and again. "We had," Reverend Morris recalls, "to present a strong front and expect the whole bag. We kept a discipline on, in spite of our fears that we were asking for too much." Rauh advised them to hold out publicly and privately for the entire bloc of Georgia seats, an audacious stand to take, in view of the rumors swirling through the hotel that only the Mississippi challenge had a chance of getting anything substantial as a settlement and that, at best, the Georgia insurgents could hope for only a token seating of two members.

The job of maintaining a façade, outwardly, at least, of determination to get all the seats, had been made more difficult by the conciliatory tone of Ben Brown's remarks to the credentials committee. He had expressed the hope that some of the worthier men on the regular delegation might be allowed to keep their seats at the convention—a hands-across-the-border gesture that opened the way for Governor Hughes's first compromise solution. Early Friday morning shortly after midnight, in the Hilton's basement press room, Hughes announced that the credentials committee was attempting to settle the dispute by offering half the Georgia seats—and half the votes, too —to each of the rival delegations. Maddox, a presidential aspirant, would not be seated as a delegate. The challengers gave no public indication of their reaction, but "secretly," said Al Horn afterward, "we were elated." All the more so because it quickly appeared as though the Georgia regulars, half their seats all but lifted by the committee, were near to abandoning the remainder in a fit of high pique. Maddox bitterly assailed the Hughes announcement as a personal and prejudiced attack that would wreck the party; state chairman Gray was polling his delegation to determine whether they were ready for a floor fight—or whether they would just rather go home. Sensing a windfall in the offing, the challengers began lobbying hard for any seats left open by homeward-bound regulars, and started work on their own cut-down list of delegates, to occupy the twenty-one seats they would get whatever the regulars did—*if* the compromise went through.

The growing street army of uninvited delegates was arriving from a shadowy plebescite beyond Chicago. Conventions are always lodestones, attracting all manner of spirits somehow politicized by the energy in them, the inherent suggestion and premise being that here things get settled, courses decided upon. Chicago was in that sense no different: the Reverend Ralph David Abernathy was getting his trusty mule train ready for a pointless drive down Michigan Avenue on behalf of his Poor People's Campaign, a crusade that had been born of promise and died in its muddy cradle at Resurrection City in the spring; the self-styled Captain of the Hippie Hair Farce sewed—or got his anguished mother to sew—toy airplanes on his war-surplus flight jacket as a pair of jaunty and sardonic epaulets.

It was a Secret Serviceman's nightmare as the candidates began arriving in town; was the young man arriving without announcement to present the candidate with his strikingly ugly tempera of the brothers Kennedy just a well-meaning fan, or was he someone more sinister? Was the shadowy figure out on the Hilton Hotel marquee just a tipsy delegate trying to get some fresh air or a bird's-eye view of the crowd to take back to Dubuque—or was he, perhaps, a sniper? The agents— including Treasury Department desk types pressed into security work just for the convention, crew-cut young lawyers and accountants self-conscious with their walkie-talkies and little lapel-buttons—lived on vitamin pills and snatches of sleep, the memory of Dallas still hideously fresh in their minds . . . as it was in everybody else's. The convention, really, should have been held on an aircraft carrier in Lake Michigan, if it was held anywhere at all, with the delegates and the candidates marooned there until it was over. Then and only then would there have been the kind of security that Daley and the Administration wanted, from assassins—and from the eyes of the United States of America and the world.

But it wasn't held on a carrier, and so the folks started rolling into the big town over the weekend, from all across the country. Whole busloads from New York, come to watch, and to raise a little hell. Up in Brewster, N.Y., the best telephone-tapper and eavesdropper and electronic surveillance man in the country and maybe the world, Bernard Spindel, got his little bags of transistors and his suitcases full of radio beam sweepers ready. He was going to the convention, too, to work for Senator Eugene McCarthy just as not too many years before, in Chattanooga, he worked for Teamster Union boss Jimmy Hoffa when Hoffa thought that he was under the probing eye of the U.S. government. Frazzled by a bus strike and a taxi strike, fraught with apprehension over the inpouring hordes of long-haired kids bent on God-knows-what, smirking, yet frightened, too, by the massed soldiers bivouacked along the roads leading into the Loop, Chicago braced itself for the convention.

The credentials committee, in the limelight until the main proceedings were gaveled into life at the Amphitheater, wrestled through the weekend with the staggering problem of the 5,611 seats that were being fought over in the challenge proceedings, which it had to adjudicate. Mississippi in '64 had unlocked a floodgate of challenge; how the committee handled their claim—and Georgia's, and Texas's and Alabama's—might have a lot to do with the outcome of this convention, both inside the Amphitheater and outside, too. Governor Richard Hughes wearily set up a conference for Sunday night with former House Speaker and now Lieutenant Governor George T. Smith of Georgia, a man recognized as a moderate and likely to listen to the merits of a compromise.

Meanwhile, Bond had left his tiny room in the YMCA to move into one at the Hilton. His wife, Alice, was joining him in Chicago—bringing with her some replacements for the one shirt Bond had packed back when he thought his trip was going to be a brief one. Even Bond's reserved skepticism was beginning to buoy now, under assurances of the McCarthy and McGovern supporters on the credentials committee that they would support him down the line, even if he wanted to hold out for a floor fight over the Georgia seats. It was an incredible assurance to make and it in fact did not hold all the way, to the challengers' bitter disappointment: some of the McGovern-pledged members of the committee were among the leaders, in the heated executive session which eventually yielded the compromise, of the move to accommodate both delegations. But it nonetheless was an unmistakable signal that whatever the challengers had going for them, it was working far beyond their wildest hopes back in Macon fifteen days before.

Bond himself is laconic in explaining just what it was that he and the other members of his challenge group did that turned the trick in Chicago: "We found out that the difference between that jury and a regular jury is, that this jury is not locked up at night. You can talk to them and lobby with them and you can meet 'em in the hallway and have breakfast with them at six o'clock in the morning, and we did that."

Negaro is more lavish in his evaluation, saying, "Once they got to Chicago, this delegation was unique, not only because it had a symbol, Julian Bond, leading it, but because it had the greatest sort of public relations going in this guy, whom the news people love and who is just extremely sharp and articulate: it could really capture the hearts of America. Bond was a Fannie Lou Hamer! A much different type, but Bond was the Fannie Lou Hamer of 1968! He became a television idol overnight; there was no one else on the delegation who could have done that."

Ivanhoe Donaldson pinpoints as the reason for the challengers' success in Chicago that symbolic value which a civil rights movement background and the unseating from the Georgia House had infused in Bond. "He might have been a maverick in Georgia," Donaldson says, "but to the reform movement in the Democratic party, Julian is a hero; he represented to New York, California, Washington, D.C., Massachusetts, Oregon, delegations which were fairly strong, were antiwar forces, what they wanted to epitomize. You see, Julian represented a difference from any number of other people who *could* have co-chaired that operation: when you see Julian, *you know what he stands for*. At least in terms of rhetoric, you have an idea. When you see other people, you don't know whether they're coming or going.

"How do you win a challenge with people that no one ever heard of? That was one of the problems that Alabama faced. Julian at least had a public name. You say, 'Julian Bond would like to speak to your delegation for five minutes about the challenge,' and people would make space. It would have been impossible for the Georgia delegation to have done as well as they did with anybody else, even though the challenge would have been the same, just as legitimate and just as honest. But the nature of American politics is half personality-geared and personality-based. It's kind of dishonest, but it's true."

The Sunday evening conference with Lieutenant Governor Smith left Hughes without a compromise satisfactory to both sides in the Georgia dispute; with the opening of the convention just twenty-four hours away, the credentials committee chairman dispatched Furman Templeton, a young Negro aide, to the challengers' headquarters at the Hilton. Both sides now were hardening; one Georgia regular was heard, as he arrived in Chicago, to remark to his companion, "Let's find a bar—after that, we'll look for a plane ticket home."

On a quick plane trip back to Atlanta to get a legal effort started to ensure the convention nominees would be on the Georgia ballot regardless of how well the regular delegation did at the convention, Al Horn, the Atlanta attorney serving as counsel to the Bond delegation, had discovered that Democrats back home were sorely upset by the wrangling at the convention. The prospect of lining up eighty thousand signatures on petitions necessary for listing the Chicago nominees on the November ballot if Maddox did not choose to list them himself seemed unlikely to Horn's allies at home—especially if the McCarthy workers dropped out of the party ranks after a McCarthy defeat. Their reasoning would surely be a factor in the decision of the party's leaders. It therefore was not surprising that Hughes's new compromise, related by Templeton, suggested a way out that would save face for both sides and give both sides a voice in the selection of the party's nominees:

under the plan, both entire delegations would be seated in the Amphitheater but each side would cast only one half of Georgia's votes. Uncertain what the regulars might be goaded into doing by the anger of Maddox and Gray, and utterly convinced they *ought* to get the entire Georgia total ballot—forty-one votes—and all the seats, the challengers tried to keep a poker face, although they were seething inwardly at the off-handed way the offer had come.

"They really tried to mess over us," Bond said later, "sending this guy Templeton over to ask us if we would accept the compromise. Our position was that we would not. Our *private* position was, we would take it, if that was the best we could get. But our public opinion was that we would not take any compromise: we were all right, and they were all wrong. It was just a black-and-white issue . . . we were the good guys and they were the bad guys. But we told him we wouldn't, and we didn't want to negotiate with him—we would talk with Governor Hughes, but we didn't like people sending messengers to us, trying to feel us out. The Humphrey people were doing the same thing all the time."

Having thus spurned the compromise offer publicly, and having assured themselves privately that they were within grasping distance of an incredible victory, Bond and his delegates sat back to await the next move from the party officials. It wasn't long in coming. The Bond delegation was in a private caucus the next day, the convention scheduled to begin in just a few hours, when they were interrupted by a telephone call, from Templeton. "He asked me," Bond says, "whether I would walk out of the convention, even if we didn't get *any* seats, or if we got a bad compromise. I told him, 'No, I am committed to stay here.'

"He said, 'Do I have your permission to go before the credentials committee and tell them that?'

"I said, 'Yes, you do.' " Also, Bond recalls, Templeton extended an invitation from Hughes to come to the Hilton and discuss a settlement. Bond agreed to come. But while en route from the Del Prado where his delegation was staying, a long cab ride up the Lake Michigan shore and even more time-consuming in the now-jammed city, a mix-up occurred that Bond believes was not only deliberate but that also cost a possible total victory.

With Bond's assurance that he and his delegation were in Chicago to the finale, Templeton, Bond says, "went before the credentials committee and said, in so many words, 'Julian Bond has agreed to accept the compromise and he will not walk out.' Someone on the committee challenged him and said, 'I know that's not so because I talked to Bond this morning. They're not taking a compromise!'

"And," says Bond, "Templeton, according to what we heard, said, 'Well, it's not really so—he really didn't say that.' But nobody caught his denial, or his correction of his earlier statement.

"While I was in the damn cab on the way over to the hotel, they [the credentials committee] were voting on it! And I went up to the floor where the credentials committee had all their offices and sat in the room with Furman. While I was sitting talking to him, Hughes was having his press conference down below, announcing the settlement. I kept waiting and waiting, and you know how you gradually realize you're being screwed? I kept saying, 'Where is he? He couldn't be stuck in the elevator an hour and a half!' And, finally, the whole thing just dawned on me: while we were sitting there in Furman's office, he had his secretary typing out Hughes's announcement of the settlement! We couldn't see what he was typing. I noticed he was a little secretive with it, but not enough so I would become suspicious. We had just been had."

Given another day—as the schedule had originally given them—to lobby with more leaning delegations, and to go back and put more pressure, use more coaxing, on delegates they had already spoken with, the Georgia Loyal National Democrats, as they called themselves, might have won out, might have persuaded Governor Hughes to come forth with still another decision, to seat only them. Or, they might have dislodged a minority report from the credentials committee that would have thrust the question out on the floor. Then, given the extra lobbying time, they might have won their case there. At least, that is what they believe. There wasn't time, however, because the convention officials, anxious to get the troublesome and embarrassing seating squabbles out of the way in plenty of time for discussions and voting on the party's platform, decided to settle the Georgia question by Monday evening, the first session of the convention. Miffed at having the credentials committee decision made on the basis of what they felt was false information, the Georgia challengers might nonetheless have settled for even that compromise without a battle were it not for some further unpleasantness that confronted them soon after their arrival at the Amphitheater.

Told that Georgia's seats would remain empty until the compromise was accepted by the convention, the Georgia Loyalists were up in the balcony, gloating over their apparent defeat of Maddox when, to their shock and chagrin, they saw the regulars file out onto the floor. Where they, the challengers, had been issued mere visitors' passes, they quickly learned the regulars had been given official convention credentials—plus twenty extra passes. Says Bond with indignation, "They screwed us from our seats! They told us that both delegations would be seated up in the gallery until the question was settled, so we didn't mind that. We were sitting up in the gallery, having a good time, and I look down, and here *they* come, in on the floor! Boy, that pissed us off! I ran down to McCarthy headquarters and got a floor pass and I zipped down on the floor." There, Bond implored Governor Harold Hughes of Iowa to help.

"He got us down on the floor," Bond says. "He got very angry and he called Governor Richard Hughes and appar-

ently said something to the effect of, 'Get those people down
on the floor!' Hughes of New Jersey then called somebody
on the platform and said, 'Quick, give me forty floor passes'—
and he got them."

Passes in hand at last, Bond and his delegation filed down
out of the gallery, their hands raised aloft in the V-for-victory
symbol as the enormous amphitheater erupted in applause for
them. Once down on the floor, however, they still could not
claim their seats, for all of the chairs in the Georgia section
were occupied by their rivals, the regulars. As they milled
about, Bond was interviewed by television and other newsmen
anxious to have him explain what was happening to his challenge effort, which by now had become one of the best side-
bars to the convention story. It was Bond's cool poise then, as
he answered their questions, more than anything else in the
whole complex business of the convention challenge by the
Georgia loyalists, that won for him the national attention and
acclaim that were to follow. The challengers had not only
won a considerable victory, but they and their leader had won
it with grace.

Much later, with his curious ability to look at himself with
some degree of detachment and objectivity, Bond said, com-
menting on one piece of fan mail which congratulated him for
his "performance" at Chicago: "It *is* an arena; it is a show. I
didn't feel like an actor, but when John Chancellor comes up
to you and there are 6 million people looking at you . . . I
thought what I was doing was very complicated. The whole
challenge—people don't understand these things, unless you
take time to explain, so people who were looking would know
what we were doing. You know, they see us coming down
from the gallery and Chancellor comes up and says, 'I see
you're walking down from the gallery, Mr. Bond—what's
up?' Then, you have to tell the people what's up; you can't
just say, 'Well, we're walking down from the gallery.' It's sort
of an education process for people."

To their astonishment, the challengers heard Georgia's forty-three votes announced in support of upholding the unit rule, which bound dissident members of delegations to abide by the majority's will on questions. Al Horn, along with Bond's co-chairman, the Reverend James Hooten, hustled off to the Georgia regulars' area—the site of the delegation's microphone; Horn stayed, one hand gripping the mike, while Hooten went off to protest the Georgia vote to National Committee Chairman John Bailey, who decided neither delegation would get to vote on anything until the convention had settled the compromise issue. Meanwhile, Bond was circulating about the crowded floor, spreading the word that he and his delegates had not, in fact, accepted the Hughes compromise; at the same time Joe Rauh wandered about, making a finger-in-the-wind assessment of how a floor fight might turn out.

"When you walked the floor," Rauh recalls, "you just knew that you couldn't win a vote. You could go as low as eight hundred to as high as eleven hundred. You just knew that, rock bottom, there was no vote you could win. I knew that, really, before I got on the floor, but it got clearer and clearer. When I would talk to Negro delegates from the North who would just laugh at me, when I said the civil rights issue is a political issue, 'HHH has our votes,' you know that you can't get it. The unions were absolutely firm against it. When you lose civil rights issues in Pennsylvania, Ohio, Indiana, New Jersey, you *lose*. I mean, you can't carry a convention that's strung that way."

Impatiently, the convention voted down a motion to throw the credentials battle over until the following evening, swamping it by 11,691½ votes to 875, and then impetuously took up a motion to give Bond and his delegation *all* the Georgia seats. It lost by a narrow margin, just 1,413 votes to 1,041½; but the Amphitheater again burst into applause for the challengers, rocking to the chanting shout, "WE WANT BOND—WE WANT BOND!"

The convention had spun out of control—on the floor one Negro delegate, from California, tried to set fire to his magnetic floor pass, calling the vote an affirmation of "the racist nature of this country." At 3:45 A.M. temporary chairman Daniel Inouye of Hawaii adjourned the convention until the next day, but the amplified pounding of the gavel did not silence the pandemonium inside the Amphitheater.

It had been a serious test of Humphrey's strength and although the Administration line had not broken, it had bent, visibly and publicly, under the momentum the Georgia challenge had acquired behind it; somehow the name Julian Bond had become infused with all the pent-up urges there in the Amphitheater to join the spirit of those outside the Amphitheater.

Next morning, Georgia party chairman Gray told a reporter, "I guess we all feel a little like I do this morning, sore and baffled. The white conservative vote in the South is not wanted by the present leaders of the Democratic party. I guess we are going to have to go home and make some other arrangements. Georgia has a score to settle." Governor Lester Maddox was less eloquent, more blunt; the compromise that seemed almost certain, he said, constituted "an affront to the integrity of the citizens of our state." Julian Bond, Maddox said at an airport press conference upon his arrival back home, was a full-fledged Communist, or at the very least a Communist dupe. Maddox no longer a candidate for the White House himself, announced that he was forthwith joining the Wallace campaign.

Back in Chicago, their passions apparently spent in the ruckus the night before, the delegates, in an orderly voice vote, allocated the Georgia vote evenly to both delegations, and set about the business of settling on Hubert Humphrey as its candidate for President of the United States—without the support of several other Georgia regulars who had stayed on for the outcome. Said Jack Gunter, secretary of the regulars, as he left the Amphitheater, "We decided to get up and get the hell out of this. We're going to pack our bags and get the first plane we can. We don't want to be anywhere near this man, Bond. It will destroy the Democrats in Georgia and in the South."

The selection of Humphrey, of course, was not immediate nor unanimous; there was first the matter of eliminating McCarthy, who, in the days before the convention, had done much of the work himself toward making that a fairly easy chore; with a lackadaisical series of less than half-hearted performances before state delegations, he had demonstrated that he, if nobody else, knew his game was over. This quiet, gray, introspective, wryly humorous, earnest man, who had stirred in so many what was probably their first genuinely impassioned concern for politics, seemed to lose passion and turn away from the fight toward some inner concern. Asked what his qualifications were to be President by some member of the California delegation, for example, he declined to answer, kissing the question off with a harsh crack about the number of bathrooms in the White House and suggesting the best candidate might be a plumber. Venturing across Michigan Avenue one bright afternoon during the convention to address the adoring crowd of youths gathered there waiting for just a sight of him, McCarthy ignored the mauling they had been getting from the Chicago police altogether and spoke vaguely of other things.

Just the same, Bond stuck with McCarthy—despite some heady urgings from the Kennedy Fifth Column working in Chicago to keep alive the barely articulated hope of a nod from Hyannis Port. Armed with a nominating statement in behalf of the Senator from Massachusetts signed by an Alabama delegate, some Kennedy representatives had approached Bond in the Del Prado bar about seconding the nomination. He and Al Horn had been talking over the possibility of rekindling the floor fight on Tuesday afternoon. Bond declined the

Kennedy bid, saying he owed too much to McCarthy to shift his allegiance—unless McCarthy released him without being asked to do so. In spite of Bond's refusal to back Teddy, the Kennedy men contributed $2000 to the challenge cause before they left the Del Prado bar.

The next evening, Bond told the convention that McCarthy should be their choice, because he was "the only candidate who can win for us in 1968," and called McCarthy "the only candidate whom the American people can believe in."

The convention rejected Bond's seconding of McCarthy, but the following evening the delegates roared their approval when a forty-one-year-old Wisconsin lawyer, Ted Warshafsky, standing not at the podium but on the convention floor, entered Julian Bond's name in nomination for Vice-President, and called for a seconding speech by New York Congressman Allard Lowenstein. The move was merely a device to get Lowenstein up in front of the mike to give the White House more hell about the war in Viet Nam, but that didn't matter.

Bond had won his fight and he had won more than anybody had ever expected him to win. Warshafsky's nomination pulled in twenty-one votes for Julian Bond from the District of Columbia, one from Arizona, five from Florida, and even one-half vote from the Georgia regulars, before the twenty-eight-year-old Bond, as the members of his own embattled delegation announced their twenty-one and one-half votes for him, stepped to the microphone to say:

"I deeply appreciate the honor of having my name placed in nomination. Unfortunately, I have not yet reached the age and must therefore ask that my name be removed."

The first black man in the history of the country to be proposed for the job of Vice-President had just turned the job down on Constitutional grounds; convention chairman Carl Albert, House whip, intoned into his microphone: "Without objection, the removal is agreed to." The convention never did get to hear what it was that Allard Lowenstein was going to say.

Walking back to their room in the Hilton that night, Julian and Alice Bond stepped carefully down the corridor, taking care not to step in the wet bloodstains on the carpet. The war that Lowenstein had intended to talk about was not the only one America had on its hands now. Another had started out on Michigan Avenue.

VIII

IN the days and weeks following the Chicago convention Bond discovered, when he went out on the front steps to pick up his mail, when he went to the telephone that now seemed never to stop ringing, that he had touched a nerve somewhere out there in the fiber of America. There came pouring into Atlanta a flood of acclamation, of praise, of thanks, and of pleadings, too, from people who had seen and heard of his performance there in the convention city, and who had sensed some outstanding promise in this audacious and poised young black man from Georgia.

Hardly had the cathode tubes begun to cool when those earnest souls began to write. From distant parts of the U.S., two of them told Bond that his actions in Chicago had evoked in them feelings of wonder that they had not experienced since they had watched a young John Kennedy at the Democratic convention of 1956. From Seaford, Long Island, came the word that "yours was the most refreshing of the faces at the convention, that of a great American leader of the future." From Berkeley, someone wrote, "If I lived in Georgia, I'd be out ringing doorbells for you . . . our country desperately needs people like you." A viewer in Sanford, Florida, wrote in admiration of "your undaunted courage, forthwith judgment and your raw integrity." A Texan wrote from Houston, "Thank you for giving the Democratic convention a touch of dignity." Lyndon Johnson's one-time assistant Secretary of Labor, Esther Peterson, said, "We wait for the day you will be old enough!" A twenty-six year Army veteran, a lieutenant colonel bound for Viet Nam, wrote to Bond to tell the young legislator, "I only hope I can be half as successful as you were at the convention. I am as white as it is possible to be, but I would be proud to have you as a brother . . . we all need you." Bond had, a Notre Dame freshman told him, "re-established hope in our hearts." A breezy Kansas housewife sat down, moved by the same impulse as had the others, and wrote, "We met rather suddenly and briefly on TV and I would like to let you know how grateful I am . . . you were a source of light in dismal proceedings. We have lost so many of our heroes we are ready to grasp any hand offered. . . . The phone rang for three days with the query, 'Who is Julian Bond?' We are impressed. If your follow-through comes anywhere near that first pitch, I have a feeling a lot of people will soon know who Julian Bond from Georgia is."

There even came a letter all the way from Washington, from the Democratic nominee himself, written to congratulate Bond on the appearance of a feature story about him and his family in the *Washington Post*. In his brief note, the Vice-President extended an apology and an invitation. "I am sorry," he said, "we didn't have a chance to talk at the convention. I do hope that you may be able to be of help to me in the campaign."

While Julian Bond pondered what to do with the inrush of support—sitting there in his little house or in the cramped office of the Fulton County delegation at the Georgia capital, riffling it through his fingers, thrusting bales of it across his desk to visitors so they too could marvel at it—he was emphatically certain of one thing. He was not going to be able to be of much help to Hubert Humphrey in the campaign. He answered as many of the requests for him to come and give a speech as he could, even signing on with a speakers' agency (the same one, ironically, that represents Strom Thurmond) to help smooth the problems of logistics created by the deluge of requests; but that request from the Vice-President was one that went largely unheeded. And when Bond did speak of the Vice-President, it was not so often to help him as it was to mock him, to deride Humphrey as a pale shadow of the man he had served.

As he traveled about the country, Bond enjoyed telling reporters and editors, in intimate office conferences and luncheons high up in the publishing houses, his view of the differences among George Wallace, Richard Nixon and Hubert Humphrey: "If you lay down in front of George Wallace's car," Bond said, "he'll run over you. And if you lay down in front of Richard Nixon's car, he'll tell his chauffeur to run over you. Hubert Humphrey will cry as he watches George Wallace and Richard Nixon run over you." Hysterical, Bond hinted: that's what he thought of Hubert Humphrey now in the last weeks of the campaign. Talking, talking, talking; underlying all the talk, however, was a shrill confusion about what to do, which course to take, what to advocate, how to regard his recent past, how to break off from the lingering aura of the Great Society to suggest somehow that things would be different in the administration of Hubert Horatio Humphrey. Campaigns, of course, are always talk, and vice-presidents nearly always have to worry about how they will wear their tail, nattily tucked into their striped trousers or daringly aflutter; but Humphrey's was a special dilemma. He had been a figure of considerable stature in the Senate, always gabby, but a rich source of ideas and ideals. He had come out of his tenure in the White House less than he went in. And nobody seemed to realize it more keenly, seemed more upset about it, than Hubert Humphrey.

When Bond did venture out of Georgia to campaign, it was on behalf of a few Senate and Congressional candidates who had caught his fancy as being worthy of his support. In New York, for example, he spoke for Paul O'Dwyer, a Senate candidate, outspoken champion of the anti-Viet Nam war cause and one of the first white Northern lawyers to volunteer his work in the South. He campaigned from the bed of a truck in Brooklyn, under a lawn-party pavilion in Westchester County (where he also endorsed a Congressional aspirant, Paul Davidoff) and on the stage of a packed and screaming auditorium in Scarsdale, with a brief stop for lunch at a Black Muslim restaurant in Harlem. There, Bond smiled as a grim-faced young black wearing a Malcolm X pendant told him, "At the convention, it would have been a hell of a thing if you hadn't got your seat—we would of had a riot right here in New York."

How many of those in the audience at those places had come out in support of the candidates is moot—both O'Dwyer and Davidoff lost the elections—and how many of those who cheered for Bond stayed home on election day, or decided not to vote for Humphrey, or not to work for him, is also undeterminable. But his remarks about the national elections and the Democratic party's nominee were hardly calculated to whip up any frenzied support for Humphrey. On the contrary, Bond dismissed the national elections as a circus, saying, "We are now passing through the annual American political season. There are two road shows on tour. There are two main attractions, produced by two companies—but they speak from the same script. The title of this year's extravaganza is 'Law and Order, or How to Sell Out to the South Without Saying "Nigger." ' One play is directed by Strom Thurmond and the other by Richard Daley. In one play, Mr. Thurmond also acts, to remind the hero of his lines. In the other, the prompter from Texas is always in the wings, to remind the leading man if he forgets his part."

The obvious urge, Bond recognized, was to spurn this sea-

son's crop of presidential candidates. It was precisely this, he
told his listeners, that he feared. Whichever side, Republican
or Democrat, won the 1968 Presidential election, Bond told
his audiences, the right wing of the country's political spectrum would really be the winner. "Those on the left," he
said, "can either choose or make no choice at all. To do the
latter would make one feel pure, of course, but to opt out
altogether leaves something to be desired." To opt out, he
said, would be to leave unanswered a crying desire for change
in the course of the United States. This longing, Bond said,
was shared "not just by black people in the cities and by students on the campuses, but by millions of housewives and
laborers and farmers and others. The job of the liberal and the
job of the radical is to put these people and their longing
together."

If that conjunction would not happen in November of
1968, Bond was counseling, then the thing to do was not
despair, but to work hard so that 1968 would never be repeated. Standing under the garden-party pavilion, he implored
his audience not to decide that, because politics had a reputation for being dirty and unsavory, they themselves would
not work to improve it. "It is important that people like yourselves," he told them, "if you are dissatisfied with the results
of the convention, don't say, 'Well, I'm just not going to have
anything to do with it. I'm not going to vote and I'm through
with it. It's all corrupt and it's evil.' Because, you can see that
there is *some* good on the ballot in November."

Not only had one candidate been murdered and another
defeated in Chicago, Bond was suggesting; something almost
equally sinister was occurring, too: a deepening of apathy and
cynical alienation and disinvolvement by the very people who
now should be taking up the causes of Robert Kennedy and
Eugene McCarthy. "When Robert Kennedy announced his
candidacy," Bond said, "some of us cringed. 'He's ruthless,'
we said. Or, 'He's a bad attorney general,' we said. Or, 'It's

a plot by President Johnson.' But none who saw black people scrambling in Watts for the touch of his hand, or saw white farmers in Alabama smiling at his jokes would believe that for long. None who saw the miles and miles of mourners from New York to Washington would remember old tales or harbor old grudges. . . ."

The cavernous Westchester Community Auditorium was nearly silent as several thousand suburb-dwellers, well-off commuters and their wives and many children, leaned forward to hear this thin and intense Negro man try to brave them into not giving up the fight he knew must be waged. "When Eugene McCarthy, months before Kennedy, announced his candidacy, we said, 'It's only a trick.' We said, 'He only wants to get us off the streets—and into the system.' We said, 'He just wants to kill the peace movement or the student movement.' But no one who saw the students in New Hampshire would believe that student movements are dead, and no one who saw the battle at the Conrad Hilton in Chicago can believe that McCarthy got the students off the streets."

Surely no one could know more keenly than Bond how difficult it was to keep hope alive, to sustain faith in the American system in the face of rebuke after rebuke. While he could not, would not stand there and urge these people to go home determined to vote for Hubert Humphrey, he would do his most eloquent damndest to persuade them that, despite Humphrey, despite Nixon, the causes their candidacies had defeated were not lost; were, still, worth pursuing, even without a Robert Kennedy or a Eugene McCarthy to lead the way.

Why?

Bond told them. "Those two candidacies," he said, "for all their failures and their tragic losses, brought to this country the fervor and the feeling that had not existed in this country since the Freedom Rides of 1961, that had not existed since the sit-in demonstrations of 1960, that had not existed since the march on Washington in 1963. Those moments of history, representing no particular accomplishment, but only people in motion, signify the beginning."

Then Bond, whose speech, with its cadenced words and suggestive ambiguity, had glinted with easy poetry, quoted another poet, Margaret Rigg, to tell about the beginning he wanted them all to see:

FACE POSSIBLE END OF BUSINESS AS USUAL STOP WHITE SILENCE
IN AMERICA STOP KIDDING STOP KILLING STOP RIOTS STOP MACE
STOP FOAM STOP POLICE ARMS RACE STOP NAPALM STOP BOMBING
STOP BLOODLETTING STOP CIA STOP PENTAGON HAWK POLICY
STOP NIXON STOP CYNICISM STOP SLEEPING STOP DREAMING
STOP CRYING STOP MUMBLING STOP NOW BEGIN AGAIN BEGIN
BEGINNING BEGIN KERNER REPORT BEGIN HEARING BEGIN SEEING
BEGIN TRYING BEGIN DOING BEGIN WORKING BEGIN WORKING
HARD BEGIN TOUCH KENNEDY AND/OR MC CARTHY SUPPORT BEGIN
ORGANIZING BEGIN BEING HUMAN BEGIN LIVING BEGIN BEING
POSSIBLE BEGIN FACING THE POSSIBLE SURPRISE OF YOUR OWN
VOICE BEGIN

When the applause quieted, Bond reminded his listeners that there was more, really, to the poem than its sound, that "it requires more than just 'reading nicely.'" The poem, the times, the future, all demanded, Bond was saying, "the realization that we had *not* overcome, that our enemies are *not* against the wall, that tomorrow will *not* be a better day. It requires constant attention to the problems of today, to hunger, the war; it requires some form of unity among those who insist on a better day, rather than a hundred different drummers beating different tunes. It requires . . ."

It would require, in fact, realizing the hope of the poem, of his speech, of his work in Chicago—of his whole adult life. That was what Bond was summing up here for these affluent white folks. It would require, he said, softly, "that those least affected and least involved, the great mass of black and white middle-class Americans, involve themselves. It requires that action replace slogans, and requires that rhetoric be replaced with reality. It requires, finally, a commitment—a commitment that might have kept the South in ferment, a commitment that would have kept Chicago's policemen busy, a commitment that might have insured a choice and not an echo on top of the ballot in November.

"And," Bond said, looking out at them, "it will require that each of us keep in mind a prophecy written by the late Langston Hughes, that dreams deferred *do* explode. For, if this dream is deferred much longer, then an explosion will come, and in the words of the old song, it will be like God giving Noah the rainbow sign: 'No more water . . . the fire next time.' "

The speech had been nothing more, really, than an eloquent eulogy for the bright hopes of Chicago, and Bond's performance on the stage was poised, cool, polished, a sort of "wait till next time" locker-room cheerer-upper for the team. But the next morning, before another kind of forum, he was different, more intense, more urgent. With high school kids he visibly felt more at home, felt a sharper contact. Up there before them in an insouciant slouch, a tight little pussycat smile masking his glittering eyes, he tried to reach them, with his talk and with his answers to those questions they asked out of the naïveté of their so-sheltered, so-insulated white teen-ager lives.

"What about violence?" one of them asked him—did Julian Bond, the Quaker-trained pacifist and poet, the minstrel of the nonviolent protest movement, condone violence?

"Let me do a political thing," Bond said, "and skip around and answer that. Suppose that I were walking down a street in Harlem and saw a couple of black guys, teen-agers, with bricks in their hands and they were getting ready to throw a brick in a store window. I buzz up and I say, 'Don't do that, fellows, that's not the way—that's not the American way. . . .' "

The other grown-ups in the school auditorium seemed relieved at this counsel of moderation coming from the black visitor who looked barely older than their pupils.

Bond continued, however. "Then they'd say to me, 'Well, what is the way?' And I'd say to them, 'Do as I do: I'm in politics, and I work in the system and wonderful things are being done.'"

Bond paused, his eyes darting slyly around the audience to gauge whether this wry irony was going across, and then resumed his mock colloquy. "They'd say, 'How many jobs have you got for people since you've been in the legislature?'

"'Two or three.'

"'How many houses have you built for people to live in since you've been in the legislature?'

"I'd say, 'None, to tell you the truth.'

"'Well, how many schools have you improved so black children will have a chance to get a decent education, so they can get a decent job?'

"'Well, almost none of them,' I'd probably say . . . and then, then I'd probably turn around and say, 'Let me help you find some more bricks.'"

There was an empty silence in the auditorium then, one that lasted just long enough for Bond to insert into it an afterthought, "But," he said, "I don't condone violence—but I do understand why it happens."

The silence broke then, as the applause engulfed Bond, the white children of Westchester County, New York, approving him just as their parents had the night before. The two had touched now, Bond and these kids, and he proceeded to address them in the way they addressed themselves; not as children at all, but as people, as grown-ups.

"Regardless of who wins in November," Bond said, "the people will have already lost. And we are coming to the point in this country where the possibility of an armed confrontation between black people and white people moves closer and closer every day. I think that those of you who have a concern that that sort of thing ought not to happen—and that it ought not be stopped by policemen and national guardsmen but by some visible evidence of change in the country—remember a poem by Langston Hughes. . . ." Again he intoned the ominous lines, reminding the kids, "Young people, black people and poor white people *are* having their dreams deferred, and they are likely to explode." He asked them to keep in mind another poem by Langston Hughes, reciting it softly into the shiny microphone, "Negroes sweet and gentle, soft and kind—pity the day they change their mind. . . ."

This was fast in the wake of Chicago, and Bond felt these children badly needed a shot of confidence, not only in the American political system, but in themselves, to make up for the depression of the convention. "There are," Bond reminded them, "young people who caused the most powerful man in the world not to seek elective office—and if you can do that, then you can do anything!"

Bond urged them then to join a re-involvement in the "struggle of the South . . . in assuring that those people so unfortunate as to be beyond your imagination, those people who are so poor they don't see a nickel from sun-up to sun-down, those people who are so much a part of the dispossessed and the disorganized and disenfranchised of this country that they are utterly without hope . . ." His voice trailed off into thought, and then he spoke again: "If I could make a plea to the young people to do something, I would say, 'Among the things you do, don't forget the people of the South.' "

They were listening, keenly, as he spoke of things they would most likely never have heard from their teachers, never have read in their texts, never have experienced first-hand, letting them glimpse briefly into the world bordering the margin Bond lives in. "People who are poor, who are black," Bond told them, "want to see a difference in their lives. They want tomorrow to be better than today, and they will only see it, it will only happen, if young people and older people make the government make it happen. The government does not do things because it is the right thing to do—the government does it because people make them do it. It is only going to happen if people get themselves together and make something happen."

Then it was time for questions to come at him from the audience. Some were timid and routine—Q. "What made you become a member of the Georgia legislature?" A. "Hard work and clean living." Some cutting, with the blunt directness of youth unaware of the world outside themselves: "I saw this program on TV," said a girl into the microphone on the floor, "and they were teaching kids, Negro kids, from kindergarten on up, the idea that black is beautiful. Don't you think," she asked Bond, "that this is kind of a disillusioning concept to teach kids?"

"Why?" Bond shot back, "Don't you think it *is* beautiful?"

Then, perhaps because he wanted to save this girl from her own embarrassment, or because he had been stung and wanted to sting back, Bond machine-gunned the auditorium with bitterness such as he seldom allowed himself.

"These kids grow up," he said, "and they get a copy of a magazine, and they open it, and the only people they see in there *doing* things are white people. And they look at an ad for cigarettes and they see a pretty girl, and a man, and they're out in the country smoking Salems. And they begin to think to themselves, that the only beautiful people in the world are white people. They look at an ad for an automobile, and the guy who's driving it is white, and the pretty girl sitting next to him—not only is she white, she's blonde!

"They say to themselves, 'The only good-looking and attractive people are white people.' Look at TV and with the exception of Bill Cosby and an occasional singer or comedian, the only people they see with intelligence and talent are white people. They begin, by the time they get to be old enough to worry about lots of things, to think something's wrong with black people—they don't *see* themselves anyplace.

"Once," Bond said, "I flew from New York to Africa, and stopped in an African country to change planes. Flying Pan Am, all the crew was white; the pilot was white; and almost all the people on the plane were white. We got to the country, Senegal, and changed planes at Dakar, and all the crew was black. I had never seen a black man flying a plane. I was shocked. I was surprised. The terrible thought went through my mind: '*Maybe he doesn't know how to* fly!'

"I knew damned well he knew how to fly," Bond said grimly, when the laughter in the auditorium had ceased, "or he wouldn't have been in the plane. But you see what that can do to you—that you can be twenty-five years old and still have, for a fraction of a second, the doubt in your mind that black people can fly airplanes. It's a terrible thing to do to people. I think it is very important that young people be taught that black is beautiful, because it *is* beautiful. They may be ugly, but it is beautiful."

The blunt assertion, the painful anecdote, the cutting appraisal of the national looking-glass press, all that had been no set-piece but a trigger-quick reflexive reaction. Bond had simply responded, as he did one day not long afterward when, during an interview with a Swedish women's magazine, the lady reporter asked him, "Mr. Bond, you are part white, are you not?" and Bond had replied without a flicker of a pause, "Through no fault of my own."

Bond may be, as one close friend said of him, more comfortable around white people than around blacks—or that remark may have stemmed merely from a bitterness that in these polarized times a black leader like Bond should spend any time socializing with whites—but he knows clearly, viscerally, who and what he is. "I don't try to do it," he says, "but if you are black, you just have to be conscious of your race. You are *made* conscious of it every hour of every day, no matter who you are or where you live. And, you have to make yourself conscious of it, too, and ask yourself, 'What does this

mean racially—is it good for *us?* Racially?' That's what I try
to do. The important thing is to tell people that their whole
life is a struggle, that they have to fight inertia and racism, and
that the little things are as important as the big ones. If you see
a little Jim Crow as you are walking down the sidewalk—step
on it!"

Hard as it is—or may be—for many white Americans to
grasp, the fact is that Bond is not hyperbolizing, is not affecting a heightened awareness of race when he says his sensibilities as a black are on guard twenty-four hours a day. It is
refracted throughout his poetry, this immanent sense of not
only blackness, blackhood, but of black *versus* white. Other
eyes might perceive, imaginably, images of conflict, of some
immutable physical law or other, in a pool table, but Bond saw
there a microcosm of racial forces at work, and wrote:

> Like plump green floor plans
> the pool tables squat
> fawning mahogany Buddhas with felt heads.
> Like clubwomen blessed with adultery
> the balls dart to kiss
> and tumble erring members into silent oblivion
> Right-angled over the verdant barbered turf
> Sharks point long fingers at the multi-colored worlds
> and play at percussion
> sounding cheap plastic clicks
> in an 8-ball universe built for ivory

White Americans should find it disturbing, troubling—horri-
fying—that when Chicago exploded in a spasm of riots, arrests
and clubbings at the convention, some blacks rejoiced that, at
last, Mr. Charlie had got a taste of the policeman's truncheon.
Bond, when four Kent State students were murdered at point-
blank range in broad daylight by national guardsmen with
semi-automatic weapons, was moved to observe that blacks
and black students too, had been killed by official gunmen
many, many times. Their deaths, he said, had never provoked

a storm of national outrage such as the one that came in the wake of the Kent State massacre. That same racial perspective evoked in Bond a response far different from that experienced by most white Americans when President John F. Kennedy was shot to death in Dallas, Texas. In a poem titled "What Does It Mean?" he wrote:

In the Mississippi Delta
The night of the shooting
While we wondered (what does it mean for the Jews?)
a Negro lady, a sharecropper,
said to one of us.
"If they can do *that* to him,
what won't they do to us?"

This is not a conscious intellectualization of a position or the studied radicalism, say, of an embattled white attacking some enemy philosophy. It is instead the ingrained mental set that comes of growing up black in the U.S. Bond says that, at one time early in his life, "Race used to seem to me to be absurd, but now it seems much more important, in the negative of the way that it used to seem absurd. That is not to say that I think it is important who drinks out of what fountain or anything like that, or who goes to what school. But I think, because of a particular turn of history, that Negroes have got to use race as a *weapon*, and the only thing all of us have in this country in common is our race. I mean, some of us are very wealthy, well-educated, some very stupid, some very poor, and so forth. The only thing we have in common is race, and so I think we have to be appealed to as a race.

"And, we have to appeal to each other as a race. I think race has increased in importance, in a very positive way. I don't think white people tend to think of themslves as a race—only when they're challenged racially do white people think of themselves as a race. But we think of ourselves as a race much more often . . . not always, but much more often. We are the oppressed. The oppressed think of themselves as a class, I think, much more than the oppressor. I think white people are tired of being guilty and ashamed. They were guilty and ashamed in 1961, '62 and '63 and maybe '64. It really stopped then, and they said, 'This is it—that's enough.' "

Bond's feelings on race can be aroused to a pitch of near ferocity, as they were one fall evening in Atlanta in 1968 when he stood before a foot-stomping, clapping, whooping audience of blacks and whites who had packed into a rally in support of Atlanta's striking garbage workers. Bond walked with John Lewis, his old buddy from the Movement days, to the platform, and was introduced by Hosea Williams, a Southern Christian Leadership Council official, who was wearing a green jump suit and white basketball shoes. Outside, the pickets carried signs depicting Mayor Ivan Allen as a rat, and all in all the scene was calculated to dispel any ghosts of the old South that might yet be hovering about. The Reverend Ralph David Abernathy was thundering into the microphone, his spiel punctuated by *amens* and *say its* from the audience, in the old tradition. "We live in a sick nation," Abernathy sorrowfully bellowed, "Lord knows it's sick." Somebody up front was yelling, "Stay on the case, Doc."

Abernathy said, "There once was a time when we were down and we didn't have much sense—but we been to school and we *know*, now."

"Tell the truth, leader," somebody screamed.

"We got to fill up the city jail, the stockades, the county jail and all the jails in and around Atlanta and maybe Ivan Allen will give garbagemen what they want," Abernathy said.

"Amen!"

Then, up to the pulpit stepped the Reverend A. D. King, brother of the slain leader, and his basso voice pumped out through the church, "One day we won't come back singing 'We Shall Overcome,' because it's not just us who will have overcome—all of Atlanta will have overcome, because *we* have won a victory. . . ." Then King led the audience in a roaring chant— "SOUL POWER!—I may be black," several thousand voices cried, "but I'm *somebody!*—I may be poor, but I'm *somebody!*—I may be poor, but I'm going to get my white pay!"

Bond spoke then, telling them, when the clapping stopped, that he was sure the garbage strikers would win. He ripped into Georgia Senator Herman Talmadge, calling him "the King of Hams. He sells those hams all over the country. You can buy them out at the airport. That's the only good thing ever came off his farm. He's been in the Senate for twelve years and he's been sitting on those hams all those years. . . ." It was coarse and rough, but the attack drew cheers. Then Bond changed his jeering tone and the church quieted as he said, "I'm going to say something now that's going to make some people mad, but I'm going to say it. There's some people in this room ought not to be here. They were standing up a minute ago, and cheering, but they're not cheering now. They ran for office before, and you never gave him your vote before. He handed out one kind of literature to white people and a different kind to black people—and then he slipped up and gave some of the literature he usually gives to white people . . . to some black people!"

Bond pointed to the man, who was sitting in the front row, smiling, the smile getting tighter and harder as a chant mounted, "Go! Go! Go!" Bond then said, "He ought to get up and leave"; but the man still sat there, as heads craned and people stretched and leaned to see who this interloper might be. "I'm not going to say his name," Bond said, "but he *ought* to go."

Some people yelled to Bond, "Call his name," and at last, in a split-second of exasperation, when, one old friend said, "Julian was as mean as I've ever seen him," Bond leaned across the pulpit and pointed straight down at the man and roared, "There he is!"

The man, Congressional candidate Wyman C. Lowe, a white political perennial in the Atlanta lists, got up and, without a visible trace of embarrassment, made his way toward the microphone. But the audience wasn't having any of it, despite the entreaties of Reverend Abernathy, who implored them, soothingly, "He is a stranger in our midst, and my mother taught me a long time ago, to always be nice to strangers."

On the stage, Lowe tried to talk, rambling into a campaign speech as though Bond's invitation to leave had never reverberated through the church, telling the angry audience—which was chanting "SIT DOWN!"—that if he were elected to Congress, he would work for a minimum wage law. A black man got the microphone from Lowe and exhorted the shouting, departing audience to remember that democracy should prevail, but in the back of the hall, another Negro said, in disgust, "Meeting *over!*" and the audience kept moving out. As Bond walked down the side of the hall, a man laughed and said to him, "The saber-toothed tiger! You've done it again!"

Outside on the church steps, people grabbed his hand, and chuckled, and said hello, and wished him well in his own election campaign. But one man cautioned Bond to beware of the wrath of Lowe's supporters in Atlanta. Already in the heated race for the Congressional seat, Lowe's Democratic opponent, Charles Weltner—who had once occupied the seat until he declined to run again rather than share the ticket with Lester Maddox—had seen his campaign headquarters firebombed. Bond later that evening, after downing a few bourbon-and-ginger-ales with some reporters, picked up a shotgun from his brother-in-law, Howard Moore, and parked it under his bed before going to sleep. It was the first time he had ever had a gun in his house.

By the end of the decade he had begun by joining the civil rights movement, Julian Bond thought he had worked out a philosophical position on race. It not only satisfied his own personal needs, but seemed to accommodate the pressures outside him, too—pressures from a vague and amorphous national constituency to assume some kind of leadership role among American black people, pressures from the weighers and analyzers of the press to become definable somewhere on the spectrum from Uncle Tom to Brother Cleaver. He found something of a position in "racialism" as opposed to racism, and if that seemed like so much semantical toe-dancing, it satisfied Bond. "Racism," said Bond, "is evil, I think, and wrong, and racialism is the opposite: it's good, and it's positive." Bond traced the notion of racialism to an African poet, Léopold Senghor, who is the premier of Senegal and who had served in the French national assembly. "He has," says Bond, "a philosophy he calls 'non-racist racialism.' It may seem—I think it does to a great many people—like splitting hairs, but I think there is a difference between racism and racialism. Racialism says you are a certain thing and that you are proud of it, and that you don't think anyone is lesser or greater than you are because they are different from you—but just that you are different and that there is something *good* about your difference. There is nothing necessarily bad about the other man's difference, but there is something *good* about yours."

This distinction that he makes in his own mind between racism, which he condemns, and racialism, which he fancies is not only acceptable to an educated man, but to a large degree desirable in a Negro, enables Bond to look upon black-power advocates with equanimity, although some of them go much further in their advocacy than he would. Everybody, says Bond, has his own definition of what black power means—or should mean. "I think," says Bond, "that it means what Carmichael says it means in his book—it means black people uniting so they can have economic and political power. I'm all for that. If people think it is menacing, I think that's because they have some kind of insecurity or guilt or something, because I don't think it menaces anybody. It menaces those people who have been gouging in the slums, and it menaces those politicians who have been running the slums like little colonial outposts. But it ought not to be menacing to anybody else, and it is not. It is, as Rap Brown says, as American as apple pie!

"Carmichael and the Panthers now say that political power comes from the barrel of a gun. My position is that, first, we are such a small minority in this country that we only have two things going for us: our numerical superiority in some parts of this country—and some of these counties in the South —and our ability to be a swing vote in other places in the South. In this city, for instance, our ability to throw an election one way or the other. And—there seems to be a lot less of it than there was a few years ago—sympathy among white people in this country. The only thing we are losing is the sympathy. People now say, 'Well, they have got the right to vote, and they can be at lunch counters. Now they want everything—they want to live, too.' "

It is, of course, that very failure of the American system to permit black people to live in the same fashion as it allows whites to live that has driven men like Bond into holding a philosophy like racialism. Bond traces its evolution in his thought to twin urges, one toward a position he calls "assimilationist," and another he calls "the separatist." His stance on the side of racialism, he says, was reached as a "gradual, evolving philosophical position—when it became obvious that the other wasn't working." One major difference between Bond and the more extreme disciples of black power is not only that he still believes in the value of the existing governmental framework, but that he concedes the need to coalesce growing black political power with other groups in *ad hoc* political cooperatives. But make no mistake: Bond appears as a black man, speaking for black men, working for black men. That sure and certain self-knowledge of who he is and what he stands for is at the core of that vaunted cool and that poise which so appeals to so many who see and hear him, and he presents his case to whatever group cares to listen.

He lined out the facts of the case, for example, for an audi-

ence of psychiatric workers in a New York hotel early in
1969, telling them that controversy still raged within nonwhite
communities over whether to fight, as the Indians once had,
or to permit the system to redress their grievances. "It rages,"
Bond said, "because two hundred years after the founding
fathers proposed to establish a melting pot, the only thing
which has not melted is us. Now we no longer wish to melt,
to be absorbed, to fit in, to join up, to enter into the mainstream. Our job, from now into the future, is to carve out our
own place, separate, but a part of the whole."

Accomplishing that, Bond told the predominantly white
group, would not only require a dedication to the notion that
black power must become more than economic and political
rhetoric, but a clear recognition "from a great many people
that it is both evil men and an evil system that we deal with,
a system that rumbles, beastlike, over every aspiration of these
groups. It will take the recognition that this system, representative democracy, has yet to win major victories for these
groups."

The victories that had resulted from years of work from
sacrifice and from beatings endured and lives lost were goading
taunts. "It has," Bond said, "won some small victories. It has
won free access to lunch counters, providing potential steak
dinners for a people with hot-dog pocketbooks. It has won
for us the right to sit in the front of the bus, a hollow victory
for a people whose longest trip is from the feudal South to
the mechanized poverty of the North. It has won the right to
vote for a people who seldom see a candidate for whom they
could honestly vote."

This kind of rhetoric comes easily to Bond, and he can
spiel it off hour after hour, in speech after speech, with undi-
minishing passion. It is not the professional ardor of an actor
or the persiflage of a demagogue, but the indignant impatience
of a human being who is convinced he is being treated un-
justly.

When, after reading a draft of the speech from which these

words were excerpted, a white secretary to his House delegation, a Southern belle, wailed that he sounded so *angry*, Bond
snapped, "I think you *have* to be angry—*always* angry."

But the remedies lie not in anger alone, or in angry acts,
but, for Bond, in carefully aimed *work*. "It will be up to us,"
he told the New York audience, "to tackle the twin evils of
Twentieth Century America: racism and militarism. We have
to begin to do that by making our own communities as strong
as they can be. They have to exercise control over all of the
resources and institutions of our community. We have to say
to ourselves that, if something operates in the black community, then black people ought to run and control it. Secondly, we have to get our politics together and get together
with others, no matter who they may be . . . to form shifting
alliances.

"This means if the labor movement wants something that
we want, too, then we support labor—and labor must support
us. It means that if the white suburbs join us in supporting
opposition to American imperialism abroad, then we join in
that struggle, too. It does not mean that labor and suburban
whites remain our allies forever. Their interests and ours cannot coincide always, and we must be careful to separate coin-
cidental interest and coalition from foolish subjugation to
strange bedfellows."

Those, Bond said, were ordinary tactics, and if they did
not prove effective, after a fair trial, then black people and
poor white people and Indians and Puerto Ricans and their
supporters ought to be ready to consider other means toward
their liberty. "In addition to doing the ordinary things," he
said, "we ought to consider always and be ready always, for
the extraordinary things. Extraordinariness, of course, assumes
that if regular and responsible and democratic and fair and
ethical methods don't work for us, then others must be considered.

"The possibility of violent revolution must not be dismissed, although prospects for it are doubtful at present. It is

unrealistic to expect that a small percentage, poorly organized and poorly armed, can overthrow a massive government with vast police powers at its disposal. It is particularly unrealistic when one considers that the war in Southeast Asia might end, and with it will end a large part of the white radical movement that might be expected to join in such a movement. And it is also unrealistic when one considers that those who order society are usually able to keep it stable by allowing minimal reforms, so that even oppression can become bearable.

"But," Bond said, "one can imagine that day might come. Until it does, one ought to work toward building a movement powerful enough to either operate without it, or powerful enough to take advantage of the moment when it arrives. That movement can have many constituent parts, and it ought to be a political movement. It ought to be political because politics in 1969 ought to stop being the art of compromise and the art of the possible—and will begin being the art of seeing who gets how much of what from whom."

He called for a fusion of constituent groups, none of whom was strong enough to stand alone, drawing heavily from young people, all working toward building a machinery "powerful enough to take control in a peaceful, orderly fashion—or to take control following the example of those who now exercise great power."

When the applause was over and the audience milled toward the stage for autographs, for a touch, for a private word, one elderly white man had a harsh question for Bond. "If blacks do what's good for blacks," he asked, "and whites do what's good for whites, and Jew for Jew, won't we all wind up in a hell of a mess? Wouldn't it be nice if somebody would do what's good for *people?*"

Shot back Bond: "We're people—aren't we?"

And the old man said, "But you don't formulate it that way, and it leads to a certain divisiveness. . . ."

Far more than whatever "divisiveness" may arise as a by-product of black politicization, Bond fears that stifling that process may lead to general civil uproar. He foresaw in early 1969 the student-police clashes like the ones that wracked Chicago during the Weathermen's "Days of Rage," and said then, "I think you're going to have a lot more such clashes, and I think you're likely to have a lot more terrorism, sabotage and stuff like that. I don't think you'll have loss of life in it, but you'll have people blowing up power plants and blowing down utility lines. And you're going to have more and more police riots, off-duty police charging a group of people. Just a lot of turmoil from now on. And the South has escaped a lot of it up until now, but I think it will start happening down here. You don't have the same type of way-out white groups here that you do in a place like Baltimore, where you have white vigilantes. You have the Klan here, but it is largely disappearing, except in North Carolina. You don't have, in the cities, these organized groups of white people who strongly resist desegregation. There are white people who resist integration, but they are not organized. I think things are going to get tighter down here—they are very loose now. And almost anything can be done politically or any other way."

Bond hopes to see the development of hard-driving black political groups working Southwide for political gains. "I think," he said, "if that's what you want black people to become, then you have to talk about black people as a unit, realizing there is no monolith. You have to talk about blacks as a unit because we are treated as a unit. We are not treated as individuals: Jackie Robinson is Jackie Robinson the Negro ball player, not Jackie Robinson an ex-baseball star. He's always Negro first. I think we have to have a group view of ourselves. I am very much concerned with white attitudes. White people control, and it's their attitudes that have to change." The best hope for Julian Bond and other blacks is there, too, ironically enough.

"Because," he said, "you have the largest concentration of

black people in this region, because I'm interested in politics, and in black politics and interracial politics, this is the part of the country I have to be in if I want to do what I'm interested in. I couldn't do it in Omaha. And, it may be that things are possible here. You once had a very, very vibrant Movement in the South, and you could build that kind of Movement again, I think. The Movement had all these young people coming in who were working very hard; it had old people, residents, working very hard in their own communities. You have to propose new obstacles; you have to draw new lines. The whole shift of the Movement has changed from physical problems like lunch-counter integration to economic problems like people living and dying and eating: hunger. You have to find a way to propose that problem. You have to continue the pressure from below. Where people once could get aroused in Jackson, Mississippi, about being refused the right to eat at lunch counters, now you've got to arouse them about the fact that children are starving in Jackson, and build a movement around that issue."

When the Chicago convention was just a few months in the past, the Nixon era just a few months old, Bond could talk about a newborn coalition of the oppressed with considerable hope, the possibility of a new Movement with some optimism—even if the future was murky. Things would work out, he felt, one of two ways. "Either this country is going to approach concentration camps, and I don't mean with barbed wire fences and guards, but the ghettos of the big cities are going to be like concentration camps. With people leaving only to work, if they work at all, and if they don't work, subsisting on welfare and their own mother wit.

"Or, in what people call brotherhood, peace and light. One or the other.

"And I don't know which is more likely. I think the next few years are going to be more important than the last few have been. Because everybody is angrier now than they were then. The whole mood of the country is sort of angry. Black people angry, white people angry, students angry, politicians angry—it's an angry country."

Then, Bond could say, "I am sort of a manic-depressive; in some ways, I am just as happy as I could be, and others. . . . You know, I think you are carried along by the euphoria of the moment. When King was killed, I just felt so bad . . . and when Kennedy was killed, very depressed. Other times, like when we won that thing in Chicago, there was this very quick feeling of euphoria, that everything was going to be all right, everywhere. I knew damn well it wasn't. But just for a few seconds, or a couple of minutes, or an hour, you feel, 'Well, things are not so bad after all!' And then you just step out of the Amphitheater, and they are just as bad as they ever were."

But early in 1970, less than a year later, Bond felt that things were so bad as to make his candidacy for the U.S. House of Representatives—one of the few political moves he had ever really planned—unwise, and so he delayed it. Making a run for Congress had long been on his mind, but white feelings on school desegregation, he felt, had been so aroused by the Nixon Administration's startling go-slow and even go-in-reverse policies that Julian Bond could not get any substantial white support.

And, while he still talked of the need for a coalition—even broadening it to include the blue-collar folks who voted for George Wallace—Bond's words were more bitter, more cynical, wearier, more defiant, than they had ever been before. Bond began his speeches with an ugly, crude parable, designed to shock his audiences now into looking, really looking at what was happening to them and to their country.

"It is the custom," he would say, leaning casually on the podium, speaking in his low, laconic voice, "for speakers on a university campus to give a little advice, and so I would like to pass on this old Eskimo adage, which is one of the first things Eskimo mothers teach their children as soon as they are able to walk." The audience, baffled, would be quiet, straining to catch this bit of wisdom, wide open for it when it came.

"Don't eat the yellow snow!"

There would be a long pause, and a longer silence, and then nervous, embarrassed laughter, and some time later the meaning of Bond's harsh joke would sink in.

His words now in the early days of the new decade are hard words, without much hope. "There can be no denial," he tells his listeners, "that we are a generation of people who may be without a future; we may be living on the edge of domestic as well as world-wide revolution that may destroy us all." The danger domestically, Bond says, "is not the obviously absurd threat that a minority of black people will somehow overthrow the government of the United States, but the real fear that the age-old division of black and white and rich and poor will become so pronounced that no bringing together will be possible; that the two separate societies so long in existence in this nation will continue indefinitely, with one more closely resembling the colonizer and the other the colonized."

The time has come, Bond is saying, to turn America off its deadly course, and the answer he proposes is as awesome as are the prospects if it fails. "From lunch counters to bus seats to voting booths to student confrontations to the McCarthy campaign to convention demonstrations—these," he says, "have been the manifestations of citizen involvement on the left hand of the spectrum. On the right we have seen the people's politics in the campaign of the hillbilly Hitler from Alabama; the growing militance of white firemen and policemen, the reactionary resistance to job equality from white workingmen. In the middle of the spectrum, we have seen the growing consumer awareness of the American housewife; the frustration of the small farmer; the new aggressiveness of middle- and low-income workers.

"All of these people differ in their motives and goals. Some are driven by fear and selfishness, others are caught in an economic system never meant for their benefit, but all are caught up in believing with every good reason that government does not care for them or listen to their opinions; taken together, although their political differences argue against their ever being together, they constitute a noisy American majority of people, who, if they acted together, could shake the foundations of the nation.

"The problem for those interested in political change achieved through political action is how to get these people to act in concert—to vote together, let us say, or to march together, or to demonstrate in unison that they seek common solutions to their common problem, the inhumanity of Twentieth Century American life and the domestic brutality which results from a brutal and bankrupt foreign policy.

"To suggest that there is an easy answer to the problem of bringing these together is to constitute a fraud. It will not be done by dismissing blue-collar workers as simple racists who vote for George Wallace; a great many voted for Robert Kennedy as well.

"It will not be done by suggesting that one group, America's black people, acting alone, can bring about its own deliverance; no group of people with our social identification and lack of power can accomplish that task.

"It will not be done by engaging in debate of the relative revisionism of Ho Chi Minh while babies starve in the streets, or by suggesting that the security of the campus is the proper place from which to engage in social criticism of people who never see a book from year to year."

But, says Julian Bond, it might be accomplished, this unlikely welding-together of America's discontented populations, if they would remind themselves of the kind of cosmic vision perceived by George Wald, Nobel laureate in biology, who said in an historic speech, "This has become one world, a world for all men. It is only such a world that can now offer us life and the chance to go on."

Bond now is tired, and although national fame has brought with it a considerable improvement in his life-style—he has been able to move out of the tiny house on Euharlee Street with the office on the front porch to a larger and more com-' fortable one with the proceeds from his speaking tours—he is certain that he does not want to spend the rest of his life in politics. He sees himself as working best as a definer of issues, and wants to wind up in a position from which he can observe, think about and write about public affairs—with freedom to become involved in an active way if he wants to do so.

Politics is not only wearing, it can be disillusioning, as Bond found the election of Richard Nixon, but he can say nonetheless, that "even if what we call the system failed in an attempt to elect a decent man as President, it still has a workability lower down," and he isn't yet ready to write off the possibility of remaining active in regional politics. "I might," he jokes, "end up dying in the well of the House, might cave in as I make my 'basic speech' on the floor of the Georgia legislature at age eighty. I just like it; I think you're more on your own there." Running for mayor of Atlanta, he says, is out of the question because "I feel much more on my own being a member of the House than I would being a single man— they're much freer to operate."

And, while it seems logical to expect that someday Bond might want to try to cash in the attention his career has brought him, call in all those political IOU's from candidates he has helped, and requite those political mash notes he gets from star-struck fans across the country, he is not ready yet. "I don't believe, I just really don't believe . . . I'm not trying to be modest . . . I don't believe I will ever be a serious candidate for national office, other than Congress. I just don't see it happening. Really, it's just beyond my comprehension that it would. I really don't. It might happen," he says, "but it might just as easily happen to Ben Brown . . . or you."

All of which, of course, sounds like the same kind of aw-shucks-who-me disavowal of anything as unseemly as political ambition that can be heard from any politician practically up to the moment he is sworn into office. Public offices rarely go begging for lack of aspirants, although men immodest enough to declare their lust for them are rare.

But Bond does have some convincing arguments against his being sought for high office by kingmakers bent on using those IOU's even if he isn't interested himself. "No," he says, "I can't see that day. Put it in its most cynical light: the trouble with that is, that these guys would then have to say, 'Well, we need somebody who will go along with most things. Who will go along with us?' Get along and go along, yeah! And they would *not* choose me. I can go along with *some* things—and I imagine, faced with the prospect of being the Vice-Presidential nominee, there might be *other* things I might go along with; who knows what a man will do when faced with an opportunity like that? But there *are* some things I would not go along with, and I don't think I would be the choice. Too undependable. I don't see that happening."

If his end goal is not high elective office, then what, to Julian Bond, is the point of it all, where is he aimed, what does it mean, or do we just have to wait and see?

"I don't know what the point is," Bond says. "I don't like to . . . like that stuff in Chicago, when everybody started shouting, 'Julian Bond! Julian Bond!' I felt very funny. Sort of embarrassed, and on the other hand, I didn't know *how* to feel—what should I do, have gone up to the front and said, 'Here I am, people?' Then, on the last night, when Humphrey was nominated, and all those people wanted to pick me up on their shoulders—I don't know why, I wasn't doing anything at the time, Humphrey had just won—and I had to lock my legs under the seat! You know, I do not *know* what the point is. I don't like to be personalized, to have people say, 'He feels this way,' or 'He feels that way; this is what he does.'

"I just like to be out there."

What that will add up to is, of course, impossible to say now. What Bond has already added up to in his short life is impressive indeed; the obstacles ahead, should he decide to try for national office, are large. But whether he makes his play in politics, at the typewriter or simply on the lecture platform, his contribution will be a valuable one, as a black man who can tell the old sad story and as a black man who won't scare the white folks so badly that they won't want to do anything about the old sad story.

As Charlie Weltner, who has himself found out what obstacles face a man who gets too close to the truth in Georgia, said one night as we toured Atlanta in his car, Julian Bond—power base or no power base—has a great future ahead.

Yeah, somebody asked, but as *what?*

"Oh," Charlie said, "I don't know—maybe just as Hero-at-Large!"

EPILOGUE

JULIAN BOND has five children now—Horace Mann, Jeffrey, Michael, Phyllis, and Julia Louise—and at a slightly paunchy thirty-plus he can no longer really be considered an *enfant terrible*. Even the big yellow brick house which he bought for her with the proceeds from his speechmaking, his partnerships in a few Dairy Queen and Wishbone Fried Chicken shops and a consulting firm has not made Alice Bond any happier with her husband's vocation as a politician.

The little boy who wrote verses about how far it was into town, and who delighted in making up playlets for his older sister and his younger brother to join in presenting, the high school boy stung by sharp white jibes, the gaunt and earnest civil rights worker so nervous on the picket line that he broke into hives, so intense that he never dreamt of the reaction his own sharp words against a far-off war would have, those separate Julian Bonds have become a man now, but they linger on in him, too. He considers himself a Southerner of course, by right of his birth in Nashville and by virtue of the years he has given to working in the South. But his old Yankee fear of the South is still in him: there is the shotgun he keeps under the bed, a sad thing for a pacifist to have to do.

Being Julian Bond is certainly no easy assignment in life. There are those demands imposed upon any man with a wife and five children, not only simply to house, feed and clothe them all, but to join with them in the business of life. "Daddy," his oldest son, Manny, asked one night, "why do you have to go out every night?" That's a hard question to answer, and Bond finally replied, softly, "That's the way it is when you're famous, right?" Manny said, with utmost earnestness, "I want you to stay home every night. Sometimes Mommy won't let me do things and you will. I don't want to look at TV—I want to do something." Manny's harried father tries, he really does, to join his kids for walks, for rides over to Grandma's; he has missed more than one important meeting because Alice has run into a hot sale downtown, which is a difficult thing to imagine happening, say, to John V. Lindsay of New York or Charles Percy of Illinois. But it is exactly the sort of thing that Alice Bond had in mind when she married Julian: a nine-to-five sort of life, with her husband home a lot. Where, she wonders, is all this politics business leading them?

Julian Bond wonders about it, too.

Try as he might to concentrate on the present, to just get through what he has to do, he is constantly plagued by people who want to know what, in effect, he is going to do when he grows up. They aren't seeing his name in the papers too much any more, they say—what is he up to? Will he, as a good many seers predict, eventually don the mantle once worn by the late Dr. King? How does he really get along with other black leaders? How, really, does he stack up against them?

"I don't know," Bond says wearily, "what they want."

Nearly seven hundred times since the Chicago convention, from the fall of 1968 until the early summer of 1970, this quiet and introverted young man, who was once so shy he could scarcely bring himself to speak to his parents' dinner guests, has got up before some audience or other, in auditoriums all across this vast nation, to try and tell his listeners how things look to him. It is a kind of vision, as Charles Negaro once put it, that could only be achieved by somebody who grew up black in the United States, somebody able to cut through all the bullshit.

"As long as I'm a state legislator," Bond says, "I'm just sort of in limbo." His grandfather called it life on the margin. So there he is, stranded himself in a kind of political margin, and fixed within a social margin that really has not changed all that much since Jim Bond's day.

For another man, that might be a paralyzing, despairing latitude and longitude upon which to find oneself. But Bond, to the contrary, has chosen to go ahead and make those seven hundred speeches; the strain of doing so, of living on the road for weeks at a time, of living out of his suitcase in motel rooms, eating restaurant food, rushing to meet plane schedules, crossing off pages in his datebook, has left him drained. Worse, the moral and political lethargy he has encountered out there has left him saddened and bitter. But he plans to stay at it because he is committed to staying within the system and this is what he thinks he should do.

The effort has changed him from committed zealot to hopeful seeker of bright new coalitions among the poor, the black, the Spanish-American, the Indian, and then to a tired and less optimistic advocate of an even broader and less likely coalition. No less committed than the younger Julian Bond, this one now advocates a desperate coalition of all Americans toward making the nation what its charter documents declared it would become.

Blackstone Ranger, Black Panther, SNCC worker, CORE demonstrator, NAACP field worker, Urban League member, Urban Coalition contributor—all bespeak merely degrees of alienation, degrees of dissatisfaction. They indicate, too, degrees of visibility, from the other side, through that one-way glass wall that separates black from white America. Through it could be seen, dimly, a Martin King, and certainly Huey

Newton, too. But somehow that glass screens out what made them what they were, what propelled them into leadership, and what it was and is they were and continue to be to their people. To perceive that, Julian Bond is saying, one must position oneself on the other side of that one-way glass wall.

The times have changed over there, too. The Movement, it turned out, wasn't about a hamburger. Not just about segregation, nor just about voting, but about a whole system. Even when other issues came along to claim the energies and attentions of the youth who once marched so devotedly behind the reverend from Birmingham, issues like Viet Nam and poverty and hunger and ghettos and environment, they too turned out to be, really, about that system. Bond, from his position out there on the margin, could perceive that they were all just quivers, twitches, responses, urgings, pleadings, assaults, attacks —provoked unmindfully by a system that just simply didn't care. That sad fact could hardly be understood by the good people with the cemetery lawn furniture out in the front yard, by the people who had won the point victory in Miami, in Chicago, or by those who actually won in November of 1968. The one-way glass, the barrier of consciousness, of simple basic awareness of social injustice, prevented it—just as it could make the slaughter at Kent State seem a senseless and brutal mass murder to those on one side of it, and a "valuable object lesson" to those on the other; just as it could make the Jackson State carnage, the Augusta murders, seem hideous to some and not so hideous at all, hideously enough, to others in this land.

But.

The growing awareness that the Movement was really about a multiplicity of wrongs, and, in the end, about the system that was doing, could be doing, so little to right them, brought more different kinds of people into its ranks. As it grew and probed in so many different directions, took up so many varied causes, the Movement became a more difficult vehicle for one man to control, until it has become nearly impossible to thrust with any seriousness upon any one man the mantle that was presumed to have belonged to Martin Luther King.

Yet it is that broad and disparate group that Bond keeps trying to reach, urging them to realize their strength. And it is those on the other side of the glass, the one-way barrier, that he is reaching, too, urging them to try and understand, to try and help shatter the barrier forever.

Bond's effort is the kind of spanning no politician would ever attempt, the kind of unmanageable assembly no practiced leader would ever dare trumpet.

But that hopeful sharing of a vision of things is just what is most desperately needed. Leaders, after all, must have some road down which to go with their bands, some visible barricades to assault. Politicians can only legislate piecemeal remedies to neat problems. Men like King cracked the visible barricades; the resulting appropriate and tidy legislation abounds to attest to that. But America is still not together; that chasm dividing it still yawns. First it has to see itself clear.

Only a poet would try something as audacious as that.

Beyond the preposterous difficulty of his· goals, however, other hazards beset Bond as he gropes toward his future.

Beyond all the persiflage, the blandishments, and the ringing words expended in winning the seat, and the drudgery of the job once in it, the pursuit of success in politics is essentially the pursuit of power. The rewards, the accolades, the tributes, and the perquisites of being an American politician all pale in comparison to the simple heady sensation of being one who decides, or helps decide, the shape of public policy and the course of events. Much more than any mere and puny business of deciding who gets how much of what from whom, politics on any level is really an extension of one's self into the future—and men have always been willing to take all sorts of risks, pay all manner of savage prices, if only they might have a stab at the future.

But it is precisely in this context, in the arena of politics, that the motives and aims of Julian Bond are most enigmatic, and therefore any consideration of his own future must necessarily be extended with the utmost caution. Bond seems, in his daily life, as he goes about his business as a legislator in the Georgia House, or as he goes about the United States as a modern-day goliard of the Movement, scarcely concerned at all with the pursuit of power. Nothing he has done or does makes any sense if considered as part of some covert strategy aimed at drawing to him the accouterments and trophies of political power.

Can a man who cares as little about power as Julian Bond succeed in any real sense in American politics? More important: should he?

Why is Bond in it—and what's in it for him? Americans, after all, have long accustomed themselves to just about every kind of politician imaginable, and for them the game holds few surprises any more. We have as a people always held in sharp and righteous suspicion those among us who decide to seek to govern, and that suspicion is now ingrained in our society, written directly into those charter blueprints which neatly compartmentalize the legislative from the executive and both of them from the judiciary. No politician, however, has aroused more fearful apprehension—or deserved it more —than those men who tried to govern without the solace and comfort of a deep-seated lust for power. That mystical sense of self-declared mission which impelled an Eisenhower, which glisters from a Lindsay, is a fearsome thing, because it so often results in a governor who has no real interest in the dreary business of governing and hence creates a vacuum that will quickly fill with all manner of nuisance and trouble. The good people who live in that part of Texas which gave the world Lyndon Johnson, for instance, wink and giggle at what a rounder he was when it came to what he got for himself along the way to getting there. But it didn't really matter to them, because in the process he got a good deal for them, too, by way of electric lights and dams to power them, roads and other plums from the public orchard. Johnson knew what power was all about in a way few men ever have.

But then, Lyndon Johnson grew up in a culture steeped in the lore of power, himself infused as much as anybody with the pain that comes from the lack of it. Johnson studied under Franklin Roosevelt to get it and did another apprenticeship under old Sam Rayburn before he got it. There have been no such tutors for Julian Bond to follow. Bond's main political hero is Adam Powell, that lonely old barracuda of the House of Representatives, a man with no empire to share whatsoever and no mantle to bequeath. Bond's own solitude of nature would undoubtedly have prevented him from joining a black political apparatus even if one had been available, just out of character. Bond's very uneasiness at being hoisted aloft, at being lionized, at being made a spokesman, a figurehead—at being, in other words, *followed*—bespeaks a loathing for leadership.

Moreover, there is about Julian Bond absolutely none of the straightforward single-mindedness of the black leaders of his time, men who have attempted, from outside the political apparatus, to wrest the rights that apparatus should have upheld. Bond has little in common with such men as the Reverend Ralph David Abernathy, the Reverend Jesse Jackson, with Eldridge Cleaver, or Stokely Carmichael, with the Black Panthers, or even with the softer-spoken Whitney Youngs and James Farmers—save the color of their skins and their shared appellations as "black leaders." These men have all taken up positions of attack, have aligned themselves with forces of protest and dissent, have joined their energies to an assault on a society which has injured and cheated black men. For their efforts, they have been variously regarded as heroes, saints, or enemies of the republic, depending upon who has done the regarding. Bond, on the other hand, has for most of his public life been an integral, sworn, elected member of a unit of the governing apparatus directly responsible for the continued existence of racial injustice. Now isn't it curious that he has chosen to do so seemingly little from his seat in the Georgia Legislature about that situation? Is it really fair to the people who elected him that Julian Bond has not pressed unstintingly for passage of that legislation—against capital punishment, for a minimum wage, etc.—that he promised he would seek when he sought their votes? His critics say that it is not fair and that Julian Bond is thereby cheating his constituents of their trust. Bond's defenders, of course, simply point to his touchy situation there in the House, and say there is little else he might do except work quietly at those aldermanic chores he can carry out without harassment from his enemies.

Both sides miss the larger point, however, which is that Bond is a Georgia black man, and that, with no tradition of black political involvement in Georgia, the South—or, on any significant scale, in the entire nation for that matter—Bond and the others of his political generation are pioneers of a kind, proceeding with caution, trying not to exacerbate old enmity and trying quietly to stake out new alliances—and at the same time, managing to get reelected again and again. Bond's approach is one which seems sound merely on the face of the situation: blacks constitute only about 11 percent of the national population, just 39 percent of the voting population in the city of Atlanta, and are outnumbered almost three-to-one in terms of voting-age population in the state of Georgia. The fact of the matter is that twenty-two million black Americans are not going to get anything that one hundred and seventy-two million white Americans don't want to give away without some mighty shrewd dealing. Consider that, as long ago as 1875, the Congress of the United States of America passed a civil rights act declaring that, henceforth, the law of the land absolutely forbade discrimination against any citizen in public places, and then consider that it was not until August of 1968 that the first Negro American was nominated for Vice-President of the United States. That Negro American, Julian Bond, thrilled to the roar of the delegates applauding him, but a part of him knew, too, that those delegates were applauding something else—their own magnanimity.

By accident of time of birth, then, Julian Bond is a kind of advance scout in politics, but he is one by dint of his own nature, too. That same reserve that precludes total joy at being nominated to run against Spiro Agnew also prevents Bond from joining *any* endeavor with wholehearted singlemindedness. He maintains a reserve, a distance between himself and the events swirling about him. Call it "aloofness," "cool," or "poise," or whatever, but some part of Bond is always on watch, considering and evaluating. Perhaps this comes from having been a professional writer—or, rather, perhaps it was this predilection for distanced observation that led him into writing in the first place. At any rate, it is the essential ingredient for style, for artful expression and persuasive action, and it precludes, in the mature Julian Bond at least, the sort of impetuousness which might lead another person down vainglorious blind alleys.

By sitting in the Georgia House, Julian Bond at least retains the possibility of participating in the decisions that will affect the people who sent him up to the big golden-domed capital building. Being Julian Bond is enough. He has to prove nothing, to his colleagues or his constituents. He retains, too, the ever-present opportunities to make end-runs around the men who stymie him in the House, venturing out frequently to carry his messages to the other people in the country.

That those messages so frequently deal with the need to work on a prosaic local basis is not surprising. Nor is it surprising that Bond spends so much of his time out of the House speaking to predominantly white audiences—a fact that leads some of his friends as well as his enemies to speculate whether Julian Bond in fact does not like being around white people better than he does being around black, whether, really, Julian Bond does not wish he *were* white.

These are silly, irrelevant speculations. Bond, part white, part Cherokee, part Negro, is irrevocably, by dint of color, black, and proud of that birthright. He is, as well, a keenly intelligent, sensitive man, who knows more acutely than most that the United States, his country, is a white society, and that the white man's game is—presently, he emphasizes, *presently* —the only game in town, and that any efforts to avoid that central fact are doomed to heartbreaking frustration. Blacks can petition, cajole, demand, rampage, march, riot, sit in, burn and weep their hearts out, but the country won't change until the white man changes. Legislative record in the Georgia House aside, Julian Bond *can* step through that one-way glass and be seen by white people, can step through that trick looking glass that divides us and stir *not* only conscience but thought, too.

America is a white man's game, always has been, but Bond knows, too, that it is a game that black men can play, and play well, and that black men like himself *will* be playing in ever-increasing numbers and to which they will have much to contribute by way of energy and insight, tolerance and com-passion. But it is a game which will continue, with happy suc-cess for all the players, only if Julian Bond, all the Julian Bonds, are heeded.